THE BLACKBERRY FARM COOKBOOK

THE BLACKBERRY FARM COOKBOOK

FOUR SEASONS OF GREAT FOOD AND THE GOOD LIFE

SAM BEALL

INTRODUCTION BY MOLLY O'NEILL

CLARKSON POTTER/PUBLISHERS

NEW YORK

www.blackberryfarm.com

All rights reserved.
Published in the United States by Clarkson Potter/Publishers, an imprint of the Crown
Publishing Group, a division of Random House, Inc., New York.
www.crownpublishing.com
www.clarksonpotter.com

CLARKSON POTTER is a trademark and POTTER with colophon is a registered
trademark of Random House, Inc.

Library of Congress Cataloging-in-Publication Data is available upon request

ISBN 978-0-307-40771-9

Printed in Hong Kong

Design by Stephanie Huntwork

4 6 8 10 9 7 5

First Edition

TO MY PARENTS, SANDY AND KREIS BEALL,
who founded this incredible place called Blackberry Farm
and who have always given me unconditional support
while I chased my dreams and continued the work they
began: creating a gracious and unique respite for the world

CONTENTS

The Poetry of Possibility on a Farm in Tennessee by Molly O'Neill 1

A Letter from the Innkeeper by Sam Beall 7

SUMMER ∼ John and His Beanstalks

DINNER IN THE GARDEN
LEMON CUCUMBER SOUP *19*
PEA SHELL AND CHEESE CURD SALAD *19*
BEET CARPACCIO WITH SUMMER CHANTERELLES
   AND CHIVES *20*
OIL-POACHED SALMON WITH RADISH SALAD
   AND PARSLEY COULIS *23*
BLACKBERRY COBBLER *24*

BARBECUE: PURE AND SIMPLE
SWEET AND SPICY FOOTHILLS COLESLAW *33*
SAM BEALL'S BAKED BEANS *33*
MR. FEATHERS'S ONION RINGS *34*
SUMMER SQUASH SALAD *34*
PEACH-GLAZED BABY BACK RIBS *36*

A BARBECUE FOR COMPANY
HEIRLOOM TOMATO TERRINE *39*
BARBECUED QUAIL WITH BLACK-EYED PEA SALAD *40*
ROASTED PEACH TART *43*

THE FOURTH OF JULY
GREEN GODDESS POTATO SALAD WITH GARDEN
   RADISHES *49*
KREIS'S TENNESSEE FIRE-FRIED CHICKEN *53*
BUTTERMILK BRINED FRIED CHICKEN WITH SAGE *54*
SWEET TEA-BRINED FRIED CHICKEN *55*
SMOKY MOUNTAIN SKILLET-FRIED CHICKEN *56*
CHILI-CURED, BATTER-FRIED CHICKEN *57*
WHITE CHOCOLATE ICE CREAM SANDWICHES *58*
TOASTED WHITE CHOCOLATE ICE CREAM *58*

FIRST CORN SUPPER
CHILLED CORN SOUP WITH GARLIC CUSTARD *65*
GRILLED CHILI-RUBBED RIB ROAST *66*
GRILL-ROASTED POTATOES *69*
SKILLET OKRA *69*
SUMMER SQUASH CASSEROLE *70*
PEACH SHORTCAKE *72*

FALL ⁓ The Amber Days

YALLARHAMMER NIGHTS
AUTUMN LAMB ROAST *93*
WINE-ROASTED DUCKS *94*
ROASTED BELL PEPPER SALAD *94*
EGGPLANT MOUSSELINE WITH ROASTED TOMATOES *96*
SKILLET APPLE CRISP *99*

QUAIL HUNTERS' DINNER
BACON-GLAZED CARROTS ON WILTED ROMAINE *107*
BUTTERED QUAIL WITH PAN-ROASTED HOMINY, GIBLET,
  AND BLACK TRUMPET RAGOUT *109*
BOURBON APPLE FRIED PIES *110*

WHEN BLACK WALNUTS FALL
BLACK WALNUT SOUP *119*
COFFEE-RUBBED DUCK BREAST WITH WINE
  MARMALADE *121*
PECAN BRUSSELS SPROUTS *121*
APPLE STACK CAKE *122*

FATHERS FRYING TURKEYS WITH SONS
PEANUT SOUP *134*
DEEP-FRIED TURKEY *135*
ROAST TURKEY WITH CORN BREAD STUFFING
  AND GRAVY *136*
STEWED SPICED APPLES *138*
DRIED CHERRY AND CRANBERRY SAUCE *138*
BEALL FAMILY OYSTER DRESSING *139*
SAM'S CARROT SOUFFLÉ *140*
WHIPPED MASHED POTATOES *140*
SWEET POTATO PIE *142*
PECAN TART WITH SORGHUM *143*

WINTER ❧ Smoke and Fire, Sausage and Ham

A COZY COMPANY MEAL FOR WINTER
TENNESSEE CORN AND TRUFFLE FLAN *161*
COUNTRY HAM–WRAPPED STURGEON WITH FENNEL AND
  SUN-DRIED TOMATO WHITE BEAN RAGOUT *162*
ROASTED PINEAPPLE UPSIDE-DOWN CAKE *165*

MIDWINTER DINNER
BUTTER LETTUCE WITH SHEEP'S MILK DRESSING *169*
BOURBON-BRAISED PORK BELLY ON GRITS WITH
  CARAMELIZED ONIONS *170*
COCONUT CAKE *173*

SUNDAY SUPPER
RAW WINTER VEGETABLE SALAD *175*
POUSSIN ROASTED WITH SUMAC-GINGER BUTTER *176*
WINTER SQUASH PURÉE *179*
BAKED BUTTERSCOTCH PUDDING *179*

DINNER IN DEER SEASON
SUNCHOKE SOUP *185*
CIDER-BASTED VENISON *187*
SKILLET SLAW *188*
ROAST PARSNIPS *188*
FIG TART *191*

SHORT RIBS FOR A LONG WINTER NIGHT
BRAISED SHORT RIBS *199*
CELERY ROOT AND POTATO PURÉE *199*
CITRUS CARPACCIO WITH CHOCOLATE-COVERED
  CLEMENTINES *200*

SPRING ～ An Appalachian Spring

SPRING PICKIN'S
WILD MUSHROOM SOUP 213
OVEN-BAKED TROUT WITH RAMPS AND MORELS 213
RHUBARB TART WITH WILD RASPBERRY CREAM 214

AN EXPRESSION OF PLACE
TEN-HOUR BRAISED LAMB NECK WITH WILTED CREASY
   GREENS AND CRISP-ROASTED MORELS 223
HERBED SPOONBREAD 224
BUTTERMILK PANNA COTTA WITH WILD
   STRAWBERRIES 224

IN PRAISE OF THE RAMP
RYE WHISKEY–CURED TROUT WITH FRESH AND PICKLED
   FENNEL 229
SMOKY MOUNTAIN RAMP RISOTTO WITH
   JACK DANIEL'S 230
BOURBON ZABAGLIONE 231

SPRING CHICKEN
ASPARAGUS AND COUNTRY HAM SALAD WITH MUSCADINE
   VINAIGRETTE 235
HERB-ROASTED SPRING CHICKEN 236
WARM CAFÉ-AU-LAIT SABAYON WITH CREOLE KISSES 237

THE PIG IN SPRING
BRAISED RABBIT WITH DANDELION GREEN SALAD 245
STUFFED PORK ROULADE 246
LEMON CHESS PIE WITH OPAL BASIL SYRUP 249

A COMPANY DINNER FOR A VERNAL EVENING
ROASTED HEN-OF-THE-WOODS WITH CORN PUDDING 251
FRICASSEE OF RABBIT IN MUSTARD CREAM 252
BUTTERMILK SORBET 253
CHOCOLATE SORBET 253

TENDER COALS
GREEN TOMATO SKILLET CAKE 259
WOOD-SMOKED VEAL BREAST 260
SALAD OF PEA TENDRILS WITH WILD GARLIC
   VINAIGRETTE 263
FRENCH FRIES 263
SPICED CUPCAKES WITH BROWNED-BUTTER
   FROSTING 264

SOME BASICS ～

DOWN TO THE BONES
CHICKEN STOCK 268
VEGETABLE STOCK 268
HAM HOCK STOCK 269
BEEF OR VEAL STOCK 269

THE FOOTHILLS PANTRY
BASIC PASTRY 270
SWEET PASTRY 270
BLACKBERRY VINEGAR 271
GREEN TOMATO MARMALADE 271

MUSCADINE GRAPE MARMALADE 272
CLOVED WATERMELON PICKLE 272
GREEN TOMATO PICKLE 273
PRESERVED LEMONS 273
PIMIENTO CHEESE 274
SPICY PIMIENTO CHEESE 274
CORNMEAL LAVOSH 275
BLACK-EYED PEA HUMMUS 275

Resources 277
Acknowledgments 281
Index 283

The Poetry of Possibility on a Farm in Tennessee

The local Cherokee say that the wing of a giant eagle swept across the land of eastern Tennessee, scraping out gorges, etching rivers and creeks, sweeping rock up, up, up to form the Great Smoky Mountains in the Appalachian mountain range. Geologists take a different view of the events that occurred six hundred million years ago. Tectonic plates collided, they say, shattering a single landmass into three discrete continents, pushing mountains twenty thousand feet above sea level and emptying shallow lakes like the one that once occupied West Millers Cove twenty-five miles south of Knoxville, Tennessee.

Perched on the southwest bank of that cove, Blackberry Farm, one of the leading small hotels in America, presides over nine thousand acres of the extraordinary landscape that resulted from these primordial events. Through the inn's dining room windows, white rail fences follow rolling hills and frame flat pastures; outside the fences, the land scrambles up rocky hillsides. Bounded by mountains, a gorge, and a river, the view from Blackberry Farm is too dramatic and singular to have sprouted gently. Be it eagle's wing or tectonic shift, some cataclysm carved this cove. Today, its pastoral tranquility seems like an armistice, a fiercely knit peace between vestigial forces, a lull.

But look again. Mythic and geological forces have simply given way to human ones, specifically to the never-ending questions of what it means to be ourselves at this moment in history and how to live fully and well.

Since 1975, when the Bealls purchased their home, a dilapidated stone and clapboard manor in the midst of a hardscrabble, overgrown farm, the family has steadily been creating a land trust, a cultural preserve, a working farm, and a small country inn. By 1994, when the inn was admitted into the prestigious Relais & Châteaux organization, Blackberry Farm was known as a place where the plaids and chintz of the British country style melded with the bent-twig furniture and feather beds of the Appalachian idiom. By then, the "Foothills Cuisine" minted in the kitchen at Blackberry Farm had long been viewed as the cutting edge of the new Southern cooking movement.

In the last several years, the Beall family has turned Blackberry back into a working farm. Today, a herd of East

Friesian sheep supply the milk for the cheese that is made in the farm's creamery and a passel of Tamworth hogs provides more than enough pork to keep the farm's salumeria stocked with six sorts of ham, up to three dozen different sausages, and enough peppery, cured and smoked slabs of pork to strike envy in the heart of the Bacon Belt. There are laying hens, chickens, beef cattle, and a garden planted with enough indigenous heirloom vegetables to supply nearly seventy percent of the produce served in the two restaurants at Blackberry Farm.

Blackberry's synthesis of land, history, culture, and place is both a remarkable and a prescient accomplishment. Nevertheless, the Beall family's real legacy may not be about buildings or land use or even hospitality. Instead, their greatest accomplishment may be the zone of possibility they created along the way.

Somewhere between the tidy pastures and the wooded mountains at Blackberry Farm, the capacity for doubt got

lost. Once one arrives there, time moves as slowly as the smoke at a Tennessee barbecue and it is possible to imagine a new way of being in the world. This sense of boundless possibility affects people of the farm as much as it does those who stay for just a spell. Most recently, it has prompted a new approach to cooking and eating.

As the gardens and artisanal food making took root at the farm, the definition of *foothills cuisine* became more expansive. In the original dining room, *foothills cuisine* means the flavors and cooking of the mountainous south. In the big red nineteenth-century barn, however, foothills cuisine also signals that the chefs and artisanal food producers who have gathered at the farm are not cooking from recipes or trends. Rather, they are studying what the land offers each day through the prism of extensive training, travel, talent, and knowledge with one thing in mind: to help the food be what it wants to be and to use that essence to create a dish that expresses a particular place on a particular day.

A memory of a favorite family dish or something eaten in a restaurant might be stirred by considering, say, a fat heirloom carrot; the cook may recall a song, a painting, a feeling, something from a cookbook. Any of these things can affect what a chef does with the day's harvest before calling it dinner. But it begins with what is.

Cooking this way reverses the modern relationship between a chef and an ingredient. Rather than writing a menu and then going shopping, the chef walks through a garden or market; goes foraging, fishing, or hunting; and cooks what is. This approach can deliver vibrant flavors and lively meals. Responsive cooking is not only a way to approach dinner. It is a way to approach life, grounded in what is, eyes wide open to what could be.

—MOLLY O'NEILL

A Letter from the Innkeeper

BY SAM BEALL

Blackberry Farm is my home. Between the day I was born and the day I left for college, our family lived in twenty-eight houses and five different states. My father, Sandy Beall, founded Ruby Tuesday's, and in its early years, the business demanded a lot of relocation. Additionally, my parents shared an unwavering commitment to improvement and movement. Once they've resurrected and perfected a house, my parents have no choice, they *must* move on. When my parents bought Blackberry Farm in 1975, they didn't imagine that the place would provide enough opportunities for improvement to fill a few lifetimes. Nor did they imagine it would become home, which in our family means "the place we return to." But Blackberry Farm has always been generous. It has never stopped offering my mother, Kreis Beall, chances to exercise her infallible sense of design. And this, in turn, continues to give my father a steady supply of new reasons to admire my mother, which is his favorite thing to do. In the early years, rooms would rise from decades of neglect to become glowing little masterpieces. We were awed by their beauty and awed by the fact that the beauty had been there all along, unrealized. My mother has a magical ability to coax spaces into what they were meant to be, capturing their light and shadows, their mood and function.

ABOVE LEFT: Two generations of Bealls pick ingredients for dinner. **ABOVE RIGHT:** Preparing a wine tasting in the cellar.

By the early 1980s, Blackberry was a nine-bedroom gem. Friends and then friends-of-friends claimed the extra rooms. Soon, one houseguest decided that he wanted his own private country manor for a weekend and asked to rent the entire house. An inn was born. My mother turned her attention to cooking and creating parties and events. When my parents entertain, everyone at the table seems to feel a magic that is so welcoming and inviting.

That feeling infused our everyday life, as well. Even as a teenager, I often chose dinner at home over going out and getting stupid with my friends. My father and I often cooked together. I always knew what I wanted to be when I grew up. I started bussing tables at Ruby Tuesday's when I was twelve and soon moved into the kitchen and started to cook. After college, I relocated to San Francisco to study at the California Culinary Academy and my real education began. Over the next three years, I worked at several vineyards, a creamery, and, finally, in both the dining room and

the kitchen of the French Laundry. In the process I learned, again and again, that the most glorious flavors come from gorgeous ingredients that are allowed to be what they are. I also realized that I was supposed to do more than merely maintain the family inn.

My mother had turned a dilapidated old house in an unlikely location into one of the finest luxury inns in the country. I wanted to turn Blackberry back into a working farm. Rather than having a single chef, I dreamed of assembling a team of chefs and culinary artisans who approach growing, making, and cooking food as I do. I knew that this approach could require an unconventional staff, people who didn't want a job as much as they wanted a way of life, a constant challenge; brilliant, creative people whose quest for "the best" could mean that they might not stay in one place for more than a few years, but people who would pour their lives into their craft with passion. I knew that assembling such a cast would be an ongoing effort: food artists, like

ABOVE LEFT: Kreis and Sandy Beall began creating Blackberry Farm thirty years ago. **ABOVE RIGHT:** Father and daughter making pies.

most artists, are restless sorts; our team would shift and change. But I was willing to take on that challenge. At a time when food was increasingly being described in terms of its molecular components, I wanted to create cuisine in a larger context, to serve food that reflected place and time and the mood of the day.

Having helped develop a cellar of 160,000 bottles, I also wanted to approach wine in a similar, holistic way. When a guest asked us to suggest a wine for one course or another, I tried to consider the person, what his or her particular sense of "perfect" might be, at the same time pairing the flavor elements of wine with those of the meal. I wanted, in other words, to do with food and wine what my mother can do with a room, an occasion, a table.

In the kitchens at Blackberry Farm, the response to ingredients can be complex and highly refined. But in the evening, when I walk across the field to my home and begin fixing dinner with Cameron, my oldest daughter and num-

ber one sous chef, my response to the same ingredients is simpler, quicker, less fussy, even more direct. Both iterations spring not from a style of cooking, but from a way of living.

In the following pages you will find effortless, down-home dishes as well as some favorites from our more complicated and demanding repertoire. You will find menus for celebrations and for family dinners and quiet suppers.

Like everything we do at Blackberry Farm, creating this book was a collective experience, and an instructive one: we had to find words for what we know in our hands and our hearts. We did this by reflecting on the seasons, and by describing the sights, sounds, folk history, and characters in our particular patch of the world. We also tried to communicate the style in which we've chosen to live by doing what we do: creating meals. You can trust our ideas, but all of us really hope that our recipes and menus will inspire you to savor your own region, meal by meal.

SUMMER ≈ John and His Beanstalks

The garden at Blackberry Farm sits on a five-acre plot on the south slope of Chilhowee Mountain. There, the sandy loam is the color of a weathered barn, of bleached and wind-worn pine. John Coykendall, the gardener who tends this plot, often references its various moods when describing one or another of his shell beans. The coat-pattern of the Milk and Cider, he says, resembles the turned dirt beneath the low-lying mist of a Smoky Mountain morning. And the deep purple frosting on the grayish Rose Bean brings to mind the mauve light of dusk creeping over the furrows in his garden. He does not make these comparisons lightly. Mr. Coykendall (pronounced "cur-ken-DOLL") has been collecting beans in the mountains and hollows (or, as he says, "hollers") of eastern Tennessee for more than half of his life. He has saved 175 varieties of the region's legumes and sees each one as a work of art.

He also views his beans as a lyrical tribute—a history lesson and an homage to place. When he calls them by name—Cades Cove Cut Short Greasy Back, Cherokee Cornfield Bean, Turkey Craw, Red Goose, Thweat Family Red Calico, Reverend Taylor, Whippoorwill Pea, the Pigott Pea—Mr. Coykendall makes each sound like a phrase from

ABOVE LEFT: John Coykendall and Jeff Ross harvesting field peas. ABOVE RIGHT: Heirloom beans from the garden (*from top*): Rose Bean, Cherokee Turkey Eye, and Georgia Millhouse Butterbean.

an Appalachian folksong. The gardener's unflinching fidelity to his straw hat and well-worn brogues, to his light blue chambray shirt and overalls, also contributes to the sense that he just might be too good to be true.

But anyone who has accompanied the master gardener and his constant shadow, a fourteen-year-old Manchester terrier named Nicholas, through the garden in June knows that John Coykendall is the real thing.

At sixty-five, Mr. Coykendall is a sturdy man with a ruddy face and hardworking hands. But his reaction to the sight of the yellow flowers opening on the pale young zucchini plants and to the widening leaves on his sweet and hot chili pepper plants makes him look like a little boy. His blue eyes widen. He smiles large; "I must look like a mule

with a mouthful of briars," he says as he lopes from row to row, registering the garden's changes.

Every one of the 110 varieties of vegetables that he and his staff nurture at Blackberry Farm tells a tale, and Mr. Coykendall is happy to serve as translator. But early in the morning there are tomatoes to be staked, lettuce and green onions to be picked, and weeds to be weeded. A morning with Mr. Coykendall shows two things that a farmer must have in order to keep at it: an absolute belief that next year will be better and an endless capacity for wonder.

"I'd like to tell you that I came by it all by birth. I'd like to tell you that I was born up there, up on top of one of those hills that's too steep for a mule to plow," he says, "but I wasn't. I was born in Knoxville and there was no farming

in my family. My grandfather was a congressman, John Jennings, Jr. My father was a banker, my mother taught school. For reasons that nobody understood, I was born to farm. Maybe I'm some sort of throwback. I always dug around in the dirt."

When other kids spent summers at summer camp, Mr. Coykendall's parents allowed him to head for the hills southeast of Knoxville. He helped the old mountain farmers plow and plant, hoe and thresh, and when the shadows grew long across the fields they invited him back for a plate of whatever their wives were fixing on the wood-fired stove. And later, sitting on the front porch as a Mason jar of moonshine was passed from rocker to creaking rocker, he listened to the mountain people's stories.

"They were seventy, eighty, ninety years old," he says. "Their isolation had preserved their culture. Up in those mountains, it was still the early nineteenth century. They spoke Elizabethan English, they grew their own food, made their own bacon, distilled their own booze, and concocted their own medicines. They dried corn and crushed it for flour. They dried beans in the shell and stitched them together to make 'leather britches' that they cooked—dried shell and bean together—deep in the winter when the wind blew through the corn crib. They knew people who had fought in the Civil War."

The stories were as singular as the beans were diverse, and Mr. Coykendall started collecting both without really knowing why. Today he tells students and other seed-savers:

"If you collect a bunch of beans and you don't find out where they came from or who grew them or what they were used for or why somebody loved them, then all you have is a bunch of beans."

But back when he was a strapping teenager, still blond and not yet attached to overalls, the beans and their tales were more like trophies. He stored them in glass jars, and in the winter, when the mountain roads were impassable, he spent hours staring at his collection and hours more drawing them. He'd always been as keen on art as he was on growing things, and he found the dried beans of summer irresistible. They were red and lavender, cream, mottled, frosted, spotted, and filigreed. His beans were oblong or squared or perfectly round; they were as fat as limas and as small as ticks; flat and smooth as little skipping stones, round as BBs.

It was the variety that grabbed Mr. Coykendall, that sense of being part of an ever-expanding world that was never without surprise. "It took ahold of me and it never let go," he says.

When it was time for college, Mr. Coykendall went to the Museum School in Boston, and after graduating, he spent sixteen years teaching graphic arts at the school while working on his own lithographs. "I'm only drawn to work that you can't make a dime doing," he says. "Art and farming." In 1986, he returned to eastern Tennessee.

He bought a farm and raised heirloom vegetables and worked as a landscaper to support his habit. The walls of his home were soon lined with jars of specimens, and the ungainly towers of notes and drawings rose steadily on every flat surface. Seed-saving wasn't noble yet; it was still considered weirder than weird. Among the nation's seed-savers, however, Coykendall was legendary. They called him "John Bean" and "the Michelangelo of Appalachia."

Nevertheless, even after he married his sweetheart, Karen, she refused to move in with him. She said that there wasn't a house big enough for the three of them: herself, her husband, and his bean collection.

So imagine the sense of destiny that filled Karen's hair salon when, in 1999, one of her clients, Kreis Beall, described her son's plan for turning Blackberry Farm back into a working agricultural enterprise. Mrs. Beall was worried that finding a master gardener familiar with indigenous antique vegetables might prove to be impossible.

"Unlikely," admits Mr. Coykendall ten years later, as he stands under a massive persimmon tree and surveys the garden that he and his staff have expanded year after year. His eyes move past the stands of cosmos here and the thatches of Mexican sunflowers there, past the bent-twig trellises and rows of corn, the humps of onion and potato plantings, and come to rest on the freshly dug patch where hazelnut and oak trees, whose roots have been inoculated with Périgord truffle spores, will soon be planted.

"Unlikely," he says, "but not impossible."

A steady stream of callers wander into Coykendall's garden shed throughout the year. During the cool months that begin in November, the period locals describe as "down in the shanks of the year," there is a fire in the cast-iron stove. The workbenches are lined with drying beans and gourds. Bundles of globe amaranth and cockscomb and sumac hang from the rafters. They make the place smell like a drying shed and prompt Mr. Coykendall, who holds court from a rocking chair, to talk about the many uses of the dipper gourd, to give lessons in stringing leather britches, and to nudge his three helpers to start bending twigs and creating winter wreathes from crimson berries, corncobs, deeply red dried peppers, tawny dried okra pods, and golden sheaths of wheat. There is a Christmas tree fashioned from dried okra and decorated with the ribbons that the gardeners have won in past years at the Tennessee Valley Fair. There are endless debates over which varieties

should be planted when it warms—or, as locals say, "come grass."

When the grass returns in late winter, the cozy, spicy smells inside the shed give way to the smell of green things and, in a world that now smells like loose mud and quickening creeks, the chosen seeds are planted.

By mid-July, the dirt in the garden has become hard-packed; inside the shed, John's world is cucumber-moist and cool. The smell of baked earth forms the base note in a cacophony of peppers and herbs and lettuces and tomatoes that are stacked in wooden crates. Sweet tones broadcast from the bundles of large, vivid flowers—old-fashioned zinnias and hollyhocks and Mexican sunflowers that are plunged into buckets full of water. It is the height of the summer and the variety is too profuse and persistent to be ignored, the vegetables so full of themselves that they are in danger of bursting.

Mr. Coykendall's face is a deeper shade of red now, and his overalls have begun their annual fade. He can't imagine a better life than the one he has. When he is asked whether he has gardened this way his whole life, Mr. Coykendall does not miss a beat.

"No," he says, "not yet."

DINNER IN THE GARDEN

Wooden planks resting on sawhorses, checkered tablecloths, buckets of flowers, and nothing but candlelit lanterns to dispel the indigo darkness that creeps down the mountain and rolls across the farm: dinner in the garden is the essence of Blackberry Farm, a deep accord between place and taste.

This is the sort of menu we might serve, a celebration of the midsummer garden. It is designed as a multicourse feast, but we often mix and match the dishes to create fewer courses. When doing this, we increase the recipe for larger serving sizes.

ON WINE *When selecting wine for a menu, we think about the flavors of the dishes and also the mood and feeling of the menu. This meal has an Italian feel, and its flavors demand something that is both fresh and muscular, such as the wines from the central part of that country. One great choice would be Valentini Trebbiano d'Abruzzo to complement this al fresco menu.*

LEMON CUCUMBER SOUP

SERVES 4 GENEROUSLY

Lemon cucumbers are a small, brownish yellow heirloom cucumber we grow in our garden. Their delicate, lemony aroma can be approximated by tossing two regular cucumbers with 1 teaspoon finely grated lemon zest before assembling the soup.

1 TABLESPOON EXTRA-VIRGIN OLIVE OIL

1 VIDALIA OR OTHER SWEET ONION, CHOPPED

2 CLOVES OF GARLIC, CHOPPED

5 LEMON CUCUMBERS, SEEDED AND DICED

1 CUP VEGETABLE STOCK (PAGE 268) OR LOW-SODIUM
   VEGETABLE BROTH

2 CUPS BUTTERMILK

1/3 CUP LIGHTLY PACKED FRESH MINT LEAVES

1 TABLESPOON SHERRY VINEGAR

1/8 TEASPOON CAYENNE PEPPER

1 TEASPOON FINE SEA SALT, PLUS MORE TO TASTE

1/4 TEASPOON FRESHLY GROUND BLACK PEPPER,
   PLUS MORE TO TASTE

FINELY DICED CUCUMBER OR CUCUMBER FLOWERS,
   FOR GARNISH (OPTIONAL)

1   In a large skillet, warm the olive oil over medium-low heat. Add the onion and cook, stirring frequently, for 3 to 5 minutes, until the onion is soft. Add the garlic and cucumbers and cook 1 minute more. Add the vegetable stock and increase the heat to medium-high. Simmer for 5 to 7 minutes, until the vegetables are tender.

2   Remove the skillet from the heat and stir in the buttermilk and mint. Working in batches, transfer the soup to a blender and blend until smooth. Pour through a fine-mesh strainer, pressing on the solids with a spoon to extract as much liquid as possible. Stir in the vinegar, cayenne, 1 teaspoon salt, and 1/4 teaspoon black pepper. Refrigerate until chilled.

3   Ladle the cold soup into bowls and garnish with diced cucumber or cucumber flowers if desired.

PEA SHELL AND CHEESE CURD SALAD

SERVES 4

We always seem to eat the pods when we are shucking sugar peas. Their snap and sweetness is too difficult to resist. Slicing the shells fine and creating recipes from them was the next logical step. In a larger portion, this can be served as a salad course, or even a light lunch.

1/4 CUP PINE NUTS

2 TABLESPOONS GRAPESEED OR VEGETABLE OIL

4 CUPS SUGAR SNAP PEAS

1/2 CUP CHEESE CURDS OR RICOTTA SALATA, CUT INTO
   1/2-INCH CUBES

1/2 CUP THINLY SLICED RADISHES

1/2 CUP LIGHTLY PACKED MINT LEAVES, FINELY CHOPPED

2 TABLESPOONS WHITE BALSAMIC VINEGAR

1 TO 2 TEASPOONS KOSHER SALT

1   Preheat the oven to 350°F. Spread the pine nuts on a baking sheet and toast until golden, 3 to 5 minutes. Meanwhile, pour the oil into a small bowl. Stir the warm nuts into the oil and set aside to cool to room temperature.

2   Bring a small saucepan of salted water to a boil and have ready a bowl of ice water. Add the peas to the boiling water and cook just until they turn bright green, about 1 minute. Use a slotted spoon to transfer the peas to the ice water. When cool, drain the peas and pat them dry. Cut the peas into thin slices on the bias and place them in a large bowl.

3   Add the cheese curds, radishes, mint, vinegar, and the reserved pine nuts and oil to the bowl; toss to coat. If using cheese curds, add 2 teaspoons of salt; if using ricotta salata, use only 1 teaspoon. Serve immediately, or cover and refrigerate for up to 4 hours.

BEET CARPACCIO WITH SUMMER CHANTERELLES AND CHIVES

SERVES 4

The beets in our garden vary in size, shape, and color. We like to use an evenly divided combination of red, white, and yellow beets in this recipe, but a single color can also be used. Try to select beets of similar size for even cooking. Dried chanterelles can be substituted for the fresh, but they have a stronger taste; soak in boiling water until tender, then drain and cook briefly in a little olive oil over medium-high heat.

6 RED, YELLOW, OR WHITE BEETS

1 POUND KOSHER SALT

2 TABLESPOONS VEGETABLE OIL

3 TO 5 CUPS CHANTERELLE MUSHROOMS, WIPED CLEAN AND TRIMMED

¼ CUP GRAPESEED OIL

1½ TABLESPOONS FRESH LEMON JUICE

1 TEASPOON FINE SEA SALT

½ TEASPOON FRESHLY GROUND BLACK PEPPER, PLUS MORE TO TASTE

8 FRESH CHIVES, CUT INTO ¼-INCH SEGMENTS (ABOUT 2 TABLESPOONS)

2 TEASPOONS EXTRA-VIRGIN OLIVE OIL, PLUS MORE FOR DRIZZLING OVER THE SALAD

1   Preheat the oven to 400°F.

2   Remove the greens from the beets and save for another use. Moisten the skin of the beets and place them in a small roasting pan. Cover them completely with the kosher salt, place in the oven, and roast for 35 minutes. Check the beets for doneness by inserting a knife into each; they are done if there is hardly any resistance. If they are not done, continue to cook and check again at 5-minute intervals.

3   When the beets are done, remove them from the salt; discard the salt, or save it for roasting potatoes or other root vegetables at another time. Keep the different colors of beets separate so that the colors do not bleed and, using a towel, rub the skins off the beets. (Use a dark-colored kitchen towel to avoid staining.) Set the beets aside to cool completely.

4   Using a mandoline or a very sharp knife, slice the yellow beets and then the red beets, about 1/16 inch thick. Continue to keep the various colors separate and set the beets aside. Cut the white beets into ¼ × ¼ × 2-inch batons. Reserve until ready to serve.

5   Place a large skillet over medium-high heat. Add the vegetable oil and let it heat for a few minutes, until it just starts to smoke a little. Add the mushrooms and cook, stirring occasionally, 6 to 8 minutes, until the mushrooms are browned. Remove from the heat and set aside.

6   In a medium bowl, whisk together the grapeseed oil, lemon juice, ½ teaspoon of the sea salt, and ¼ teaspoon of the pepper. Add the chives and mushrooms and toss to coat. In a small bowl, toss the white beet batons with the olive oil, ¼ teaspoon of the sea salt, and the remaining ¼ teaspoon pepper.

7   To serve, on salad plates, lay the yellow and red beet rounds in circles, overlapping them and alternating colors. Place a small pile of white beet batons on top. Drizzle with additional olive oil and sprinkle with the remaining ¼ teaspoon salt. Serve immediately.

OIL-POACHED SALMON WITH RADISH SALAD AND PARSLEY COULIS

SERVES 4

The rivers, streams, and lakes of the foothills may be thick with trout, pike, and walleye, but salmon is a stranger to these parts. The fine, rich fish is one of the few nonlocal ingredients that we serve. We figure that we can fly ourselves to the fish, or we can fly the fish to us. The second option, which involves flying many fish to many people, leaves, clearly, a worthier carbon footprint.

FOR THE SALMON

1 CUP KOSHER SALT

1 TABLESPOON FRESH THYME LEAVES

1 TEASPOON WHOLE WHITE PEPPERCORNS

4 5-OUNCE SKINLESS WILD SALMON FILLETS

4 CUPS MILD OLIVE OIL (NEED NOT BE EXTRA-VIRGIN)

4 CUPS GRAPESEED OR VEGETABLE OIL

FOR THE PARSLEY COULIS

2 CUPS LIGHTLY PACKED FRESH FLAT-LEAF PARSLEY LEAVES

1/4 TEASPOON FINE SEA SALT

FOR THE RADISH SALAD

20 RADISHES, TRIMMED

2 TABLESPOONS GRAPESEED OR VEGETABLE OIL

1 1/2 TEASPOONS FRESH LEMON JUICE

1 TEASPOON KOSHER SALT

1/4 TEASPOON FRESHLY GROUND BLACK PEPPER

1   To make the salmon, in a medium saucepan, bring the salt, 4 cups water, thyme, and peppercorns to a boil over high heat, stirring to dissolve the salt. Pour into a large bowl and stir in 2 cups ice cubes to cool and dilute the salt brine. Lay the salmon in the brine and let soak for 15 minutes. Remove the salmon, pat it dry with paper towels, and set it aside. Discard the brine.

2   In a heavy saucepan large enough to hold the oil but just large enough that the fillets are in a single layer, heat the olive oil and grapeseed oil over medium heat until they reach a temperature of 160°F on a deep-fry thermometer, or until the surface begins to simmer and a pinch of flour dropped into the oil floats. Adjust the heat to maintain a steady 160°F for 5 minutes. Submerge the fillets in the oil. Continue to adjust the heat as needed to keep the oil as close to 160°F as possible. Poach the salmon for 10 minutes, until it is warmed through but still pink and glossy in the middle. (An instant-read thermometer inserted into the center of each piece should read 145°F.) Use a slotted spatula to gently remove the salmon from the oil and set aside on a plate.

3   To make the parsley coulis, bring a large pot of salted water to a boil. Have ready a bowl of ice water. Add the parsley leaves to the boiling water and cook for 7 to 8 minutes, until the leaves are so soft they dissolve if rubbed between your fingers. Strain the leaves and place in the ice water to cool. Strain the leaves again, place in a blender with the salt and 1 tablespoon water, and purée. Add a little more water if needed. Cover and refrigerate until ready to serve.

4   Twenty minutes before serving, make the radish salad. Combine equal amounts of water and ice in a large bowl. Using a mandoline or a very sharp knife, slice the radishes paper thin; place in the ice water and let sit for 15 minutes. Drain the radishes and whirl them in a salad spinner or pat between paper towels to remove all the water. In a large bowl, whisk together the grapeseed oil and lemon juice. Add the radishes and toss to coat. Toss again with the salt and pepper.

5   When ready to serve, spread 2 tablespoons of parsley coulis in a small pool in the center of each serving plate. Top with a piece of salmon. Spoon the radish salad alongside the salmon and serve.

BLACKBERRY COBBLER

SERVES 8

By late June, the blackberries on the farm have arrived at their peak. The berries here are half the size of commercially grown berries; and they are purple-black and juicy, with tiny seeds and crisp skin, which makes them stand up well in desserts such as cobblers. We like making the biscuit-dough version of cobbler; it allows us to use more berries and the dough soaks up more berry juice than other pastry does. We like using a cast-iron skillet, but this cobbler can also be made in any oven-proof dish. Serve with vanilla ice cream or whipped cream.

8 CUPS FRESH BLACKBERRIES

1¼ CUPS SUGAR

ZEST AND JUICE OF ½ LIME

1 TABLESPOON CORNSTARCH

1¼ CUPS ALL-PURPOSE FLOUR

1¼ TEASPOONS BAKING POWDER

¼ TEASPOON BAKING SODA

⅛ TEASPOON FINE SEA SALT

6 TABLESPOONS (¾ STICK) UNSALTED BUTTER, CUT INTO SMALL CUBES AND CHILLED

¼ CUP BUTTERMILK

1   Preheat the oven to 350°F.

2   In a large bowl, toss together the blackberries, 1 cup of the sugar, and the lime zest. In a small bowl, whisk together the lime juice and the cornstarch until smooth. Drizzle the lime juice mixture over the blackberry mixture and toss to combine. Scrape the blackberry mixture into a 10-inch cast-iron skillet and set aside.

3   In a medium bowl, whisk together the flour, baking powder, baking soda, salt, and the remaining ¼ cup sugar. Use your fingertips to rub the butter into the flour mixture until it is the texture of coarse meal. Make a well in the center of the dry ingredients. Pour the buttermilk into the well and stir with a fork until the mixture comes together. Crumble the dough evenly over the top of the blackberry mixture.

4   Bake the cobbler for 40 minutes, or until the blackberry filling is bubbling and the topping is golden brown. Let the cobbler rest for 10 minutes before serving.

SAM ON SMOKE

I'VE BEEN FASCINATED BY SMOKE SINCE I COULD WALK. MY FATHER IS AN EXCELLENT COOK, AND IN THE SUMMER, WHEN MOST FAMILY GATHERINGS CENTERED AROUND OUR STONE CHIMNEY GRILL, MY FATHER WAS KING. I LOVED WATCHING HIM ADD WOOD TO THE PIT UNDER THE GRILL, AND I WAS MESMERIZED BY THE WAY THE

wood flamed, glowed, and turned white. When I was fourteen, I spent a summer working in a restaurant where ribs were a signature item and I took a special interest in cooking them. My interest may have been sparked by the fact that ribs were the easiest thing on the menu to cook. But the fact that we cooked them over a fire figured in my need to be the number one rib man in Blount County. It also launched me on a quest to master smoke.

Cooking over a wood fire is almost a sacrament below the Mason-Dixon Line. The particulars are intensely debated. I've heard people argue types of wood, cuts of meat, varieties of seasoning, and the finer points of the cooking vessel as if there is only one way and as if the fate of one's mortal soul rested on making that choice. But these issues pale next to the importance of smoke.

It may be cool or hot, fast or slow, it may give a subtle wood character to food or become overwhelming and pervasive. Every ingredient and every person has different needs in smoke. Smoke connects one region's barbecue to another, one man's shiny, hooded grill to another guy's old charred pig cooker. Tennessee doesn't have a sole barbecue style. The state is a repository of several barbecue philosophies, and smoke serves as the common thread.

The earliest barbecues in our part of the world must have been Cherokee, a fire in a pit banked by river rock, topped with a large joint of meat, and buried, to save the heat. Later came wood-fired clay ovens, brick ovens, fireplaces, and smokehouses, each offering a different intensity of smoke.

Of course, not many grills or ovens in a restaurant can compete with wood fires in the great outdoors. I started experimenting with smoke in covered grills and by the time I was in high school, I had progressed to balancing the air and heat in an old stone chimney grill in the backyard of the bunkhouse at Blackberry Farm. It comes down to

this simple fact: the more smoke there is and the longer an ingredient is surrounded by it, the heavier the smoky taste will be. There is an art to regulating the mix of smoke and air in a cooker.

For me, mastering that touch required many steaks and pork butts, many spare ribs and short ribs, many legs of lamb. The pig cooker that I had fabricated by a welder on the other side of the mountain is built to go from 0 to 800 degrees F in a few minutes and it gives a great sear or initial crisping to food. Then, when the heat is dropped to a temperature of 200 to 250 degrees, it creates a gentle and enveloping heat—this temperature is crucial—that allows layers of smoky flavor to build in the meat. The kettle grills we have outside the kitchen door, designed to sear and smoke quickly, work best for small cuts of meat. The Kamado, a clay and ceramic tandoori-style cooker from India, maintains heat for hours after it is fired and a simple adjustment to the damper regulates its intensity.

I have so many types of wood cookers at the farm that we joke about "the smoke of the day." But each is like a child, each is a different character, each presents a different challenge.

At least once a summer, we build a pit down by the creek, line it with river rock, build a fire, make a spit from green wood, and go primal with a suckling pig. A pit gives an earthy, highly nuanced smoke. I like a more delicate smoke than many. But then, I'm using the best ingredients, not the lesser cuts of meat that were traditional, cuts that needed to be cooked forever and just had to have a strong smoke.

Every few years there is some "new" barbecue trend. But the truth is, there are no secrets to barbecue and there is nothing new about it. Barbecue is, as my father says, as old as smoke. It's about love and patience and the sort of knowledge you can only get from experience.

BARBECUE: PURE AND SIMPLE

Traditionally, *barbecue* was a noun, the name of something to eat, preferably with baked beans and onion rings and coleslaw. These days, the word *barbecue* is being used as a verb and refers to an activity that occurs on a grill in the backyard. Well, that just isn't right. Following is one of our favorite menus for barbecue, the noun. In addition to peach-glazed barbecued baby back ribs and the sides we love, we've also included recipes for some of the other sauces we like most. The yields vary—we love leftovers—but each can be doubled or cut in half to accommodate the size of the party.

ON WINE ⤙ *The floral and spicy quality in Gewürztraminers from Alsace is a wonderful complement to the sweet-spicy flavors of the baked beans and Peach-Glazed Baby Back Ribs in this menu. A favorite is Zind Humbrecht Clos Windsbuhl because we find it has an intensity that stands up well to bold foods.*

SWEET AND SPICY FOOTHILLS COLESLAW

SERVES 6

For maximum crunch, this zippy variation on classic coleslaw should be made no more than two hours before serving. This also makes a fine companion to fried chicken or burgers.

3 TABLESPOONS DIJON MUSTARD

¼ CUP (PACKED) LIGHT BROWN SUGAR

3 TABLESPOONS MALT VINEGAR

1½ TEASPOONS MUSTARD SEED OIL OR VERY SPICY
   MUSTARD SUCH AS ENGLISH OR GERMAN

1½ TEASPOONS KOSHER SALT, PLUS MORE TO TASTE

¼ TEASPOON FRESHLY GROUND BLACK PEPPER,
   PLUS MORE TO TASTE

1 CUP MAYONNAISE

3 CUPS THINLY SLICED RED CABBAGE

3 CUPS THINLY SLICED GREEN CABBAGE

1½ CUPS SHREDDED CARROTS

¾ CUP SHREDDED RED ONION

1   In a large bowl, whisk together the Dijon mustard, brown sugar, malt vinegar, mustard seed oil, 1½ teaspoons salt, and ¼ teaspoon pepper, whisking until the sugar dissolves. Whisk in the mayonnaise.

2   Add the red and green cabbages, carrots, and onion and toss until the vegetables are coated. Cover and refrigerate for 30 minutes.

3   Strain the coleslaw. Taste and season the coleslaw with more salt or pepper if desired.

OPPOSITE, LEFT: Sandy digs into barbecue.

SAM BEALL'S BAKED BEANS

SERVES UP TO 12

This dish relies on fresh shucked or recently dried beans—and the difference shows. After assembling the pot of beans, we like to cover it loosely with foil and put it in the smoker or cooker or grill, which adds a smoky flavor that can't be matched on the stovetop.

1 POUND RECENTLY DRIED (OR FRESH SHUCKED)
   PINTO BEANS

1 HAM HOCK

1 TABLESPOON VEGETABLE OIL

1 MEDIUM WHITE ONION, DICED

2 CLOVES OF GARLIC, MINCED

1½ TEASPOONS MUSTARD SEED

1 TEASPOON DRY MUSTARD

1 TEASPOON GROUND GINGER

½ TEASPOON FRESHLY GROUND BLACK PEPPER

3 CUPS COLD WATER

¾ CUP HONEY

2 TEASPOONS MALT VINEGAR

1   Place the beans in a large bowl, add enough water to cover them by about 3 inches, and soak overnight.

2   Four hours prior to serving, place the ham hock in a tall pot of cold water and simmer for ½ hour, until the meat is tender. Drain and cut the meat into bite-sized pieces. Drain and rinse the beans and place them in a large bowl with the ham. Preheat the oven to 250°F.

3   In a large skillet, heat the oil over medium-low heat. Add the onion and cook, stirring occasionally, about 10 minutes, until softened. Add the garlic and cook for 2 more minutes, then add the mustard seed, dry mustard, ginger, and pepper and cook for 5 more minutes to allow the flavors to bloom.

4   Scrape the mixture into the bowl with the beans and stir in the water and honey. Transfer to a 9 × 13-inch baking dish or other large casserole, cover with foil, and bake for 4½ to 5 hours, until the beans are tender. Remove from the oven and stir in the vinegar. Serve warm.

MR. FEATHERS'S ONION RINGS

SERVES 4 TO 6

Josh Feathers, a cook here at the farm, grew up hunting, fishing, and cooking in the backcountry of northeastern Tennessee, and he is a fierce guardian of the state's traditional mountain cooking. He calls his home state "the melting pit" of barbecue. Eastern Tennessee unquestionably favors North Carolina–style, vinegar-based pork barbecue, he says, while the western part of the state champions the Texan-style barbecue, which highlights beef brisket or ribs seasoned and slathered with tomato- and coffee-based sauces. According to Mr. Feathers, onion rings are a must with barbecue. His recipe is addictive.

2 LARGE WHITE ONIONS, PEELED AND CUT INTO
  ½-INCH-THICK SLICES

4 CUPS BUTTERMILK

2 CUPS MASA HARINA OR CORN FLOUR

1 CUP ALL-PURPOSE FLOUR

1½ TABLESPOONS OLD BAY SEASONING

½ TEASPOON GARLIC POWDER

1 12-OUNCE BOTTLE LIGHT BEER

1 CUP CLUB SODA

1½ TEASPOONS KOSHER SALT, PLUS MORE FOR SPRINKLING
  ON THE ONION RINGS

½ TEASPOON FRESHLY GROUND BLACK PEPPER

6 CUPS VEGETABLE OIL

1   Separate the onion slices into rings, place them in a large bowl, and add the buttermilk. Let soak at room temperature for 1 hour.

2   To make the batter, in a large, shallow bowl combine the masa harina, flour, Old Bay, and garlic powder. Whisk in the beer, whisking just until combined. Whisk in the club soda, 1½ teaspoons salt, and the pepper. Set aside.

3   Pour the oil into a large cast-iron skillet and heat over high heat until a pinch of flour sprinkled into the oil immediately bubbles (but doesn't spit) and slowly begins to brown, or a deep-fry thermometer registers 350°F.

4   Strain the onion rings into a colander; discard the buttermilk. Place a few handfuls of rings in the batter and stir with a fork to coat them completely. One at a time, pick the rings up with the fork, let excess batter drip back into the bowl, and slide the rings into the oil; add only as many rings as will comfortably fit on the surface of the skillet. Maintain the heat of the oil as close to 350°F as possible and fry the rings, turning them once or twice, until they are crispy and golden brown, about 3 minutes.

5   Remove the onion rings from the oil with a slotted spoon and place on a platter lined with paper towels. Continue battering and cooking until all the rings are fried. Sprinkle them lightly with more salt and serve hot.

SUMMER SQUASH SALAD

SERVES 4

For this simple recipe, wafer-thin slices are key, so use a sharp knife. Because the salt will immediately begin pulling the liquid from the squash, this is best made just before serving.

4 SMALL TO MEDIUM YELLOW SUMMER SQUASH

2 TEASPOONS COARSE SEA SALT, PLUS ½ TEASPOON MORE
  IF NEEDED

Cut the squashes in half lengthwise, and then cut them into ⅛-inch-thick half-moon slices. In a large bowl, toss the squash with 2 teaspoons of the salt. Serve immediately, or cover and refrigerate. If serving after chilling, taste the salad and add the remaining ½ teaspoon of salt if needed.

PEACH-GLAZED BABY BACK RIBS

SERVES 4 TO 8

There are two methods for cooking these ribs. We prefer using a smoker or a kettle grill with a tight-fitting cover and an adjustable vent. If using a kettle grill, you will need to regularly bank the fire with additional fuel in order to maintain a steady temperature. The second method involves long, slow cooking in the oven, which produces fall-from-the-bone ribs, but without the wood-smoke flavor.

Whichever method you choose, here are a few more of our favorite barbecue sauce recipes. They will keep refrigerated for one week or frozen for three months.

1 CUP KOSHER SALT

4 RACKS BABY BACK RIBS (2½ TO 3 POUNDS EACH)

¼ CUP DRY MUSTARD POWDER

½ CUP CHILI POWDER

2 TABLESPOONS GROUND TURMERIC

1 CUP (PACKED) LIGHT BROWN SUGAR

3 TABLESPOONS FINE SEA SALT

1 TABLESPOON GARLIC POWDER

3 CUPS PEACH BARBECUE SAUCE (AT RIGHT)

1   In a large bowl, stir together the kosher salt and 16 cups (1 gallon) water until the salt dissolves. Add the ribs and refrigerate for at least 4 hours or overnight. Remove the ribs, discard the water, and pat the ribs dry with a clean kitchen towel.

2   In a small bowl, combine the mustard powder, chili powder, turmeric, brown sugar, sea salt, and garlic powder. Coat each rack with the rub. Cover and refrigerate for an additional 2 hours.

3   Five hours before dinner, remove the ribs from the refrigerator. If cooking in an outdoor smoker or a lidded grill, prepare the fire, and when all coals are white, place the ribs either inside the smoker or on the grill, close or cover, and cook for 3 to 4 hours. Check occasionally to assure that the temperature of the smoker or lidded grill is about

250°F—warm, but not hot. If cooking the ribs in the oven, preheat the oven to 250°F. Place the ribs on baking sheets that are covered in aluminum foil and cook, turning once, for about 4 hours. The ribs are done when the meat easily pulls away from the bone.

4   Brush the racks generously with the peach sauce and cut into individual ribs. Place the ribs on individual plates or mound on a platter, and serve, passing the remaining sauce on the side.

PEACH BARBECUE SAUCE

MAKES ABOUT 1 QUART

We like this sweet, sour, salty, and hot sauce on pork and chicken.

1 TABLESPOON VEGETABLE OIL

1 VIDALIA OR OTHER SWEET ONION, FINELY CHOPPED

1 JALAPEÑO PEPPER, SEEDED AND FINELY CHOPPED

6 PEACHES, PEELED, PITTED, AND CHOPPED

½ CUP BOURBON

½ CUP CIDER VINEGAR

⅓ CUP HONEY

¼ CUP DIJON MUSTARD

2 TEASPOONS CHILI POWDER

1   In a medium skillet, heat the oil over medium-low heat. Add the onion and jalapeño and cook for 8 to 10 minutes, until the onion is very soft. Increase the heat to medium-high and stir in the peaches, bourbon, vinegar, honey, mustard, and chili powder. Bring to a boil, lower the heat, and simmer, covered, for 10 to 12 minutes, until the peaches are tender.

2   Transfer the mixture into a food processor and process until very smooth. Cool to room temperature before using.

BLACKBERRY BARBECUE SAUCE

MAKES ABOUT 3 CUPS

This sauce, which is great on quail (see page 40), pork, chicken, or duck, burns easily, so it is best brushed on the meat in the final moments of cooking and then generously slathered on just before serving.

2 CUPS BLACKBERRIES

¼ CUP SUGAR

I TABLESPOON UNSALTED BUTTER

½ VIDALIA OR OTHER SWEET ONION, FINELY CHOPPED

2 CLOVES OF GARLIC, FINELY CHOPPED

I JALAPEÑO PEPPER, SEEDED AND FINELY CHOPPED

6 TABLESPOONS TOMATO PASTE

⅔ CUP STRONG BREWED COFFEE

¼ CUP SORGHUM

¼ CUP CIDER VINEGAR

2 TABLESPOONS BALSAMIC VINEGAR

2 TABLESPOONS WORCESTERSHIRE SAUCE

I½ TEASPOONS SOY SAUCE

I TABLESPOON CHILI POWDER

1   Place the blackberries, ¼ cup water, and the sugar in a blender and purée. Strain through a fine-mesh strainer into a medium bowl. Press on the solids in the strainer with a wooden spoon to extract as much of the juice and pulp from the blackberries as possible; you should have about ½ cup of purée. Set aside.

2   Place a medium saucepan over medium heat and add the butter. When the butter starts to bubble, add the onion and cook, stirring occasionally, for 10 to 12 minutes, until golden brown. If the onion begins to stick or brown too quickly, add a tablespoon of water.

3   Add the garlic and jalapeño and cook, stirring, for 30 seconds. Add the tomato paste and continue to stir for 2 to 3 minutes more, until the paste turns brick red. Stir in the blackberry purée, coffee, sorghum, cider vinegar, balsamic vinegar, Worcestershire, soy sauce, chili powder, and 2 tablespoons water. Bring the mixture to a boil, lower the heat, and simmer for 30 minutes, stirring occasionally.

4   Strain the sauce through a fine-mesh strainer, pressing down hard with a spoon to extract as much liquid as possible. Discard the solids. Cool to room temperature before serving.

COFFEE BARBECUE SAUCE

MAKES ABOUT I QUART

We love using this bitter, sour, sweet, and piquant sauce to tenderize large cuts of meat; brisket, beef ribs, lamb, and pork are some of our favorites.

3 CUPS STRONG BREWED COFFEE

I½ CUPS BALSAMIC VINEGAR

⅓ CUP SORGHUM OR MOLASSES

¼ CUP WORCESTERSHIRE SAUCE

4 TABLESPOONS (½ STICK) UNSALTED BUTTER

2 TABLESPOONS TOMATO PASTE

4 TEASPOONS DIJON MUSTARD

2½ TEASPOONS HOT SAUCE

I½ TEASPOONS KOSHER SALT

2½ TEASPOONS FRESHLY GROUND BLACK PEPPER

In a large saucepan, combine the coffee, vinegar, sorghum, and Worcestershire. Cook over medium-high heat for 15 to 20 minutes, until the sauce reduces by about two thirds. Stir in the butter, tomato paste, mustard, hot sauce, salt, and pepper and cool to room temperature before using.

A BARBECUE FOR COMPANY

There is an old saying in the South: "Get ten people together and where the Irish will start to fight, the Southerners will start a barbecue." Before we consider the differences between meats, smoke, and sauces, it is important to understand that barbecue, the event, occurs in one of two ways: with paper towels or with nice linen napkins.

The earliest account of a barbecue in America is of an afternoon festivity thrown by George Washington in an outdoor pavilion in the woods to which wagons of china, glassware, and linens were hauled. However, it is barbecue, the paper-towel event, that is central to the Southern sense of self. The linen-napkin barbecue is simply a refined version invented for the convenience of those who prefer to dine on a comfortable chair indoors, preferably with air-conditioning, or fancy a fine wine. And sometimes, we do.

ON WINE *Red wine with Old World subtlety stands up best to this full-flavored quail and with the tomato terrine is a gentle evocation of southern France and northern Italy. For this menu we particularly like wines made with the Dolcetto grape. A favorite producer is Pecchenino.*

HEIRLOOM TOMATO TERRINE

SERVES 8

This terrine should be made at least one and up to three days in advance and kept well chilled until serving. For neat slices, use a sharp knife that has been warmed under running water and then wiped dry.

6 LARGE YELLOW TOMATOES

6 LARGE RED TOMATOES

¼ CUP LIGHTLY PACKED FRESH BASIL LEAVES

2 TABLESPOONS KOSHER SALT

4 ¼-OUNCE PACKETS POWDERED GELATIN

2 CUPS RED AND YELLOW CHERRY TOMATOES

1 TABLESPOON EXTRA-VIRGIN OLIVE OIL

⅛ TEASPOON FRESHLY GROUND BLACK PEPPER

1 To peel the large tomatoes, cut a shallow X through the skin at the top and bottom of each tomato. Bring a large pot of water to a boil and have ready a bowl of ice water. Working with one or two at a time, lower the tomatoes into the boiling water and heat them for 20 seconds at most. Immediately transfer the tomatoes to the ice water, let them cool, and then peel off and discard the skins.

2 Cut each tomato into sixths. With a paring knife, trim away the inner pulp and seeds, leaving shells of tomato flesh that look like petals. Set aside the pulp and seeds in a bowl and place the petals in a single layer on a baking sheet lined with paper towels. Cover the petals with another layer of paper towels and refrigerate overnight.

3 Meanwhile, place the tomato pulp and seeds, basil, and salt in a food processor and process until the mixture is smooth. Line a fine-mesh strainer with cheesecloth and place the strainer over a large bowl with room enough for the liquid to collect in the bowl without touching the bottom of the strainer. Pour the tomato mixture into the strainer and let sit, refrigerated, overnight.

4 The next day, discard the solids in the strainer. Place 2 cups of the collected tomato water in a small saucepan. (Discard the remaining tomato water, or reserve for another use.) Stir the gelatin into the tomato water, let it sit for 2 minutes, and then heat over medium heat, stirring to dissolve the gelatin. Remove the pan from the heat and set it aside.

5 Lightly oil the inside of an 8 × 3-inch (5-cup) terrine mold. Line the mold with plastic wrap, pressing it firmly and smoothly against the insides and letting 3 or 4 inches hang over the top to fold over the terrine after it is filled.

6 Beginning with the yellow tomato petals, dip a petal into the gelatin mixture and place it in the bottom of the mold against one short side. Repeat with enough petals to cover the bottom of the mold, placing each new petal parallel to the one before. If necessary, trim petals to make them fit snugly against the sides of the mold.

7 Repeat with a layer of red tomato petals. Continue making layers, alternating colors, until the mold is filled within ¼ inch of the rim. (If the gelatin in the pan starts to become thick, place the pan over low heat and stir until it liquefies.)

8 Slowly pour gelatin over the assembled terrine, letting it fill in any spaces between the tomato petals; you may have gelatin left over. Fold the plastic wrap over the terrine and lightly press the top to remove any air bubbles that might be trapped inside. Place two 1-pound boxes of butter (or other objects of similar weight and size) on top of the terrine and refrigerate it until set, at least 8 hours or overnight.

9 Just before serving, cut the cherry tomatoes in half, place them in a small bowl, and toss with the olive oil and pepper. To serve, fold the plastic on top of the terrine down and carefully invert it onto a cutting board. Remove and discard the plastic wrap and use a sharp, dry knife to cut the terrine into 1-inch slices. Serve the slices garnished with the cherry tomatoes.

BARBECUED QUAIL WITH BLACK-EYED PEA SALAD

SERVES 4

Cooked fresh field peas or dried pigeon peas can be substituted for the dried black-eyed peas. For tasty and tender peas, make them several days in advance, but do not combine them with the vegetable vinaigrette until thirty minutes prior to serving. Allow them to come to room temperature.

FOR THE SALAD

2¼ CUPS DRIED BLACK-EYED PEAS

3 TABLESPOONS CHAMPAGNE VINEGAR

3 TABLESPOONS MALT VINEGAR

½ CUP EXTRA-VIRGIN OLIVE OIL

¾ TEASPOON CHOPPED FRESH TARRAGON LEAVES

½ TEASPOON MINCED FRESH THYME LEAVES

1¼ TEASPOONS FRESHLY GROUND BLACK PEPPER

1 TEASPOON FINE SEA SALT, PLUS MORE TO TASTE

1 RED BELL PEPPER, CORED, SEEDED, AND DICED

1 GREEN BELL PEPPER, CORED, SEEDED, AND DICED

1 YELLOW BELL PEPPER, CORED, SEEDED, AND DICED

2 SCALLIONS, WHITE AND GREEN PARTS, THINLY SLICED

½ TEASPOON FINELY CHOPPED GARLIC

2 STRIPS OF BACON

6 CUPS CHICKEN STOCK (PAGE 268) OR VEGETABLE STOCK (PAGE 268), OR LOW-SODIUM CHICKEN OR VEGETABLE BROTH

FOR THE QUAIL

4 QUAIL

2 TEASPOONS KOSHER SALT AND FRESHLY GROUND BLACK PEPPER

2 TABLESPOONS VEGETABLE OIL

½ CUP BLACKBERRY BARBECUE SAUCE (PAGE 37)

1 To make the black-eyed pea salad, place the beans in a large bowl, add enough water to cover them by about 3 inches, and soak overnight at room temperature.

2 In a large bowl, whisk together the vinegars, oil, tarragon, thyme, pepper, and ½ teaspoon of the salt. Add the bell peppers, scallions, and garlic and toss. Cover and refrigerate overnight.

3 The next day, drain the peas and place them in a medium pot with the bacon and stock. Bring to a boil, then lower the heat and simmer the peas for 30 minutes, or until tender. Stir in the remaining ½ teaspoon salt. Strain, discard the bacon, and add the peas to the vegetable vinaigrette. Toss to coat and let sit at room temperature for 30 minutes. Taste and add more salt and pepper if desired.

4 To make the quail, preheat the oven to 375°F. Have the quails at room temperature and sprinkle them with the salt.

5 Heat a medium ovenproof skillet over medium-high heat and add the oil. When very hot, add the quail and cook for 1 to 2 minutes per side, until browned. Transfer to the oven and roast for 6 to 8 minutes, until the breast meat is slightly resistant when you poke it with your finger and the juices run clear if the thickest part of the thighs are pricked with the point of a paring knife.

6 Remove the quail from the oven, brush with the barbecue sauce, and let rest for 3 minutes.

7 Place a generous scoop of the pea salad on each of 4 plates. Brush the quail with additional barbecue sauce and place one on top of each serving of salad.

ROASTED PEACH TART

SERVES 6

Using sea salt brings out the tang beneath the deeply floral notes of the caramelized ripe peaches.

FOR THE PASTRY

1¾ CUPS ALL-PURPOSE FLOUR

2 TABLESPOONS SUGAR

¼ TEASPOON FINE SEA SALT

12 TABLESPOONS (1½ STICKS) UNSALTED BUTTER, CUT INTO
   SMALL CUBES AND CHILLED

2 TO 3 TABLESPOONS ICE WATER

FOR THE PEACHES

1 TABLESPOON LIGHT CORN SYRUP OR HONEY

½ CUP SUGAR

½ TEASPOON FINE SEA SALT

1 TABLESPOON UNSALTED BUTTER

1 TABLESPOON HONEY

5 MEDIUM PEACHES, PEELED, HALVED, AND PITTED

1   Preheat the oven to 350°F. Position a rack in the center of the oven.

2   To make the pastry, place the flour, sugar, and salt in a food processor and pulse to combine. Sprinkle the cubes of butter over the flour mixture and pulse until the mixture resembles coarse meal. Add the ice water a tablespoon at a time and pulse until the dough just begins to pull away from the sides of the bowl.

3   Scoop the dough out of the processor, place on a floured surface, and knead a few times, just until the dough is smooth. Pat the dough into a disk, wrap in plastic wrap, and set aside to rest in a cool place for 1 hour. To roll out the dough, lightly flour a rolling pin and the work surface and roll out to a circle 10 inches in diameter. Set aside.

4   To make the peaches, in a 10-inch skillet, stir together the corn syrup and 3 tablespoons water. Sprinkle the sugar evenly over the corn syrup mixture and cook over medium heat without stirring for 11 to 12 minutes, until the sugar melts and turns deep amber in color.

5   Immediately remove the skillet from the heat and stir in the salt, butter, and honey. Arrange the peaches, cut side up, in the hot caramel, positioning them very close together to cover the bottom of the skillet. Place the pastry over the peaches and tuck the edges into the pan with a small spatula or the tip of a knife.

6   Bake in the center of the oven for 35 to 40 minutes, until the pastry is golden brown.

7   Place the skillet on a wire rack to cool for 10 minutes. Cover the top of the skillet with a large dinner plate or round platter a little bigger than the skillet. Protecting your hands with oven mitts, grasp the skillet and plate on both sides and, in one swift motion, invert it and place it on the counter. Carefully lift the skillet off the plate; if any of the peaches stick to the bottom of the skillet, just use a spatula to loosen them and then replace them on the tart. Let the tart cool a few more minutes, just until the caramel firms a bit, then slice and serve warm.

ICED TEA ～ A TALL GLASS OF SWEET TEA WITH A TOUCH OF BRUISED MINT SYMBOLIZES A WAY OF LIVING IN WHICH SHADY WRAPAROUND PORCHES, ROCKING CHAIRS, AND SULTRY, FLOWER-SCENTED AIR FIGURE PROMINENTLY. MANY PARTS OF THAT VISION HAVE FADED, BUT ICED TEA'S PROMISE OF A MOMENT OF EASE AND A SLIGHT COOLING

remain. It's difficult to improve on a classic, so we would never presume to try. These are simply variations on the theme that play different flavor notes—fruity and tart, spicy and sweet—while still providing an oasis of calm.

BLUEBERRY AND APPLE GREEN TEA

MAKES ABOUT 1 GALLON

8 CUPS HOT, FRESHLY BREWED GREEN TEA

3 CUPS BLUEBERRIES

1½ CUPS SUGAR

1 CUP APPLE JUICE

6 CUPS COLD WATER

GREEN APPLE SLICES, FOR GARNISH

1   In a large bowl, combine the hot green tea, blueberries, and sugar, stirring until the sugar is dissolved. Use a potato masher or a muddler to crush the blueberries. Let the mixture steep for about 30 minutes.

2   Strain the liquid through a fine-mesh strainer into a large pitcher, pressing down on the blueberries with a spoon to extract as much juice and pulp as possible. Stir in the apple juice and cold water, and serve over ice, garnished by floating the green apple slices on top or pressing them onto the rim of the glass.

RASPBERRY RED OZ TEA

MAKES ABOUT 1 GALLON

8 CUPS HOT, FRESHLY BREWED RED OZ OR RED ZINGER TEA

8 CUPS RASPBERRIES, PLUS MORE FOR GARNISH

1½ CUPS SUGAR

½ CUP FRESH LIME JUICE

6 CUPS COLD WATER

1   In a large bowl, combine the hot tea, raspberries, and sugar, stirring until the sugar is dissolved. Use a potato masher or a muddler to crush the raspberries. Let the mixture steep for about 30 minutes.

2   Strain the liquid through a fine-mesh strainer into a large pitcher, pressing down on the raspberries with a spoon to extract as much juice and pulp as possible. Stir in the lime juice and cold water, and serve over ice, garnished with whole raspberries.

STRAWBERRY-CITRUS LEMONADE

MAKES ABOUT 3 QUARTS

1 POUND STRAWBERRIES, HULLED AND SLICED (ABOUT 3 CUPS)

1½ CUPS SUGAR

2 CUPS BOILING WATER

1½ CUPS FRESH LEMON JUICE

1 CUP FRESH ORANGE JUICE

½ CUP FRESH LIME JUICE

6 CUPS COLD WATER

1   In a large bowl, combine the strawberries, sugar, and boiling water, stirring until the sugar is dissolved. Use a potato masher or a muddler to crush the strawberries. Let the mixture steep for about 30 minutes.

2   Stir in the lemon juice, orange juice, and lime juice. Strain the liquid through a fine-mesh strainer into a large pitcher, pressing down on the strawberries with a spoon to extract as much juice and pulp as possible. Stir in the cold water and serve over ice.

THE FOURTH OF JULY

Traditionally, small fryer chickens made their annual debut early in July, and we like to honor that tradition by breaking out the five different types of fried chicken in our repertoire. The chicken can be served hot or cold, and the meal can be served at midday or later in the evening before the sky explodes. We also set the table with our spicy coleslaw (see page 33) and the rich potato salad that we adore. For dessert, it's always ice cream sandwiches.

ON WINE ⌐ *Nothing is better than Champagne with fried chicken. The best bottles can complement down-home cooking as well as rarefied foods. In fact, Champagne from small growers and producers such as Jacques Selosse have enough presence and verve to elevate fried chicken, barbecue, even hamburgers.*

GREEN GODDESS POTATO SALAD WITH GARDEN RADISHES

SERVES 6 TO 8

This potato salad was the happy result of a collision of chef, garden, and tradition. It can be made up to four hours before serving and kept well chilled. The dressing is also tasty tossed with a simple salad or served as a dip for vegetable crudités.

6 CUPS (ABOUT 4½ POUNDS) NEW FINGERLING POTATOES, SCRUBBED AND QUARTERED

1 TABLESPOON KOSHER SALT

¾ CUP FRESH SPINACH LEAVES

¼ CUP FRESH TARRAGON LEAVES

¼ CUP FRESH BASIL LEAVES

¼ CUP FRESH FLAT-LEAF PARSLEY LEAVES

¼ CUP CHAMPAGNE VINEGAR

5 SCALLIONS, WHITE AND LIGHT-GREEN PARTS, CHOPPED

1 CUP MAYONNAISE

1½ TEASPOONS FINE SEA SALT, OR TO TASTE

8 SMALL RADISHES, TRIMMED AND SHREDDED

1   Place the potatoes in a medium saucepan and add enough cold water to cover by about 1 inch. Add the kosher salt and bring to a boil. Turn off the heat, cover the pot, and let sit until tender, about 10 minutes. Drain the potatoes, transfer them to a large bowl, and refrigerate until cooled.

2   In a food processor, combine the spinach, tarragon, basil, parsley, and vinegar and process until smooth. Add the scallions and process until smooth. Scrape this mixture into a medium bowl and whisk in the mayonnaise and salt. Cover and refrigerate until needed.

3   Toss the cooled potatoes with the dressing and garnish with the radishes.

FRIED CHICKEN IN TENNESSEE ～ TENNESSEE IS A TWO-TERRAIN STATE AND IT HAS TWO DISTINCT STYLES OF FRIED CHICKEN. IN THE MOUNTAINS OF EASTERN TENNESSEE, COOKS PRACTICE THE UNEMBELLISHED ALCHEMY THAT OCCURS WHEN CHICKEN PIECES ARE DUSTED IN MILDLY SEASONED FLOUR AND PAN-FRIED SLOWLY IN SHALLOW LARD.

Moving west, the land softens into the gentle hills and plains of the Cumberland Plateau and the chicken gets sassier and more "Southern." Cooks add a splash of Tabasco to the milk, powdered habanero to the flour, a dose of cayenne to the frying pan, or a shower of powdered pepper to the chicken before serving to create Tennessee's legendary "hot and spicy" chicken.

Different variations suit different days and occasions and for that reason, in addition to the batter-fried chili-cured chicken recipe, four other versions of fried chicken are served at Blackberry Farm. One is a traditional mountain recipe that was gathered from a local woman who lived, farmed, raised her family, and fried her chicken in the same Smoky Mountain homestead for eight decades. Others are variations on the classic Southern style of fried chicken that were developed by several members of our culinary team. One calls for sage as well as paprika and delivers a woodsy heat, and another uses a sweet tea brine to create the flavor of an endless afternoon of rocking in the shade.

Most cooks at Blackberry Farm have long since deferred to health concerns and rather than frying chicken in lard, they use vegetable, grapeseed, or peanut oil with a tablespoon of bacon fat for flavor. Some cooks at the farm claim that chicken is juicier when batter-fried, others prefer a crispy and more delicate crust. But all agree that only two things are, in fact, essential to the best fried chicken: drumsticks and thighs are more succulent and the best comes from chicken that's been left on the bone.

KREIS'S TENNESSEE FIRE-FRIED CHICKEN

SERVES 8

The heat and spice can be calibrated by varying the amount of Tabasco, paprika, and cayenne. This recipe yields a mildly hot and peppery version. For this recipe, the chicken needs to sit overnight before frying.

1 QUART BUTTERMILK

¼ CUP HOT SAUCE

¼ CUP KOSHER SALT

8 CHICKEN DRUMSTICKS

8 CHICKEN THIGHS

6 CUPS VEGETABLE OIL, LARD, OR BACON GREASE, FOR FRYING

4 CUPS ALL-PURPOSE FLOUR

¼ CUP SWEET PAPRIKA

3 TABLESPOONS FRESHLY GROUND BLACK PEPPER

1 TABLESPOON CAYENNE PEPPER

1   Combine the buttermilk, hot sauce, and salt in a large bowl. Add the drumsticks and thighs, cover the bowl, and refrigerate overnight, turning the chicken occasionally.

2   Place the fat in a large cast-iron skillet and heat over high heat until a pinch of flour sprinkled into the oil immediately bubbles (but doesn't spit) and slowly begins to brown, or a deep-fry thermometer registers 320°F.

3   In a medium bowl, combine the flour, paprika, black pepper, and cayenne. Working in batches, remove the chicken pieces from the buttermilk, coat them in the flour mixture, shake off the excess, and place them in the hot fat, being careful not to overcrowd the skillet.

4   Fry, monitoring the thermometer (if you're using one) and adjusting the heat as necessary to maintain the temperature of the oil; if you're not using a thermometer, look for a vigorous bubbling around each piece. Cook each batch for about 15 minutes, turning once, until the skin is crispy and golden brown all over and the juices run clear when the thickest part of each piece is poked with the tip of a paring knife. (An instant-read thermometer inserted into the thickest part of each piece should register 170°F.)

5   Transfer the chicken pieces to a wire rack to drain; blot them with paper towels. Continue the process until all the chicken is cooked. Cool for a few minutes before serving.

BUTTERMILK-BRINED FRIED CHICKEN WITH SAGE

SERVES 8

Josh Feathers conceived this chicken to make use of one of our favorite products at Blackberry Farm: the buttermilk that our friend Earl Cruze makes from his farm's fresh, full-cream milk. For those who do not live near Cruze Farm, any low-fat buttermilk will work. For this recipe, the chicken needs to sit for forty-eight hours before frying. Serve this hot with all the traditional fixings or cold with coleslaw and potato salad.

FOR THE CHICKEN

1 QUART (4 CUPS) CRUZE FARM BUTTERMILK OR STORE-
   BOUGHT BUTTERMILK

2 TABLESPOONS FINE SEA SALT

4 TEASPOONS HOT SAUCE

4 TEASPOONS WORCESTERSHIRE SAUCE

8 FRESH SAGE LEAVES, THINLY SLICED

8 CHICKEN DRUMSTICKS

8 CHICKEN THIGHS

FOR THE COATING

8 CUPS ALL-PURPOSE FLOUR

2 CUPS FINELY GROUND CORNMEAL

2 TEASPOONS SWEET PAPRIKA

2 TABLESPOONS DRY MUSTARD POWDER

4 TEASPOONS DRIED THYME

6 FRESH SAGE LEAVES, MINCED

2 TABLESPOONS FINE SEA SALT

2 CUPS CRUZE FARM BUTTERMILK OR STORE-BOUGHT
   BUTTERMILK

2 LARGE EGGS

6 CUPS VEGETABLE OIL, FOR FRYING

1 To make the chicken, in a large bowl, whisk together the buttermilk, salt, hot sauce, Worcestershire, sage, and 1½ cups water. Add the chicken pieces, stir to coat, cover the bowl, and refrigerate for 48 hours.

2 Remove the chicken from the liquid and let sit in a large strainer for 10 minutes. Discard the liquid.

3 To make the coating, in a large bowl, combine 4 cups of the all-purpose flour, the cornmeal, paprika, mustard, thyme, and sage. In a second bowl, mix the remaining 4 cups of flour with the salt. And in a third bowl, whisk together the buttermilk and eggs.

4 Dredge each chicken piece first in the flour and salt, then in the buttermilk mixture, and finally in the cornmeal and flour mixture. Transfer the pieces to a rack and let sit for 20 to 30 minutes before frying.

5 Pour the oil into a large cast-iron skillet and heat over high heat until a pinch of flour sprinkled into the oil immediately bubbles (but doesn't spit) and slowly begins to brown, or a deep-fry thermometer registers 325°F. Working in batches, place the chicken pieces in the skillet, being careful not to overcrowd the skillet. Fry, monitoring the thermometer (if you're using one) and adjusting the heat as necessary to maintain the temperature of the oil; if you're not using a thermometer, look for a vigorous bubbling around each piece. Cook each batch for about 15 minutes, turning once, until the skin is crispy and golden brown all over and the juices run clear when the thickest part of each piece is poked with the tip of a paring knife. (An instant-read thermometer inserted into the thickest part of each piece should register 170°F.)

6 Transfer the chicken pieces to a wire rack to drain; blot with paper towels. Cool for a few minutes before serving.

SWEET TEA-BRINED FRIED CHICKEN

SERVES 8

Chef John Fleer spent several years perfecting a recipe that used a Southern favorite, sweetened iced tea, to give a tart note to chicken while also tenderizing the meat. The result may be the best picnic chicken ever. The thick coating stays crisp in boxed lunches or on big buffets, and the meat stays succulent. Double-strength tea is important. To brew it, combine fourteen black tea bags with four cups of boiling water, allow to steep for five minutes, and then remove the bags and cool the tea. For this recipe, the chicken needs to sit for forty-eight hours before frying.

FOR THE CHICKEN

1 QUART (4 CUPS) DOUBLE-STRENGTH BREWED TEA

ZEST OF 1 LEMON

1 CUP SUGAR

½ CUP KOSHER SALT

8 CHICKEN LEG QUARTERS

FOR THE COATING

5 CUPS ALL-PURPOSE FLOUR

2 CUPS FINELY GROUND CORNMEAL

2 TABLESPOONS OLD BAY SEASONING

1 TABLESPOON CHILI POWDER

1 TABLESPOON FINE SEA SALT

1 TEASPOON FRESHLY GROUND BLACK PEPPER

2 CUPS BUTTERMILK

2 LARGE EGGS

6 CUPS VEGETABLE OIL, FOR FRYING

1   To make the chicken, in a large saucepan combine the tea, lemon zest, sugar, and salt. Simmer over medium heat for 2 to 3 minutes, until the salt and sugar are dissolved. Remove from the heat and pour in 4 cups of ice water. Cool completely.

2   Pour the cooled liquid into a large bowl, add the chicken, cover, and refrigerate for 48 hours. Remove the chicken from the brine and let sit in a strainer for 10 minutes.

3   In the meantime, make the coating. In a large bowl, combine 2 cups of the flour, the cornmeal, Old Bay, chili powder, salt, and pepper. In a second bowl, place the remaining 3 cups of flour. In a third bowl, whisk together the buttermilk and eggs. Dredge each piece of chicken in the flour, then dip in the buttermilk mixture, and finally dredge in the cornmeal and flour mixture. Transfer the pieces to a rack and let sit for 20 to 30 minutes before frying.

4   Pour the oil into a large cast-iron skillet and heat over high heat until a pinch of flour sprinkled into the oil immediately bubbles (but doesn't spit) and slowly begins to brown, or a deep-fry thermometer registers 325°F. Working in batches, place the chicken pieces in the skillet, being careful not to overcrowd the skillet. Fry, monitoring the thermometer (if you're using one) and adjusting the heat as necessary to maintain the proper temperature of the oil; if you're not using a thermometer, look for a vigorous bubbling around each piece. Cook each batch for about 15 minutes, turning once, until the skin is crispy and golden brown all over and the juices run clear when the thickest part of each piece is poked with the tip of a paring knife. (An instant-read thermometer inserted into the thickest part of each piece should register 170°F.)

5   Transfer the chicken pieces to a wire rack to drain; blot them with paper towels. Continue the process until all the chicken is cooked. Cool for a few minutes before serving.

SMOKY MOUNTAIN SKILLET-FRIED CHICKEN

SERVES 3 TO 4

This is everybody's grandmother's fried chicken—a classic, unembellished symphony of chicken, flour, hot fat, and a cast-iron skillet. The secret is keeping a steady heat and allowing the chicken to cook until golden on one side and then turning it. This chicken is best served hot with Whipped Mashed Potatoes (page 140).

I WHOLE CHICKEN, CUT INTO 8 PIECES

3 TEASPOONS KOSHER SALT

6 CUPS VEGETABLE OIL, FOR FRYING

¼ CUP BACON FAT

4 CUPS CAKE FLOUR

I CUP ALL-PURPOSE FLOUR

2 TEASPOONS GARLIC POWDER

2 TABLESPOONS DRY MUSTARD POWDER

½ TEASPOON FRESHLY GROUND BLACK PEPPER

1   Place the chicken in a large bowl and toss with 2 teaspoons of the kosher salt. Refrigerate for 30 minutes.

2   Pour the oil into a large cast-iron skillet, add the bacon fat, and heat over high heat until a pinch of flour sprinkled into the oil immediately bubbles (but doesn't spit) and slowly begins to brown, or a deep-fry thermometer registers 325°F.

3   Whisk together the cake flour, all-purpose flour, garlic powder, mustard powder, black pepper, and remaining 1 teaspoon salt.

4   Dredge the chicken pieces in the flour mixture, shaking off the excess, and place in the skillet. Working in batches, fry the chicken, monitoring the thermometer (if you're using one) and adjusting the heat as necessary to maintain the proper temperature of the oil; if you're not using a thermometer, look for a vigorous bubbling around each piece. Cook each batch for 10 to 15 minutes, turning once, until the skin is crispy and golden brown all over and the juices run clear when the thickest part of each piece is poked with the tip of a paring knife. (An instant-read thermometer inserted into the thickest part of each breast should register 160°F and thighs and drumstick should register 170°F.)

5   Transfer the chicken pieces to a wire rack to drain; blot them with paper towels. Continue the process until all the chicken is cooked. Cool for a few minutes before serving.

CHILI-CURED, BATTER-FRIED CHICKEN

SERVES 4

Food historians claim that Tennessee hot-and-spicy fried chicken was created in the 1940s to salve the ravages of boozy all-nighters in the blues and jazz clubs of Memphis and the country music halls in Nashville. This recipe takes the concept a step further. We cure the chicken in cayenne, then bake it in duck fat to create a confit of chicken. We then use a beer batter to help keep the meat juicy and to add a yeasty, sweet flavor that complements the pepper. Duck fat is available in specialty stores as well as from some Web-based mail-order food providers; it can be stored in the freezer. This recipe will make up to twelve pieces of chicken.

I CUP KOSHER SALT

I CUP SUGAR

¼ CUP CAYENNE PEPPER

8 CHICKEN THIGHS

5 CUPS DUCK FAT

2 JALAPEÑO PEPPERS, SLICED IN HALF LENGTHWISE

I TABLESPOON CRUSHED RED PEPPER FLAKES

BEER BATTER (SEE BATTER RECIPE IN MR. FEATHERS'S ONION RINGS, PAGE 34)

I CUP ALL-PURPOSE FLOUR

6 CUPS VEGETABLE OIL, FOR FRYING

1 In a large bowl, combine the salt, sugar, and cayenne. Add the chicken and toss until each piece is coated. Place a wire rack over a baking sheet and place the chicken on the rack. Refrigerate, uncovered, for about 4 hours. Rinse the chicken under cold water and pat the pieces dry with paper towels.

2 Preheat the oven to 250°F.

3 In a saucepan, heat 4 cups of the duck fat over medium heat until hot but not bubbling. Add the jalapeños and red pepper flakes. Place the chicken in a casserole just large enough to hold the pieces in a single layer and pour in the duck fat; if the chicken is not completely submerged in the fat, add the remaining cup. Cover the dish with foil and bake for about 3 hours, until the chicken is very tender but not falling apart. Remove the chicken from the fat and set on a wire rack to drain. Save the duck fat for another use.

4 Prepare the beer batter. Place the flour on a plate. Heat the oil in a large cast-iron skillet over high heat until a pinch of flour sprinkled into the oil immediately bubbles (but doesn't spit) and slowly begins to brown, or a deep-fry thermometer registers 325°F.

5 Dredge the chicken pieces in the flour, shake off excess, and then coat in the beer batter. Place the chicken in the skillet and fry, monitoring the thermometer (if you're using one) and adjusting the heat as necessary to maintain the proper temperature of the oil; if you're not using a thermometer, look for a vigorous bubbling around each piece. Cook the chicken for about 8 minutes, turning once, until the outside is crisp and golden brown (remember, the chicken is already cooked through, so don't overcook it).

6 Transfer the chicken thighs to a rack to drain; blot them with paper towels. Cool for a few minutes before serving.

WHITE CHOCOLATE ICE CREAM SANDWICHES

MAKES 10 TO 12 SANDWICHES

Ice cream sandwiches are great food for a crowd. They can also be prepared ahead of time and kept for up to one month in the freezer.

5 TABLESPOONS UNSALTED BUTTER, SOFTENED

1 CUP (PACKED) LIGHT BROWN SUGAR

2 LARGE EGGS

1¼ TEASPOONS PURE VANILLA EXTRACT

2 CUPS ALL-PURPOSE FLOUR

¾ TEASPOON SALT

1½ CUPS WHITE CHOCOLATE CHIPS

1 CUP MACADAMIA NUTS, CHOPPED

1 QUART TOASTED WHITE CHOCOLATE ICE CREAM
  (AT RIGHT)

1   Preheat the oven to 375°F; grease 2 baking sheets.

2   In the bowl of an electric mixer, cream together the butter and brown sugar until light and fluffy. Beat in the eggs and vanilla. Add the flour and salt and mix on low speed until just incorporated. Fold in the chocolate chips and nuts.

3   By rounded tablespoons or using a 1-ounce ice cream scoop, drop the cookie dough onto the baking sheets. Bake for 10 to 12 minutes, until they are golden brown around the edges and puffed in the middle.

4   Remove the cookies from the oven and let them cool on the pans. Set aside for sandwiching later; the cookies can be stored in an airtight container for 1 to 2 days.

5   To assemble the sandwiches, place half of the cookies flat side up on a baking sheet. Remove well-frozen ice cream from the quart container in one piece, then, using a knife, slice into ½-inch-thick slices, trimming if necessary to fit on the cookie. Place the ice cream onto a cookie and top with another cookie, flat side down. Immediately wrap in plastic and place in the freezer. Allow the sandwiches to freeze for at least 2 hours before serving.

TOASTED WHITE CHOCOLATE ICE CREAM

MAKES 1 QUART

The higher the grade of white chocolate nibs you use, the better this ice cream will be. Toasting the nibs gives wonderful caramel overtones. We use this ice cream between white chocolate chip cookies to make ice cream sandwiches. It is also wonderful on chocolate desserts and even on a full-bodied peach pie.

8 OUNCES WHITE CHOCOLATE, COARSELY CHOPPED

2 CUPS HEAVY CREAM

6 LARGE EGG YOLKS

½ CUP SUGAR

1   Preheat the oven to 375°F.

2   Spread the chopped chocolate on a baking sheet. Bake for 8 to 10 minutes, until the chocolate is golden brown. Set aside.

3   In a medium saucepan, heat the cream over medium-high heat just until it comes to a simmer. Remove it from the heat and set aside.

4   In a large bowl, using an electric mixer on low speed or a wire whisk, beat the yolks and sugar together until the mixture is pale yellow in color. Beating constantly, add the hot cream mixture to the yolk mixture in a slow, steady stream. Scrape the white chocolate into the cream mixture and stir until smooth. Transfer the yolk mixture to the top of a double boiler set over (not in) a pot of simmering water. Cook, stirring with a wooden spoon or heat-proof spatula, for 8 to 10 minutes, until the mixture is thick enough to coat the back of the spoon. Remove from the heat, pour into a clean bowl, cover, and refrigerate until well chilled.

5   Process in an ice cream maker according to the manufacturer's directions. Transfer the ice cream to an airtight container, cover, and freeze until very firm.

TENDER BISCUITS ⌒

THE EARLIEST BISCUITS IN OUR AREA, AS IN MOST OF THE AMERICAN SOUTH, WERE "BEATEN BISCUITS," A COMBINATION OF FLOUR, SALT, LARD, AND WATER THAT WAS "BEATEN" TOGETHER TO MAKE A QUICK, HARD-TACK-LIKE BREAD. IT IS NOT CLEAR WHEN THE LIGHTER AND FLUFFIER BISCUIT MADE ITS DEBUT. MANY BELIEVE,

however, that Southern civilization began at that moment. A fine biscuit is not the sort of thing that one can learn on the run, or from a recipe. "English simply does not have cooking terms with the fine shadings of meaning required here," writes Bill Neal in his book *Biscuits, Spoonbread, and Sweet Potato Pie* (1990). Tender biscuits are the result of a particular touch, and acquiring it demands practice, preferably under the supervision of a woman who can say, "I made my husband biscuits every day for fifty-two years."

The best biscuit is golden brown and just slightly crispy on the outside; inside, it is puffy, flaky, and tender. Baking powder, baking soda, or yeast leaven the combination of flour and lard, butter, or shortening to make the biscuit airier and lighter than anything so rich has a right to be. Part of the lightening depends upon the carbon dioxide that is created when baking powder (an acid) and baking soda (a base) mix it up in the bowl. Like most Southerners, we prefer to use buttermilk (sour and therefore acidic) and adjust the quantity of baking soda accordingly. (In homage to biscuits of bygone days, many people add a touch of lard to the butter or vegetable shortening in their recipe.)

In addition to the leavening process, one must work the dough in such a way that each grain of flour is encased in fat. This means reducing the amount of liquid that makes its way into the flour, which, in turn, activates less gluten. Active gluten creates a heavy biscuit, which, while not an actual felony, could be cause for ridicule, shunning, or divorce. Low-gluten flour is the only choice for biscuits. We use White Lily and believe that no other compares. In addition, we further inhibit gluten development by keeping the flour and the cooking fat cold until mixing time.

These practices serve us well when we make "angel biscuits," a slightly sweeter, yeast-leavened version. Angel biscuits are more challenging to put together, but they are the lightest of all and many people see them as the pinnacle of Southern civilization.

BLACKBERRY FARM BISCUITS

MAKES 1 DOZEN BISCUITS

1¾ CUPS PLUS 2 TABLESPOONS WHITE LILY FLOUR OR
   ALL-PURPOSE FLOUR
¾ TEASPOON FINE SEA SALT
¾ TEASPOON BAKING SODA
¾ TEASPOON CREAM OF TARTAR
¼ CUP SHORTENING
1 CUP BUTTERMILK
4 TABLESPOONS (½ STICK) UNSALTED BUTTER,
   AT ROOM TEMPERATURE
2 TABLESPOONS UNSALTED BUTTER, MELTED

1   Preheat the oven to 400°F. Lightly butter a baking sheet
    and set it aside.

2   In a large bowl, combine the flour, salt, baking soda, and
    cream of tartar. Use your fingertips to rub the shortening
    into the flour mixture until it is the texture of coarse meal.
    Make a well in the center of the dry ingredients, pour in the
    buttermilk, and stir with a fork until the dough comes to-
    gether. Turn the dough out onto a well-floured work surface.
    With floured hands, pat the dough out into a square about
    ¾ inch thick. Spread the soft butter crosswise over the center
    third of the dough. As if you were folding a letter, fold up
    the bottom third of the dough to cover the butter, and fold
    the top third down. Pat the dough out once more into a
    square that is ¾ inch thick and repeat the folding again.

3   Roll or pat the dough out to a thickness of about 1 inch.
    Cut out biscuits with a 2½-inch round cutter dipped in
    flour. Arrange the biscuits with sides touching on the
    prepared baking sheet. Gather the scraps of dough and
    gently press them together, being careful to handle the
    dough as little as possible. Pat into a square that is 1 inch
    thick. Cut out the remaining biscuits and place them with
    sides touching on the baking sheet.

4   Bake for 15 to 20 minutes, until the biscuits are golden
    brown and firm to the touch. Remove from the oven and
    brush the tops with the melted butter. Serve warm or at
    room temperature.

ANGEL BISCUITS

MAKES 2 DOZEN BISCUITS

1 ¼-OUNCE PACKET ACTIVE DRY YEAST
2 TABLESPOONS LUKEWARM WATER (110°F)
2 CUPS CAKE FLOUR
2 CUPS ALL-PURPOSE FLOUR
1 TEASPOON BAKING SODA
2 TEASPOONS BAKING POWDER
1 TABLESPOON FINE SEA SALT
¼ CUP SUGAR
¾ CUP SHORTENING
1½ CUPS BUTTERMILK
4 TABLESPOONS (½ STICK) UNSALTED BUTTER, MELTED

1   In a small bowl, stir together the yeast and warm water and
    set it aside for 10 minutes, until the mixture is foamy.

2   In a large bowl, whisk together the cake flour, all-purpose
    flour, baking soda, baking powder, salt, and sugar. Use your
    fingertips to rub the shortening into the flour mixture until
    there are no pieces larger than peas. Add the yeast mixture
    and the buttermilk, stirring just until the dough comes
    together. Turn the dough out onto a lightly floured surface
    and gently knead for 5 or 6 turns; the dough should be soft
    and moist. Place the dough in a clean bowl, cover with plastic
    wrap, and refrigerate for at least 8 hours and up to 2 days.

3   Turn the chilled dough out onto a lightly floured surface
    and gently knead 5 or 6 times. With a floured rolling pin,
    roll the dough out to a circle about ½ inch thick. Use a
    2½-inch round cutter dipped in flour to cut out as many
    biscuits as possible. Arrange the biscuits with their sides
    touching on a buttered baking sheet. Gather the dough
    scraps, knead them 3 times, and roll the dough out again.
    Cut out as many more biscuits as possible. Cover the biscuits
    with a damp kitchen towel and let them rise in a warm place
    for 1 to 1½ hours, until the biscuits have doubled in height.

4   Preheat the oven to 425°F. Bake the biscuits for 15 to 20
    minutes, until the tops are golden brown. Remove from the
    oven, brush the tops of the biscuits with melted butter, and
    serve warm.

Wild blackberries have scattered the hillsides of the farm for more than a century, giving inspiration for its name in the 1930s as well as an embarrassment of riches in blackberry jam, tea, tarts, muffins, shortcakes, and even barbecue sauce. As the berries ripen on the branch from red to blue-black, their color is reminiscent of the folk art flags and even some of the traditional Appalachian quilts that decorate the trees and rail fences around the fourth of July.

FIRST CORN SUPPER

Corn is central to Southern cooking. We use it most often dried and milled—as flour, grits, cornmeal—and most often in the cooler months. But every year, when the first edible ears begin appearing on the stalks, corn mania takes hold of the kitchen. We can't help using the small, milky nubs in as many ways as possible. For this menu, we start with a chilled corn soup garnished with a garlic custard, and follow it with a chili-rubbed rib roast, grill-roasted potatoes, and fried okra. Peach shortcake rounds out the meal.

ON WINE ⟞ *The bold flavor of a fire-roasted rib roast demands a wine that is refined without being tame. We'd choose a wine from the Priorat, a region in northeastern Spain. Elegant and rich, these wines have enough fruit to play off of the spicy seasoning as well as the richness of the meat. Alvaro Palacios offers some great choices, and who wouldn't love L'Ermita ($800!)—but, happily, Palacios has a great variety of reasonably priced wines, as well.*

CHILLED CORN SOUP WITH GARLIC CUSTARD

SERVES 4

We combine a mild corn broth with oven-roasted corn kernels that impart a toasty, caramel flavor. We like this soup so much that we've been known to add chopped cooked shrimp or cold meat to turn it into a meal.

FOR THE SOUP

8 EARS SWEET CORN

2 TABLESPOONS UNSALTED BUTTER

I ONION, CHOPPED

4 LARGE CLOVES OF GARLIC, CHOPPED

I2 SPRIGS OF FRESH THYME

3½ TEASPOONS KOSHER SALT

¼ TEASPOON FRESHLY GROUND BLACK PEPPER,
   PLUS MORE FOR GARNISH

2 TABLESPOONS FRESH LEMON JUICE

FOR THE GARLIC CUSTARD

I½ TEASPOONS UNSALTED BUTTER

2 LARGE CLOVES OF GARLIC, CHOPPED

I CUP HEAVY CREAM

½ TEASPOON KOSHER SALT

I LARGE EGG

I LARGE EGG YOLK

I½ TEASPOONS MINCED FRESH CHIVES

1   To make the soup, preheat the oven to 350°F.

2   Cut the corn kernels from the cobs. Reserve the cobs. Put the butter in a roasting pan and place it in the oven for 3 minutes, or until the butter is melted. Remove from the oven and stir in the corn kernels, onion, and garlic, spreading the mixture evenly over the bottom of the pan. Roast for about 1 hour, until the onion is soft and the kernels around the edges of the pan begin to turn golden brown.

3   Meanwhile, in a large pot, combine the reserved corn cobs, 12 cups water, and the thyme. Bring to a boil over high heat. Reduce the heat to medium and simmer for 1 hour. Remove and discard the cobs. Strain the corn stock into a large bowl.

4   Working in batches, purée 8 cups of the corn stock and the roasted corn mixture in a blender. Strain into a large bowl. Stir in the salt and the ¼ teaspoon pepper. Cover and refrigerate until well chilled.

5   To make the custard, preheat the oven to 300°F. Lightly grease four 4-ounce ramekins. Place the ramekins inside a baking dish and set aside.

6   In a small saucepan, melt the butter over low heat. Add the garlic and cook, stirring often, for about 1 minute, until softened and fragrant. Stir in the cream and salt. Increase the heat to medium and bring the cream mixture just to a simmer. Remove from the heat and let sit for 5 minutes. Strain into a small bowl and set aside.

7   In a large bowl, whisk together the egg, yolk, and chives. Whisking constantly, add the warm cream mixture to the yolk mixture in a slow, steady stream.

8   Divide the egg mixture among the prepared ramekins. Pour enough hot water into the baking dish to come halfway up the sides of the ramekins. Bake for 15 minutes, carefully rotate the baking dish 180 degrees, and bake for another 15 minutes, or until the custards are set and a thin knife inserted into the center comes out clean. Let the ramekins sit in the water bath for 10 minutes. To turn out the custards, run a thin knife around the inside edge, and invert in the center of 4 shallow serving bowls or soup plates.

10 Stir the lemon juice into the soup. Ladle the chilled soup around the custards. Garnish with a small pinch of ground pepper and serve.

GRILLED CHILI-RUBBED RIB ROAST

SERVES 8

Make sure that the butcher leaves the bones on this roast; they keep the meat succulent while it cooks. This dish sings when served with grilled potatoes topped with crème fraîche and chives.

FOR THE CHILI PASTE
12 DRIED CHILES DE ÁRBOL
12 SERRANO PEPPERS, STEMMED AND SEEDED
12 CLOVES OF GARLIC
2 TEASPOONS GROUND CORIANDER
2 TEASPOONS GROUND CUMIN
¾ CUP EXTRA-VIRGIN OLIVE OIL

FOR THE RIB ROAST
1 5- TO 6-POUND FIRST-CUT STANDING RIB ROAST
(ABOUT 3 RIBS), CHINE BONE REMOVED AND TIED TO THE
BOTTOM OF THE ROAST, AND ALL BUT A THIN LAYER OF
FAT REMOVED
2 TEASPOONS KOSHER SALT
1 TEASPOON FRESHLY GROUND BLACK PEPPER

1   To make the chili paste, place the chiles de árbol in a small bowl, cover with hot tap water, and let sit for about 30 minutes, until pliable and leathery.

2   Drain the chilies, remove and discard the stems and seeds, and place them in a small saucepan along with the serranos, garlic, and half the oil. Bring the chili mixture just to a simmer over medium heat; reduce the heat to low and let cook for about 20 minutes, until the garlic is soft.

3   Transfer the chili mixture to a food processor, add the coriander and cumin, and pulse until puréed. Drizzle in the remaining oil and pulse to form a loose paste. Transfer to a small bowl and set aside to cool. Use within 2 hours, or cover and refrigerate for up to 1 day.

4   Remove the roast from the refrigerator and let it sit at room temperature for 45 minutes.

5   Meanwhile, prepare a grill using natural charcoal. When the coals are very hot, push them to one side of the grill to create a hot zone for direct grilling and a cooler zone for indirect grilling.

6   Sprinkle the roast with the salt and pepper. Using the hot zone of the grill, sear the meat on the bone side for 1 or 2 minutes, until well browned, then turn the meat with tongs and sear it on the narrow sides of the roast for 1 to 2 minutes on each side. Finally, sear the meaty side for about 3 minutes; remember to turn the roast with tongs to avoid piercing the meat and letting the juices escape.

7   Move the roast to the cooler zone of the grill and place it bone side down. Brush the meat with a generous layer of chili paste, reserving up to ¼ cup to use prior to serving. Close the lid and grill for 1 hour 30 minutes to 1 hour 45 minutes, until an instant-read thermometer inserted into the thickest part of the meat, but not touching bone, registers 125°F for rare or about 130°F for medium-rare.

8   Transfer the roast to a cutting board and brush with more chili paste. Let the meat rest for 30 minutes before carving. Serve with the remaining chili paste on the side.

GRILL-ROASTED POTATOES

SERVES 8

Olive oil or butter is always tasty on smoky roasted potatoes, but here the rich, subtle tang of crème fraîche is enough to make you greedy. We generally make twice as many potatoes as we think we might need.

4 POUNDS RED BLISS POTATOES

I CUP CRÈME FRAÎCHE

I TEASPOON KOSHER SALT

¼ TEASPOON FRESHLY GROUND BLACK PEPPER

1   Prepare a grill using natural charcoal. When the coals are very hot, push them to one side of the grill to create a hot zone for direct grilling and a cooler zone for indirect grilling.

2   Place the potatoes on the cooler side of the grill, close the lid, and cook for about I hour, until the potatoes are tender when pierced with the tip of a knife.

3   Transfer the potatoes to a cutting board. Use the side of a large knife or the bottom of a heavy drinking glass to flatten each potato into a disk that is about ¾ inch thick. The skins will split, but the potato should stay intact. Drizzle the crème fraîche over the potatoes, sprinkle with salt and pepper, and serve warm.

SKILLET OKRA

SERVES 8

Traditionally, Southerners have either deep-fried their okra or boiled it until it is soft, but here, we cook it enough to soften the fibrous pods while preserving some of their crunch. It's essential not to stir the okra too much or it will become mushy. This okra dish also makes a fine companion to chicken, ham, or fresh pork and can be prepared well in advance of dinner, covered, and kept in a warm place without losing a bit of its appeal.

5 OUNCES BACON (4 TO 5 STRIPS), CUT INTO ¼-INCH PIECES

I LARGE VIDALIA OR OTHER SWEET ONION, DICED

I POUND OKRA, TRIMMED AND CUT INTO ½-INCH-THICK ROUNDS

1½ TEASPOONS KOSHER SALT

½ TEASPOON FRESHLY GROUND BLACK PEPPER

2 LARGE TOMATOES, CORED, SEEDED, AND CUT INTO ½-INCH PIECES

1   Preheat the oven to 350°F.

2   In a large ovenproof skillet, cook the bacon over medium heat for about 8 minutes, until crispy. Use a slotted spoon to transfer the bacon to a plate lined with paper towels; set aside.

3   Add the onion to the bacon drippings in the skillet and cook, stirring often, until caramelized, about 5 minutes, then remove and set aside along with the bacon.

4   Add the okra to the pan along with the salt and pepper. Transfer the skillet to the oven and bake for 10 to 12 minutes, stirring once gently, until the okra is tender. Add the bacon, onions, and tomatoes in the last 5 minutes of cooking. Serve warm.

SUMMER SQUASH CASSEROLE

SERVES 8

Most Southerners have their own recipe for this quick casse-role that makes use of bumper crops. Sam Beall learned this from his father, Sandy, and, based on availability, he varies the vegetables and the cheese that he uses. Traditionally, squash casserole was served as a side dish to meals of poultry, pork, beef, or trout. But now we are seeing it served as a main course, with or without a bit of meat on the side. It also makes a fine lunch when paired with a green salad or a tomato salad. Although the casserole has the best flavor and texture when served immediately after cooking, it can also be made up to two days ahead. Once cooled, the casserole should be covered with foil and refrigerated. Keep the foil in place when warm-ing the casserole for thirty minutes at 325°F.

4 TABLESPOONS (½ STICK) UNSALTED BUTTER

I SMALL VIDALIA OR OTHER SWEET ONION, FINELY CHOPPED

4 MEDIUM YELLOW SUMMER SQUASH (ABOUT 2 POUNDS
   TOTAL), CUT INTO ¼-INCH-THICK SLICES

¼ CUP GRATED PARMESAN CHEESE

I CUP GRATED MANCHEGO CHEESE

I CUP FRESH BREAD CRUMBS

2 LARGE EGGS, LIGHTLY BEATEN

I TEASPOON KOSHER SALT

½ TEASPOON FRESHLY GROUND BLACK PEPPER

1   Preheat the oven to 375°F. Butter an 8 × 8-inch baking dish and set aside.

2   In a large skillet, melt the butter over medium-high heat. Spoon off 2 tablespoons of the melted butter and set aside. Add the onion to the skillet and cook, stirring often, until softened but not browned, about 5 minutes. Add the squash and stir well. Cover and cook, stirring often, for 7 to 8 minutes, until the squash is tender but not browned. Transfer the squash and onion to a large bowl, let it cool for a few minutes, then stir in the Parmesan, ¼ cup of the Manchego, and ½ cup of the bread crumbs. Stir in the eggs, salt, and pepper. Transfer the squash mixture to the prepared baking dish.

3   In a small bowl, combine the remaining ¼ cup of Manchego and the remaining ½ cup of bread crumbs. Drizzle with the reserved melted butter and toss. Scatter the crumb mixture over the casserole. Bake for 30 minutes, until the top is crisp and golden brown and a knife inserted into the center comes out clean. Serve hot.

PEACH SHORTCAKE

SERVES 8

Fresh spearmint or peppermint can be used in place of hyssop, an herb with a licorice-like flavor. We use the same buttery dough for shortcake as we do for our biscuits, but if the fruit is slightly tart, we add a pinch of sugar to the dough. The biscuits for the shortcake can be made a day ahead of serving and kept in a tightly covered container at room temperature, but we love them best right from the oven. Serve with lightly sweetened whipped cream.

1 RECIPE BLACKBERRY FARM BISCUITS (PAGE 61)

8 LARGE PEACHES (ABOUT 8 OUNCES EACH), PEELED AND PITTED

½ CUP MUSCOVADO SUGAR OR PACKED LIGHT BROWN SUGAR

1 TABLESPOON FRESH LEMON JUICE

6 FRESH HYSSOP OR MINT LEAVES

1   Prepare the biscuits. Fifteen minutes prior to serving, cut the peaches into thin wedges, and halve each wedge crosswise. Place the peaches in a bowl, toss with the sugar and lemon juice, and set aside for 15 minutes, or until the peaches are juicy and a little tender.

2   To serve, split the biscuits, add the hyssop or mint, spoon the peaches over the split biscuit, and top with a generous dollop of whipped cream.

ICE CREAM ∕ EVEN IN THE MOUNTAINS THERE ARE A FEW BLISTERINGLY HOT WEEKS IN THE SUMMER, TIMES WHEN A COOLED BROW IS NOT ENOUGH—ONE WANTS COOL AT THE MARROW. WE MAKE GRANITÉS AND FROZEN FRUIT, SORBETS, FROZEN CREAMS, AND ICE CREAM. NOTHING SOOTHES LIKE ICE CREAM. THE FIRST SHIPMENTS OF ICE BLOCKS

to the South began arriving in the early 1800s, and from the start, frozen drinks and ice cream seemed to be the first order of business. Yankees had beer gardens, we had ice cream gardens. We still seem to have more shady patios dedicated to the delicate art of eating and savoring ice cream than other parts of the country. In addition to the need for cooling, we have so many things to make ice cream from. At Blackberry Farm, we could make a different variety of ice cream every week of summer from the local berries and tree fruit—and we do—still, there is never enough ice cream.

We eat it with pies and crisps and cobblers; with fruit, cookies, shortbread; and all by itself. These are a few of our favorite ice creams, along with several of the sauces that we find difficult, if not impossible, to resist. Also, don't miss the indulgent white chocolate ice cream (page 58) that sings with these sauces and not just in sandwiches.

BUTTERMILK-VANILLA BEAN ICE CREAM

MAKES 1 QUART

This mildly tangy ice cream is wonderful on sweet fruit pies and crisps. Great with cookies—or pressed between two cookies to make an ice cream sandwich—as well as with fruit, fudge, and butterscotch sauces, it is also delicious hugging a piece of layer cake.

1½ CUPS HEAVY CREAM

1 VANILLA BEAN, SPLIT AND SEEDS SCRAPED OUT
    WITH THE TIP OF A KNIFE

8 LARGE EGG YOLKS

½ CUP SUGAR

1 CUP BUTTERMILK

1   Pour the cream into a medium saucepan. Add the vanilla seeds to the cream. Heat the cream mixture over medium-high heat just until it comes to a simmer. Remove it from the heat and set it aside.

2   In a large bowl, using an electric mixer on low speed or a wire whisk, beat the yolks and sugar together until the mixture is pale yellow in color. Beating constantly, add the hot cream mixture to the yolk mixture in a slow, steady stream.

3   Transfer the yolk mixture to the top of a double boiler set over (not in) a pot of simmering water. Cook, stirring constantly with a wooden spoon or heat-proof spatula, for 8 to 10 minutes, until the mixture is thick enough to coat the back of the spoon. Remove from the heat, pour into a clean bowl, cover with plastic wrap, and refrigerate until well chilled.

4   Stir the buttermilk into the chilled cream mixture. Process in an ice cream maker according to the manufacturer's directions. Transfer to an airtight container, cover, and freeze until very firm.

SPICED PECAN ICE CREAM

MAKES I QUART

This ice cream has a special affinity for peach desserts but is also wonderful on pound cake, with cookies, or with butterscotch sauce.

2 CUPS HALF-AND-HALF

I VANILLA BEAN, SPLIT AND SEEDS SCRAPED OUT WITH
   THE TIP OF A KNIFE

6 LARGE EGG YOLKS

¾ CUP GRANULATED SUGAR

¼ CUP (PACKED) LIGHT BROWN SUGAR

¾ TEASPOON KOSHER SALT

⅛ TEASPOON CAYENNE PEPPER

¾ TEASPOON CINNAMON

I LARGE EGG WHITE

I TEASPOON WATER

2 CUPS PECAN HALVES, BROKEN INTO HALVES

1   Pour the half-and-half into a medium saucepan. Add the vanilla seeds to the half-and-half and heat the mixture over medium-high heat just until it comes to a simmer. Remove from the heat and set it aside.

2   In a large bowl, using an electric mixer on low speed or a wire whisk, beat the yolks and ½ cup of the granulated sugar together until the mixture is pale yellow in color. Beating constantly, add the hot half-and-half mixture to the yolk mixture in a slow, steady stream.

3   Transfer the yolk mixture into the top of a double boiler set over (not in) a pot of simmering water. Cook, stirring constantly with a wooden spoon or heat-proof spatula, for 8 to 10 minutes, until the mixture is thick enough to coat the back of the spoon. Remove from the heat, pour into a clean bowl, cover, and refrigerate until well chilled.

4   Meanwhile, preheat the oven to 300°F. Line a baking sheet with a silicone baking mat or parchment paper and set it aside. In a medium bowl, combine the remaining ¼ cup of granulated sugar, the brown sugar, salt, cayenne, and cinnamon. In another medium bowl, beat the egg white until frothy but not stiff and stir in the water. Add the pecans to the egg white and stir to coat. Sprinkle the pecans with the sugar mixture and stir to coat. Spread the pecans on the prepared baking sheet and bake for 22 to 25 minutes, until browned. Immediately pour the nuts onto another baking sheet and set aside to cool to room temperature. Break apart any pecans that have stuck together.

5   Process the chilled yolk mixture in an ice cream maker according to the manufacturer's directions. When the ice cream is nearly frozen, add the pecans. When the pecans are incorporated, transfer the ice cream to an airtight container, cover, and freeze until very firm.

PEACH ICE CREAM

MAKES I QUART

There is a certain magic that happens between a vanilla bean and a really ripe peach. Vanilla extract doesn't give the same, smooth buttery tones. This variation on a Southern classic needs fresh, very ripe peaches. It is delicious on pound cake, peach pie, cake, or cobbler—or all by itself.

2 CUPS HEAVY CREAM

I VANILLA BEAN, SPLIT AND SEEDS SCRAPED OUT WITH
    THE TIP OF A KNIFE

6 LARGE EGG YOLKS

½ CUP PLUS 2 TABLESPOONS SUGAR

2 LARGE PEACHES (ABOUT 8 OUNCES EACH)

1   Pour the cream into a medium saucepan. Add the vanilla seeds to the cream and heat the mixture over medium-high heat just until it comes to a simmer. Remove it from the heat and set it aside.

2   In a large bowl, using an electric mixer on low speed or a wire whisk, beat the yolks and ½ cup of the sugar together until the mixture is pale yellow in color. Beating constantly, add the hot cream mixture to the yolk mixture in a slow, steady stream.

3   Transfer the yolk mixture into the top of a double boiler set over (not in) a pot of simmering water. Cook, stirring constantly with a wooden spoon or heat-proof spatula for 8 to 10 minutes, until the mixture is thick enough to coat the back of the spoon. Remove from the heat, pour into a clean bowl, cover, and refrigerate until well chilled.

4   Process in an ice cream maker according to the manufacturer's directions. When the ice cream is nearly frozen, peel and pit the peaches. Place the peaches in a small bowl and coarsely mash with a potato masher or a fork. Stir in the 2 remaining tablespoons of sugar and set aside for 10 minutes. Add the peaches and the accumulated juice to the ice cream. When the peaches are incorporated, transfer the ice cream to an airtight container, cover, and freeze until very firm.

SPICED FUDGE SAUCE

MAKES ABOUT 4 CUPS

Inspired by the classic Mexican chili pepper and chocolate combination, we used various warm spices to give an edge to our fudge sauce. It's addictive whether on ice cream or on flourless chocolate cakes.

1 CUP SUGAR

⅓ CUP CANE SYRUP

2 CUPS WATER

3 WHOLE CLOVES

½ CINNAMON STICK

⅛ TEASPOON GROUND CAYENNE PEPPER

1 CUP COCOA POWDER

2 OUNCES BITTERSWEET CHOCOLATE, COARSELY CHOPPED

1   In a medium saucepan, combine the sugar, cane syrup, water, cloves, cinnamon, and cayenne. Bring to a boil over high heat. Remove from the heat and let sit for 5 minutes. Strain into a small bowl and set aside.

2   Sift the cocoa powder in a large bowl. Whisk the sugar mixture into the cocoa. Add the chocolate and stir until melted and smooth. Serve warm or cover and refrigerate for up to 1 day. Reheat before serving.

BOURBON BUTTERSCOTCH SAUCE

MAKES ABOUT 2 CUPS

Most Southerners have a weakness for butterscotch as children and bourbon as adults. We combined both to make a sauce that is delicious on vanilla ice cream, peach ice cream, pound cake, chocolate cake—or all by itself.

1 CUP (PACKED) LIGHT BROWN SUGAR

⅓ CUP LIGHT CORN SYRUP

4 TABLESPOONS (½ STICK) UNSALTED BUTTER

3 TABLESPOONS BOURBON

½ CUP HEAVY CREAM

¼ TEASPOON KOSHER SALT

1   In a small heavy saucepan, combine the brown sugar, corn syrup, butter, and 2 tablespoons of the bourbon. Bring to a boil over medium-high heat and cook for 5 to 6 minutes, until the mixture is golden brown.

2   Remove from the heat and slowly stir in the cream. The mixture will bubble vigorously at first. Stir in the salt and the remaining 1 tablespoon of bourbon, stirring until the mixture is very smooth. Serve warm or cover and refrigerate for up to 1 day. Reheat before serving.

OPPOSITE: A peck of peppers: heirloom yellow Romanians and Italian Tollis peppers. **ABOVE:** Master gardeners John Coykendall and Jeff Ross harvesting the garden under the watchful eye of Nicholas the dog.

FALL ～ The Amber Days

First you eat all you can from your garden, then you can what you can't eat. —APPALACHIAN SAYING

In late September the color begins to move down Chilhowee Mountain. The tulip poplars turn chartreuse, the maples conjugate red. The persimmons and sourwoods burst into a startling orange and look like shiny stitches in the crazy quilt that begins on the mountaintop and unfolds, down, down, down toward the garden at Blackberry Farm. At first, the cooler air is the reward we all knew would follow late summer's miasma. Then suddenly, one morning in early October, the air smells like smoke and muscadine grapes and it is fall.

Both cultivated and wild vegetables flare vivid, defiant colors. They know they are doomed and, not long after the first frost, they fade. Mountain people used to call autumn the amber days. Now well past its annual apex, the sun has mellowed. The light is golden, the shadows are more pro-nounced, and the smoky veil that drapes the mountain looks especially blue at dawn.

Scientists know that the light refracted from the hard-wood and evergreen forest gives the moist mountain air its bluish cast. But science rarely offers the satisfying scope that folk wisdom can provide. The Cherokee, for instance, don't think that the mist is something that transforms the mountains; they view the blue vapor as something that the mountains do to transform themselves. *"Jus hunk sti,"* they describe them: "the mountains that smoke."

The western side of the Smoky Mountains has always been its wild side. For the Paleo, Archaic, and Woodland peoples and, finally, the Cherokee, who arrived around 1230, the region was more of a hunting ground than a settlement.

Five centuries later, its first white settlers didn't exactly choose the remote region. Like John Hesse, who built a homestead and barn on the site that became Blackberry Farm, they were given patches of land in return for their service in the American Revolution.

The mountains separated the region from the rest of the nation and kept family farms isolated from one another. But these settlers shared a fate, and they needed to hold things in common. Before long they had developed a discrete dialect, as well as similar farm ways, foodways, and ways of getting by. They needed a barn full of guests for "corn-shuckin's," and they held gatherings first at one farm and

then at another to butcher pork and make sausages, bacon, ham, and scrapple during the "hog killin' days" of late autumn. Yes, the work was arduous and overwhelming. At summer's end there were mountains of corn to be shucked, dried, cracked, parched, turned into hominy, or milled. And, at well over seven hundred pounds, the typical hog was not something that many families could properly dispatch on their own. The people also needed the bond and the intimacy of helping to stock one another's larder for winter. It bolstered their sense of being isolated and forgotten by the world, of being "us," the hardworking innocents, so that the rest of the world could be "them."

The mountains that isolated the region also protected its culture. The quilting and spinning and woodcarving, the fiddling, flute playing, and clog dancing; the canning,

curing, pickling, ham smoking, and moonshining have not yet gone the way of the dinosaurs. Neither has the premium placed on self-reliance. A mountain that determines its own weather and smokes to its own drummer is still greatly esteemed.

The response to the seasons may have outlived its necessity, but there is still an urgency about fall's foraging and harvesting, a sense of grabbing and saving the day. The last gasps of summer—the red, yellow, orange, green, and purple sweet peppers—need to be ushered quickly into a second life as piccalilli, chowchow, catsup, or jelly. The last corn standing needs to be husked, parched, dried, made into hominy, ground into grits, milled into meal and flour—and, of course, distilled into moonshine.

Mason jars full of the fire water begin to appear in a

judge a barn by its clapboard: the larder's interior is all white ceramic tiles and polished stainless steel. Here traditional Southern mountain food preservation meets state-of-the-art technology.

The larder is the apex of three kingdoms—the jam-making world, the land of cheese, and the sovereign state of charcuterie—and each realm has its ruler. All three are former chefs who attended culinary school and have an impressive culinary pedigree. In their twenties, they were all generalists, driven to push past the boundaries of fine cooking to create an *avant*-American cuisine. But in their thirties, after marrying and beginning families, each of them became obsessed with preserving food. The larder at Blackberry Farm is an example of "build it and they will come." In the cave-cold cellar, Michael Sullivan reigns over sausage, bacon, and ham. Upstairs, Kristian Holbrook is one of the deans of cheese making at Blackberry Farm. And, in an adjoining kitchen, Haesel Charlesworth is among the empresses of jam.

Ms. Charlesworth, in fact, presides over anything that can be picked from the garden and put by in a jar. Fall is her time. When the garden exhales one final round of sweet peppers, okra, and corn, when the figs and black walnuts and hard, autumn tree fruit are ripe enough to fall from their branches, the lights in the kitchen burn from early morning to well past midnight.

The wire-mesh shelves are already stacked with jars of blackberry, strawberry, blueberry, raspberry, and peach jam, along with spiced peaches, plum conserves, quince paste, and rosemary and sassafras jellies. There are dilly beans, green-tomato pickles, pickled okra, bread and butter pickles, half sours, dills, piccalilli, and chowchow. This place has enough jars to feed a major metropolitan area.

The jars have silver lids and their contents glow like

shallow bend of Hesse Creek in the fall. No one is sure who stashes them there. Along with the empty rockers that creak on the terrace and the gauzy white nets that billow like ghosts under the persimmon trees, the jars could be apparitions. They give a shivery feeling to October nights.

There is always uncertainty between the ends and beginnings of things. Shepherding the transition offers a certain reassurance, and the result—a well-stocked larder—commands a particular respect.

The white-clapboard larder at Blackberry Farm sits adjacent to the big red barn, on a knoll that overlooks sheep pastures and the dairy. Although freshly painted, it seems like the sort of outbuilding that would have a dirt floor, a veil of cobwebs festooning its Mason jars, and perhaps an old butcher's block with dark nicks and deep valleys. Never

stained-glass windows. But at nine o'clock on an October evening, Ms. Charlesworth still has not finished saving summer and early fall. Wild grape butter is sputtering laconically in her fifty-gallon jam pot and she is considering the apples, crab apples, and pears on her worktable as intently as a post-season pitcher might stare down home plate.

Preserving food, some say, is the art of capturing an ingredient at the moment between not quite ripe and over the hill and keeping it, as one would (if one could) keep the most perfect moment of one's life: in order to return and experience it again and again. Ms. Charlesworth has about as much patience with rose-colored nostalgia as she does with limp green beans.

"Pull-leeeez," she says, her gaze still fixed on the mounds of fall fruit. "Preserving is nothing but a race against rot."

Ms. Charlesworth grew up outside Philadelphia in the Brandywine Valley and studied historical preservation and painting at the Art Institute of Chicago before becoming a pastry chef. Now in her early thirties, she often wears her curly red hair in pigtails that resemble pompoms on either side of her head. She looks a little like Pippi Longstocking. Her current vocation appeals to her sardonic side. "Yes," she said, in her most careful upper-crust accent, "I practice a form of historical preservation, darling, the one that is sealed in pretty glass jars."

Her grandmother taught her how to crochet and make jam—"the things that a well-bred young lady needed to know a hundred years ago." That basic know-how, along

OPPOSITE: Persimmons on a galvanized steel tub.

with her speed in the kitchen, served Ms. Charlesworth well on the first hot summer day that one hundred pounds of wild blackberries appeared on her worktable. But saving the berries is one thing, she discovered; turning them into something that wakes people up and shows them exactly where they are in the world is something else entirely: "That sort of jam generally happens when the jam maker has a couple centuries of jam-making history living in her hands and no other way to make art."

Traditional Appalachian cooks had a genius for putting food by. Vegetables like okra, sweet potato, corn, pumpkin, and beans, and fruits like apple and pear, were cut and air-dried, sundered, or dehydrated over faded coals. Cabbage and potatoes were buried in shallow trenches on a slope. Almost every vegetable was pickled; almost every fruit was made into jelly, jam, or preserves. A cook's jam cupboard was a measure of her worth.

The contrast between the fresh and the preserved, the fatty and the sweet or vinegary is central to the region's cold-weather cooking. After the late-summer rush ends, Ms. Charlesworth spends the winter researching local preservation techniques and studying recipes for the chowchow and piccalilli and cushaw squash butter that were made before the Civil War.

"Those women could make good from *anything*," she said. "They didn't measure, they didn't time, but they never messed up—their hands just *knew*."

People don't need that kind of hands anymore, she added. "They have freezers."

YALLARHAMMER NIGHTS

Set at a bend of Hesse Creek, the Yallarhammer is an open-air pavilion that offers warmth from the huge, stacked-stone fireplace at night. Today a bank of smokers and grills sits out back, a roasting pit in front. Even on the hottest summer nights, a breeze moves through the place, the sound of the creek is a balm, and the residual smoke in the wooden beams and ceilings makes it smell like a rustic cathedral of open-fire cookery.

There is a camp-like spirit to the way we cook and eat: family-style platters of roasted meat, vegetables, and salads appear and, without a particular plan, have become some of the best meals at the farm. We've been known to huddle by the fireplace and smokers well into December. The rustic, harvest-table feel of these meals epitomizes fall at the farm. The menu is designed to mix and match, with leftovers in mind.

ON WINE *This casual dinner set in a "secret" open-air pavilion makes us think of some of the lesser-known wine regions, such as the Roussillon, on the French side of the Pyrenees. The Grenache grape dominates the area and creates an incredibly rich, intense wine. Because these wines are still not widely known, they are also a great value. We are really excited by the modern wine produced by Clos des Fées.*

AUTUMN LAMB ROAST

SERVES 10 TO 12

For this recipe, the meat is brined a day before cooking, which adds flavor and tenderizes it. The initial browning is key: without the contrast of a sturdy exterior crust, the texture of the meat can be slightly rubbery. The Kimchee Collards (page 103), made with arugula, is a good accompaniment to this dish.

FOR THE BRINE

5 APPLES, CUT INTO ½-INCH-THICK SLICES

1 GALLON (16 CUPS) APPLE CIDER

2 CUPS SOY SAUCE

1 CUP APPLE CIDER VINEGAR

4 ONIONS, CHOPPED

½ CUP CHOPPED GARLIC

1 POUND (ABOUT 2¼ CUPS) LIGHT BROWN SUGAR

2 CUPS KOSHER SALT

2 TABLESPOONS GROUND CARDAMOM

2 TABLESPOONS CRACKED BLACK PEPPER

2 QUARTS (8 CUPS) ICE WATER

FOR THE LAMB

1 8-POUND SEMI-BONELESS LEG OF LAMB

1 TABLESPOON KOSHER SALT

1 TEASPOON FRESHLY GROUND BLACK PEPPER

2½ TABLESPOONS VEGETABLE OIL

10 SPRIGS OF FRESH ROSEMARY

1 BUNCH OF FRESH THYME

5 SPRIGS OF FRESH SAGE

1   To make the brine using an outdoor smoker, prepare the smoker and heat to 200°F. Place the apples in the smoker and smoke for about 1 hour.

2   Alternatively, if using a stovetop smoker, soak 1 cup of hickory wood chips in just enough water to cover for 1 hour.

Strain the chips and spread them in the bottom of a roasting pan. Place the pan over medium heat and watch closely until the chips start to smoke, about 5 minutes. Lower the heat to low and place a rack over the chips. Place the apple slices on the rack and cover the pan securely. Regulate the flame in order to keep it steady and low and allow the apples to smoke for 10 to 12 minutes, until slightly softened; remove from the heat and set aside.

3   In a tall stockpot, combine the cider, soy sauce, vinegar, onions, garlic, brown sugar, salt, cardamom, and pepper and bring to a boil over high heat. Add the smoked apples and boil for 5 minutes. Remove from the heat, stir in 2 quarts ice water, and refrigerate until the brine is completely cooled.

4   To brine the lamb, remove the brine from the refrigerator and submerge the leg of lamb in it. Cover and refrigerate for at least 24 hours and up to 36 hours.

5   Preheat the oven to 250°F.

6   Remove the lamb from the brine, pat it dry with paper towels, and sprinkle it all over with the salt and pepper. Heat a large skillet over medium-high heat and add 2 tablespoons of the oil. When hot, place the lamb in the skillet and brown well on all sides, using tongs to turn it.

7   Cover the bottom of a large roasting pan with the rosemary, thyme, and sage and drizzle them with the remaining ½ tablespoon of oil. Place a rack on top of the herbs and put the leg of lamb on the rack. Roast in the middle of the oven for about 2½ hours for medium-rare (an instant-read thermometer inserted into the thickest part of the leg and not touching the bone will register 130°F). Remove from the oven and let rest for 25 to 30 minutes before carving and serving.

WINE-ROASTED DUCKS

SERVES 8

As the weather cools, we start hankering for duck. This is one of our favorite recipes. We've prepared the dish in the oven, but we've also used wood-fired ovens.

I CUP RED WINE, PREFERABLY PINOT NOIR OR GRENACHE

2 TABLESPOONS HONEY

2 4½-POUND DUCKS, NECKS AND WING TIPS REMOVED

2 TABLESPOONS KOSHER SALT

½ TEASPOON FRESHLY GROUND BLACK PEPPER

2 SMALL ORANGES, QUARTERED

2 SMALL ONIONS, QUARTERED

1   Preheat the oven to 450°F. Position a rack in the center of the oven.

2   In a small saucepan, cook the wine over high heat for about 15 minutes, until it reduces to ½ cup. Stir in the honey and set aside.

3   Sprinkle the ducks inside and out with the salt and pepper. Place 1 orange and 1 onion inside each duck. Cut a small slit in the skin above the legs on each duck. Crisscross the legs and tuck the ends through the slits on the oppostite leg to hold them together.

4   Place the ducks in a large roasting pan and roast in the center of the oven for 30 minutes. Reduce the oven temperature to 250°F. Baste the ducks with the red wine mixture and roast them for another 25 minutes. Baste the ducks again and roast them, until the juices that run out of the cavities of the ducks are rosy (but not red) if you tilt the ducks with tongs, 15 to 25 additional minutes (thermometer inserted into the thickest part of the breast but not touching bone will read 150°F).

5   Remove the ducks from the oven and preheat the broiler. Broil the ducks for about 10 minutes, until the skin is golden brown. Baste with more of the red wine mixture and pan juices. Transfer the ducks to a cutting board and let them rest for 15 minutes before carving.

ROASTED BELL PEPPER SALAD

SERVES 8

Here, we created a quick, aromatic oil to give another layer of taste to the full-flavored peppers. The results were delicious— and the peppers added a bright note to the table, as well.

I LEMON

⅓ CUP EXTRA-VIRGIN OLIVE OIL

2 TEASPOONS MARJORAM LEAVES

12 RED BELL PEPPERS

12 YELLOW BELL PEPPERS

1½ TEASPOONS KOSHER SALT

1   Use a vegetable peeler to cut wide strips of peel from the lemon, making sure to take only the yellow zest and no white pith. In a small saucepan, stir together the lemon zest, oil, and marjoram. Cook the oil mixture over medium heat for about 4 minutes, until a few bubbles rise up from the bottom of the pan. Remove the pan from the heat and set aside for 4 hours. Strain into a small bowl. Use the oil within a few hours, or cover and refrigerate for up to 3 days.

2   Preheat the oven to 450°F. Core and seed the peppers, cut them into quarters, and place in a large bowl. Drizzle the peppers with 2 tablespoons of the lemon-marjoram oil and the salt; toss to coat. Divide the peppers between 2 rimmed baking sheets and roast for 25 minutes, or until the peppers are tender and beginning to char on the edges. Transfer to a serving platter, drizzle with the remaining lemon-marjoram oil, and serve warm or at room temperature.

EGGPLANT MOUSSELINE WITH ROASTED TOMATOES

SERVES 8

Indian eggplant, which is small and light purple, is rich but not bitter. If they are unavailable, Japanese eggplants can be substituted.

8 INDIAN OR JAPANESE EGGPLANTS, PEELED AND HALVED LENGTHWISE

4 CLOVES OF GARLIC, PEELED

½ CUP PLUS 3 TABLESPOONS EXTRA-VIRGIN OLIVE OIL

3 TEASPOONS KOSHER SALT, PLUS MORE TO TASTE

½ TEASPOON FRESHLY GROUND BLACK PEPPER, PLUS MORE TO TASTE

10 ROMA TOMATOES, OR ANY STURDY PLUM VARIETY

5 SPRIGS OF FRESH THYME

1 TEASPOON LEMON ZEST

1   Preheat the oven to 325°F.

2   Peel the eggplants, cut into ½-inch chunks, and place in a roasting pan along with the garlic. Add ½ cup of the olive oil and toss to coat. Roast for about 45 minutes, until the eggplant is very tender and golden brown. Add 2 teaspoons of the salt and ¼ teaspoon of the pepper and roast for 15 minutes more.

3   Meanwhile, core the tomatoes and cut them into quarters. Use your fingers to scoop out and discard the seeds from each quarter. Place the tomatoes in a large bowl and toss with 3 tablespoons of the olive oil. Add the leaves from the thyme sprigs, 1 teaspoon of the salt, and ¼ teaspoon of the pepper.

4   Place the tomatoes skin side down on a wire rack set over a rimmed baking sheet and roast for 35 to 45 minutes, until they are very soft but still hold their shape.

5   When the eggplant is tender, use a potato masher to mash it well, ensuring that there are no lumps; taste and adjust seasoning with additional salt and pepper if desired.

6   When the tomatoes are done and still warm, remove and discard their skins.

7   To serve, divide warm mashed eggplant on each of 4 plates and surround with roasted tomato quarters. Garnish with the lemon zest.

SKILLET APPLE CRISP

SERVES 8 TO 10

Cast-iron pans are perfect for making the crisps and pan dowdies of the colder weather. In apple season, we generally use as many different tart varieties as we can find so that nearly every bite tastes just a little bit different. Other times, we've found that any crisp, tart apple will make a satisfying dessert. Granny Smiths are a good choice.

6 GRANNY SMITH APPLES, PEELED, CORED,
 AND CUT INTO ½-INCH PIECES

I VANILLA BEAN, SPLIT AND SEEDS SCRAPED OUT
 WITH THE TIP OF A KNIFE

¾ CUP (PACKED) LIGHT BROWN SUGAR

I TABLESPOON CORNSTARCH

ZEST AND JUICE OF I LEMON

I TEASPOON GROUND CINNAMON

I CUP ALL-PURPOSE FLOUR

I CUP GRANULATED SUGAR

I CUP OLD-FASHIONED ROLLED OATS

½ TEASPOON BAKING SODA

½ TEASPOON FINE SEA SALT

FINELY GRATED ZEST OF I LEMON

I2 TABLESPOONS (I½ STICKS) UNSALTED BUTTER,
 DICED, AT ROOM TEMPERATURE

1 Preheat the oven to 375°F.

2 Place the apples in a large bowl. Add the vanilla seeds, brown sugar, cornstarch, zest and juice of first lemon, and cinnamon to the apples and toss to coat. Transfer the apple mixture to a 10-inch cast-iron skillet and set aside.

3 To make the topping, in a medium bowl, stir together the flour, granulated sugar, oats, baking soda, salt, and zest. Add the butter and use your fingertips to rub the butter into the flour mixture until there are no pieces of butter left larger than small peas. Sprinkle the flour mixture evenly over the apple mixture.

4 Bake for I hour, until the apple filling is bubbling and the topping is golden brown. Serve warm.

COLD-WEATHER GREENS

GREENS, LIKE BACON AND CORN BREAD, ARE MOTHER'S MILK TO MOST SOUTHERNERS. THIS SENTIMENT IS EVEN MORE PRONOUNCED IN THE REGION'S ISOLATED SOUTHERN MOUNTAINS WHERE GREENS WERE, TRADITIONALLY, A TONIC, A MEDICINE, A MEAL, A DAILY MIRACLE. EACH WEATHER HAS ITS PARTICULAR

green. Fall brings the last of the summer chards along with mustard and turnip greens. But kale (especially the leathery varieties) and collards are the biggest treats.

Almost any green can be cooked in the Southern manner—simmered forever, with a bit of water and a ham bone—but at different stages in their lives, each green lends itself to other inventions. Early kale is, for instance, so tender that it can be eaten stem, rib, and all and can be thinly sliced and turned into a salad. It can be quickly sautéed or stir-fried. Young kale is also a real treat when roasted in a hot oven; and the technique works well for midlife kale, as well. After hard frosts, as the leaves of these heartier greens thicken and become

tougher, they are best braised or cooked long and slow. In addition to heat, the other variable in cooking greens is the fat that is used for cooking them. Whenever possible, we cook greens in the fat of the meat with which they will be served. A chicken meal gets greens cooked in chicken fat and lamb gets greens cooked in lamb fat (or a little olive oil). We don't use tallow on the greens we serve with beef; instead, we use butter. For fish, or for very delicate chicken or veal entrees, we tend to use a neutral oil. Naturally, a pork dinner gets greens cooked in bacon fat. In fact, when in doubt, always err on the side of bacon. Bacon loves everything, and just about everything loves bacon.

KALE SALAD WITH BUTTERMILK DRESSING
SERVES 4

This crunchy, tangy salad has a slaw consistency and we love it with grilled meat, barbecue, or even fried chicken. It wilts and softens slowly and is a fine choice for a buffet-style party.

1½ POUNDS YOUNG, TENDER KALE, STEMS DISCARDED AND
    LEAVES SLICED CROSSWISE INTO THIN RIBBONS

½ CUP SOUR CREAM

¼ CUP BUTTERMILK

1 TABLESPOON APPLE CIDER VINEGAR

¼ TEASPOON WORCESTERSHIRE SAUCE

1 TABLESPOON FINELY CHOPPED FRESH CHIVES

½ TEASPOON SUGAR

½ TEASPOON KOSHER SALT

⅛ TEASPOON FRESHLY GROUND BLACK PEPPER

1   Transfer the kale to a large bowl, and set aside.

2   In a small bowl, stir together the sour cream, buttermilk, vinegar, Worcestershire, chives, sugar, salt, and pepper. Pour the sour-cream mixture over the kale and toss to coat.

OVEN-ROASTED KALE
SERVES 4

Quick roasting causes kale to begin to caramelize and crisp. Oven-roasted kale provides a wonderful counterpoint to steamed shellfish and braised meat. We also love to eat it with sliced sausages.

1½ POUNDS KALE, STEMS DISCARDED AND LEAVES TORN
    INTO LARGE PIECES

¼ CUP EXTRA-VIRGIN OLIVE OIL

½ TEASPOON KOSHER SALT

¼ TEASPOON FRESHLY GROUND BLACK PEPPER

1   Preheat the oven to 350°F.

2   Divide the kale leaves between 2 rimmed baking sheets. Drizzle the kale with the oil, toss to coat, and spread it evenly over the pans. Roast for 5 minutes, stir, and roast for about 3 minutes more, until the kale is crisp but not browned. Sprinkle with the salt and pepper and serve warm.

WILTED COLLARD GREENS

SERVES 6

Collards are as great when quickly sautéed—as in this recipe—
as they are when stewed. Young collards with small leaves can
be stemmed and used without additional cutting. Older, larger
collard leaves are best stemmed and then chopped. For the best
texture, collard greens should be sautéed just before serving.

1 TABLESPOON EXTRA-VIRGIN OLIVE OIL

2 POUNDS COLLARD GREENS, TOUGH STEMS DISCARDED,
   LEAVES WELL RINSED

¾ TEASPOON KOSHER SALT

¼ TEASPOON FRESHLY GROUND BLACK PEPPER

In a large skillet, heat the oil over medium-high heat for
1 minute. Begin adding the greens, stirring and adding more to
the skillet as they wilt. Cook, tossing and stirring, until the
greens are warm and slightly softened but still crunchy, about
2 minutes. Season with salt and pepper and serve immediately.

POT LIKKER COLLARDS

SERVES 8

Cold nights call for "pot likker," the flavorful "liquor" that
the leathery greens release when they are cooked slowly—
perfect for sopping up with corn bread. Slow-cooked greens
are a great choice for a crowd or a buffet and team up well
with chicken, beef, pork—or with nothing more than a hunk
of that corn bread.

¼ CUP BACON FAT

2 CUPS FINELY DICED ONION

8 CUPS HAM HOCK STOCK (PAGE 269)

4 POUNDS COLLARD GREENS, STEMS DISCARDED, LEAVES
   CUT INTO 3-INCH PIECES

2 TABLESPOONS CANE SYRUP (AVAILABLE IN GOURMET
   MARKETS AND HEALTH FOOD STORES)

4 TEASPOONS APPLE CIDER VINEGAR

1 TEASPOON KOSHER SALT

1   In a large pot, heat the bacon fat over medium heat. Add the
    onion and cook, stirring often, for about 5 minutes, until
    softened. Stir in the stock, collards, syrup, vinegar, and salt
    and bring to a boil over high heat. Reduce the heat to
    medium-low, cover the pan, and summer for 45 minutes, or
    until the collards are very tender.

2   Remove from the heat and let sit, covered, for 1 hour.
    Reheat over medium heat and serve warm.

KIMCHEE COLLARDS

MAKES ABOUT 4 CUPS

This quick, spicy pickle turns finely sliced collards into a perfect companion for fried chicken or barbecue or rich, full-flavored meat, like lamb or aged beef. The recipe needs to be made three days in advance and allowed to age and will keep up to two weeks in the refrigerator. Arugula can be substituted for the collards.

1 POUND COLLARD GREENS, STEMS DISCARDED AND LEAVES
    CUT INTO ¼-INCH STRIPS

2 TABLESPOONS KOSHER SALT

1 CARROT, PEELED AND CUT INTO THIN STRIPS

4 SMALL RADISHES, SHAVED PAPER THIN

¼ CUP SOY SAUCE

2 TABLESPOONS HONEY

3 TABLESPOONS APPLE CIDER VINEGAR

1 TEASPOON CHOPPED GARLIC

¼ CUP THINLY SLICED WHOLE SCALLIONS

1 JALAPEÑO PEPPER, SEEDED AND MINCED (FOR A MORE
    INTENSE HEAT, DO NOT SEED)

1 TEASPOON CRUSHED RED PEPPER FLAKES

1   Place the collards in a large colander set inside a large bowl. Sprinkle the collards with the salt, toss, and let sit at room temperature for 1 hour. Discard the liquid that collects in the bowl. Rinse and drain the collards, squeeze them dry, and transfer them into a large bowl. Stir in the carrot, radishes, soy sauce, and ½ cup water. Cover and refrigerate overnight.

2   Pour the liquid into a small bowl and stir in the honey and vinegar. Stir the garlic, scallions, jalapeño, and red pepper flakes into the collards. Pour the soy mixture over the collard mixture and stir to combine.

3   Cover and refrigerate for at least 2 days before serving. Store covered and refrigerated for up to 2 weeks.

QUAIL HUNTERS' DINNER

Some people eagerly await opening day of baseball season, some get restless for the first tulips or daffodils, and some live their lives, at least in part, for the beginning of bird hunting season. For most, hunting entails a long, social walk through woods and meadows or a quiet stakeout near a pond. The competition is quieter than, say, the passions that football ignites around this time of year. Dressing and cooking the catch is part of the ritual. It's a smaller task to look forward to, but one that no real hunter would fail to perform. As one begins to imagine dinner, it becomes clear just how long a day it has been and, even despite a brilliant fall sun, just how cold one is. Flushed faces abound at dinner after a hunt. As the wind-burned skin begins to fade, the evening fire lends its healing glow.

ON WINE ⌒ *A well-made Pinot Noir is subtle enough not to overwhelm the delicate quail and has enough acidity to cleanse the palate between bites. Choices from the cooler climates—California's Russian River Valley or even Mendocino County—are made to order.*

BACON-GLAZED CARROTS ON WILTED ROMAINE

SERVES 4

The first carrots of winter are sweet enough to stand up to salty bacon. We love serving them on wilted (or "kilt," in local parlance) romaine lettuce before a substantial meal.

4 TO 6 CARROTS, PEELED AND CUT ON THE BIAS INTO
   ⅓-INCH-THICK SLICES TO MEASURE 6 CUPS
3 STRIPS OF THICK-CUT BACON, FINELY DICED
2 TEASPOONS FRESH THYME LEAVES
2 TEASPOONS HONEY
1½ TEASPOONS KOSHER SALT
½ TEASPOON FRESHLY GROUND BLACK PEPPER
1 HEAD OF ROMAINE LETTUCE, COARSELY CHOPPED
½ FRESH LEMON

1   In a medium saucepan, bring 4 cups of lightly salted water
    to a boil over high heat. Add the carrots, bring back to a
    boil, and cook for 5 to 6 minutes, until tender. Drain the
    carrots in a colander and rinse under cold running water
    until cool. Drain and set aside.

2   Place a medium skillet over medium heat. When hot, add
    the bacon and cook, stirring occasionally, for about
    7 minutes, until crispy. Remove the bacon with a slotted
    spoon and set aside. Stir the thyme and honey into the fat
    in the skillet, return to medium heat, and let cook for
    1 minute. Add the carrots and cook for another 2 to
    3 minutes, tossing them in the pan so that they're well
    coated. Sprinkle with salt and pepper.

3   Remove the carrots from the pan and add the lettuce. Cook,
    stirring, for about 1 minute, until the lettuce is just wilted.
    Transfer to a platter or divide among plates, top with the
    carrots, add a light squeeze of fresh lemon over the carrots,
    then sprinkle with the reserved bacon bits and serve.

BUTTERED QUAIL WITH PAN-ROASTED HOMINY, GIBLET, AND BLACK TRUMPET RAGOUT

SERVES 4

Black trumpet mushrooms, which have a delicate butter taste and an almost fruity aroma, abound in our woods in the fall. Any firm wild mushroom will work in this recipe. If you don't have giblets, use chicken livers.

2 TABLESPOONS GRAPESEED OR VEGETABLE OIL

2 CUPS COOKED, DRAINED HOMINY

4 OUNCES BLACK TRUMPET MUSHROOMS, TRIMMED AND COARSELY CHOPPED

2 LEEKS, WHITE AND LIGHT-GREEN PARTS, HALVED LENGTHWISE AND CHOPPED

3 TEASPOONS KOSHER SALT

¾ TEASPOON FRESHLY GROUND BLACK PEPPER

6 OUNCES TURKEY OR CHICKEN GIBLETS, CHOPPED

1 CUP CHICKEN STOCK (PAGE 268) OR LOW-SODIUM CHICKEN BROTH

2 TEASPOONS FRESH THYME LEAVES

1 BAY LEAF

2 TEASPOONS FRESH LEMON JUICE

1½ TABLESPOONS UNSALTED BUTTER

4 4-OUNCE QUAIL, BONED

1   To make the ragout, in a large skillet, heat 1 tablespoon of the oil over medium heat. Add the hominy, mushrooms, leeks, 2 teaspoons of the salt, and ½ teaspoon of the pepper. Cook, stirring occasionally, for 10 to 12 minutes, until the leeks are golden brown. Add the giblets and cook for another 3 to 4 minutes, until just seared. Add the stock, thyme, and bay leaf; bring to a boil, lower the heat, and simmer for 8 minutes, or until most of the liquid has evaporated and the mushrooms are tender. Remove from the heat, discard the bay leaf, and stir in the lemon juice and 1½ teaspoons of the butter. Set aside.

2   Brush the quail with the remaining tablespoon of oil and sprinkle them with the remaining 1 teaspoon salt and ¼ teaspoon pepper. Place a medium skillet over medium-high heat; when very hot, add the quail, breast side down. Cook until the skin is lightly browned, then turn the quail and sear them, about 2 minutes, on both sides. Add the remaining tablespoon of butter to the pan; when it melts, begin basting the quail with butter every minute or so while cooking for another 4 to 5 minutes, until the breast meat is slightly resistant when you poke it with your finger and the juices run clear if the thickest part of the thighs are pricked with the point of a paring knife.

3   Remove the quail from the pan and reheat the ragout if necessary, divide it among 4 serving plates, and top each serving with a quail.

BOURBON APPLE FRIED PIES

MAKES 18 PIES, ENOUGH FOR 8 TO 10 SERVINGS

Fried pies, also called half-moon pies and mule's ears, are well loved throughout the mountain south. While people from Georgia and Alabama prefer dried peaches in their fried pies, Tennesseans want apples. The most traditional use only high-quality dried apples, but we've found that the fresh "noneating" heirloom apples (also called cider or vinegar apples) or even Granny Smiths remain so firm that they merit a break with tradition.

For best results, make the pies ahead of time and freeze them on a tray. They fry best when frozen.

1 TABLESPOON UNSALTED BUTTER

½ CUP (PACKED) LIGHT BROWN SUGAR

½ TEASPOON GROUND CINNAMON

1 VANILLA BEAN, SPLIT AND SEEDS SCRAPED OUT WITH THE TIP OF A KNIFE

½ CUP JACK DANIEL'S TENNESSEE WHISKEY OR OTHER BOURBON

6 TART APPLES (SUCH AS GRANNY SMITH), PEELED AND CUT INTO 1-INCH CHUNKS

1 LARGE EGG

½ RECIPE SWEET PASTRY (PAGE 270)

3 CUPS VEGETABLE OIL

ICE CREAM, FOR SERVING

1   In a medium skillet over medium heat, combine the butter, sugar, cinnamon, and vanilla bean seeds. Boil for about 5 minutes, until very thick and caramelized. Remove from the heat and carefully stir in the whiskey; the mixture may sputter. Return the pan to medium heat and cook, stirring, for another 3 minutes.

2   Add the apples and swirl the pan or stir gently to coat the apples with the liquid. Cook for 5 minutes more, or until the apples start to soften. Remove from the heat and let cool to room temperature; refrigerate if not using within an hour or two.

3   When you're ready to assemble the pies, beat the egg and ½ cup cold water together until smooth. Set aside. Strain the apple mixture through a fine-mesh strainer to remove any lumps and set the solids and liquid aside in separate bowls.

4   On a floured surface, roll out half the dough to a thickness of ⅛ inch. With a 4-inch round cutter, cut out circles and transfer them to a clean surface. Brush the circles all over with the egg wash. Spoon 2 apple chunks and a little sauce onto the bottom half of each circle. Fold the top of each down to cover the filling, making half-moon shapes. Using the tines of a fork or your fingers, press down on the edges to seal the pies.

5   Transfer them to a rimmed baking sheet lined with parchment or wax paper, being careful that they don't touch each other. Place the baking sheet in the freezer for 4 to 5 hours, until the pies are solidly frozen. Once frozen, the pies can either be cooked immediately or transferred to resealable plastic bags and kept frozen for up to a month.

6   When ready to serve the pies, place the oil in a large skillet and heat over high heat until a pinch of flour sprinkled into the oil immediately bubbles (but doesn't spit) and begins to brown, or a deep-fry thermometer registers 350°F. Take the pies out of the freezer and fry a few at a time in the oil, turning them once, for about 5 minutes, until golden brown around the edges and the filling is heated through.

7   Remove with a slotted spoon and drain on paper towels. Repeat until all the pies are cooked. Serve them warm with scoops of the ice cream on the side.

A CAVALCADE OF CORN

SOME SOUTHERN FAMILIES EAT CORN THAT IS ONLY WHITE, CONTENDING THAT YELLOW CORN ISN'T EVEN FIT FOR ANIMALS. OTHER CLANS THINK YELLOW CORN IS MORE FLAVORFUL. EVERYBODY ELSE THINKS THAT CORN IS CORN, STOP TALKING, LET'S EAT. REGARDLESS OF THE YELLOW VERSUS WHITE DEBATE OR THE

argument over whether butter corn is superior to sweet corn, there's no question that Southerners love to eat corn.

Traditionally, every family had its favorite corn, and there was a corn for every season.

We plant at least four kinds every year, all of them heirloom varieties that were traditionally grown in the region. There is a different sort of second life ahead of each row of corn in our garden: some will be eaten fresh, some will be milled, some will be frozen, pickled, or dried. Because it was so important historically, seasonal cooking in the foothills revolved around the sort of corn that could be counted on.

FRESH CORN
Because it should be eaten as soon as possible after picking, fresh sweet corn is sometimes called the most immediate of all vegetables.

In the advanced stages of corn-love, the truly smitten have been known to set a pot of water on the stove before venturing forth to pick or purchase their corn. Fresh corn is sometimes called green corn, usually boiled or roasted and eaten right off the cob. In the first case, even those mildly taken with it bring the corn from the field, shuck it quickly, plunged it into boiling water and cook it for mere minutes. The hot ears are served heavily buttered and salted. Roasting ears, on the other hand, are left in their shucks and roasted outdoors over a grill or campfire for an hour or so. Some people soak roasting ears in water to prevent scorching, while others like the smoky flavor that comes from the charred shucks. Like boiled corn, roasting ears are served with plenty of butter and salt.

Fresh corn kernels cut from the cobs can be creamed, skillet fried, made into pudding, or formed into fritters. Most creamed corn recipes called for thickening with milk and a roux. Skillet-fried kernels

were sautéed in fat, preferably bacon grease. Corn pudding is actually a rich and eggy custard that envelops whole or puréed kernels. For fritters, the kernels are folded into a thick batter and deep-fried by the spoonful. For any of these methods, it is important to scrape the cobs to extract the starchy, milky liquid that clings to them when the kernels are cut off.

Traditionally, a small amount of the fresh corn was pickled or put-up in relishes, especially when the harvest was large.

GRITTED CORN

Gritted corn is obscure but not without its fans. It holds an important place in households where life depended on frugality and ingenuity. Gritted corn comes from whole ears that are too old to be considered fresh, yet too green to be considered dried. The semi-soft ears were grated, or "gritted," on large pieces of tin that had been pierced with a nail to create a large, rough grater. The result was very coarse, very damp cornmeal that was most often used in corn bread, although it could also be cooked and eaten as porridge.

DRIED CORN

Fresh corn is fleeting, but dried corn keeps year around. The dried kernels can be cooked whole, ground into cornmeal, or soaked in lye made from hardwood ashes to make hominy. Although some people snack on dried corn straight from the bag, most whole kernel dried corn is reconstituted through a variety of cooking methods.

We were early devotees of John Cope's Dried Sweet Corn. Today his brand is so popular that the term *copes corn* has become a generic term for all types of dried sweet corn.

CORNMEAL

Dried corn can be ground as fine as talc or left as coarse as chicken scratch, but most cooks consider stone-ground meal to be the gold standard. Fine enough that it rarely needs to be sifted, stone-ground cornmeal is nonetheless gritty enough to add texture and flavor to a recipe. It retains the distinct nutty, intense flavor of dried corn.

More Southern recipes use cornmeal than fresh corn. Meal can be used in place of flour or cornstarch for thickening, dusting and dredging. It can be boiled into a simple mush. But the starring role for cornmeal is cornbread in its many guises: skillet cakes, sticks, muffins, dodgers, dumplings, griddle cakes, wafers, light bread, waffles, hush puppies, hoecakes, pone, dressing, and spoonbread.

HOMINY

Hominy is dried whole corn kernels that have been soaked in a lye solution to remove their husks. Hominy can be used fresh or allowed to dry. We use fresh wet hominy as a vegetable, served seasoned and warmed, or put it in soups and ragouts.

GRITS

Dried hominy is ground into one of the most iconic and misunderstood of all Southern dishes: grits. No matter how they are eventually served, grits are first cooked in boiling salted liquid until they are tender and creamy. Depending on how they were processed, that can take anywhere from five to ninety minutes. The more traditional the milling, the longer they must cook. Good grits are rich, creamy, and taste like corn yet benefit from generous seasoning. Bad grits are thin, watery, and taste of nothing, so no amount of seasoning will redeem them.

Blackberry Farm's leading chefs: Josh Feathers, Adam Cooke, and Joseph Lenn

WHEN BLACK WALNUTS FALL

No one is neutral on the subject of black walnuts. The nut has a strong, rich taste—earthy, smoky, and a little winey—that dominates nearly everything it comes into contact with, and people either adore or detest them. We love them. In the fall the nut, encased in a husk that resembles a green tennis ball and is two to two and a half inches across, falls to the ground. Under this husk is the black walnut shell, a thick carapace that is reminiscent of a petrified dinosaur egg. Traditionally, children gathered the nuts much as they would gather Easter eggs, assembled them, and stomped on them to remove the husks. The liquid from the husk is dark brown and is so saturated and intense that it was traditionally used as ink; therefore, the stomping operation left black stains on the ground and on the stompers. In an attempt to reduce staining on the hands that cracked the nut and picked its meat, black walnuts were husked and then left in their black shells to age for several days between husking and cracking.

Cracking black walnuts is not for sissies. Traditionally young people used a hammer, a vise, a block of wood, or a mallet for the job. Many housewives have a smooth, heavy river rock that they use every year to shatter the prehistoric shell; others put the nuts in a bag and run over them with trucks or minivans.

Some say that black walnuts are prized as a result of all the effort they require. But we think it comes down to taste: nothing compares to black walnuts. Here in the mountain south, the thud of a black walnut falling from a tree is the sound that distinguishes early and later autumn.

ON WINE *The deep, almost bitter flavors of the coffee and black walnut in this menu call for a wine that has an earthiness and power as well as a clean, bright fruitiness. Red wines made in the Bierzo region of northwestern Spain from the indigenous Mencía grape fit the bill nicely.*

BLACK WALNUT SOUP

SERVES 4 TO 6

This is an intense and very rich soup. English walnuts are not a good substitution.

3 TABLESPOONS UNSALTED BUTTER

I TABLESPOON MINCED SHALLOTS

I STALK OF CELERY, MINCED

3 TABLESPOONS ALL-PURPOSE FLOUR

6 CUPS CHICKEN STOCK (PAGE 268) OR VEGETABLE STOCK
   (PAGE 268), OR LOW-SODIUM CHICKEN OR VEGETABLE
   BROTH

I BAY LEAF

I TABLESPOON KOSHER SALT, PLUS MORE TO TASTE

PINCH OF CRACKED BLACK PEPPER, PLUS MORE TO TASTE

¾ CUP PLUS I TABLESPOON BLACK WALNUTS, LIGHTLY
   TOASTED

3 CUPS HEAVY CREAM

1   In a large pot over medium heat, melt the butter. Add the shallots and celery and cook, stirring, 3 to 5 minutes, until softened. Add the flour and cook, stirring constantly, for another 2 to 3 minutes. Add the stock, bay leaf, 1 tablespoon salt, a pinch of pepper, and ¾ cup of the black walnuts and bring to a boil. Lower the heat and simmer, uncovered, for about 20 minutes. Add 2 cups of the cream and simmer for 15 minutes more.

2   Remove and discard the bay leaf. Working in 3 batches, purée the soup in a blender. Taste and season with more salt and pepper if needed.

3   When ready to serve, reheat the soup. Place the remaining 1 cup cream in the blender and blend on high speed just until foamy (do not blend too long or the cream will separate).

4   Ladle the hot soup into bowls. Place a scoop of foamed cream on the top of each serving. Using a Microplane or zester, grate the remaining toasted black walnuts over the top of each serving.

COFFEE-RUBBED DUCK BREAST WITH WINE MARMALADE

SERVES 4

The rich, bitter tone of coffee works magic with duck. It offsets the fattiness of the meat, and coffee also serves as a counterpoint if one indulges in the marmalade that we suggest as an accompaniment. (We like to use one of the varietal grape marmalades that can be purchased in specialty food stores or the one we make at the farm from the local muscadines.)

4 6-OUNCE DUCK BREASTS
1 TABLESPOON GROUND COFFEE
1½ TEASPOONS (PACKED) LIGHT BROWN SUGAR
½ TEASPOON GROUND CINNAMON
1 TABLESPOON KOSHER SALT
1 TEASPOON FRESHLY GROUND BLACK PEPPER
1 TEASPOON VEGETABLE OIL
1 CUP WINE MARMALADE, AT ROOM TEMPERATURE

1   With a sharp knife, score the skin of the duck by cutting deeply (but not all the way through) a few times in one direction, then a few times in the other direction, making a crosshatch pattern. In a small bowl, mix together the coffee, brown sugar, cinnamon, salt, and pepper. Coat the breast meat (not the skin) with the mixture.

2   Place a medium cast-iron skillet over medium heat and add the oil. When hot, place the duck breasts in the skillet skin side down. Let cook for 6 to 8 minutes, until deeply browned; remove the pan from the heat and carefully tilt it to pour off the accumulated fat. Return the pan to medium-low heat and continue to cook the duck skin side down for about 15 minutes more, until the skin is very crispy and most of the fat has rendered off.

3   Raise the heat to medium, turn the breasts meat side down, and cook until browned and the duck is medium-rare, 2 to 3 minutes; if you cut into the center of a breast it should be deep pink but not raw. (An instant-read thermometer inserted into the center of a breast should read 130°F.) (Cook a few minutes longer if you would prefer your duck medium.)

4   Transfer the breasts to a cutting board and let rest for 5 minutes before thinly slicing each on the bias. Serve with the marmalade.

PECAN BRUSSELS SPROUTS

SERVES 4 TO 6

Unlike black walnuts, pecans are sweet and give a pleasant, toasty tone to the sharp and sometimes sulfurous flavor of Brussels sprouts.

2 POUNDS BRUSSELS SPROUTS, YELLOWED LEAVES AND
   STEM END TRIMMED OFF
¼ CUP PECANS, CHOPPED
1 TABLESPOON VEGETABLE OIL
1 TEASPOON KOSHER SALT
½ TEASPOON FRESHLY GROUND BLACK PEPPER
1 TABLESPOON UNSALTED BUTTER

1   Preheat the oven to 350°F and place a casserole dish inside to heat up.

2   Quarter the Brussels sprouts and add them to the hot casserole dish along with the pecans, oil, salt, and pepper. Toss the vegetables to coat and then bake for 20 to 30 minutes, until tender and very lightly browned.

3   Remove from the oven, toss with the butter, and serve hot.

APPLE STACK CAKE

SERVES 12

Stack cake, layers of thin, torte-like cake that are tiered with spiced reconstituted dried apples, was a sensible solution to the lack of fresh fruit in the cold months and the wealth of apples that were traditionally dried in the fall. Since refrigeration became commonplace, there's been no practical need for the cake, but that has not lessened the appetite for it. Apple stack cake is a point of honor in the mountains of southern Appalachia.

Our version borrows from a number of historic and family recipes to create the flavor of the mountains in the fall. Like all stack cake recipes, ours must be made at least one day ahead and wrapped in plastic to "age," and to allow some of the juice from the reconstituted apples to seep into the cake. Only home-dried or organic dried apples can be used; commercially dried apples frequently contain chemicals that make for an unpleasantly acrid taste.

FOR THE CAKE
4 CUPS ALL-PURPOSE FLOUR
1 TEASPOON BAKING POWDER
1 TEASPOON BAKING SODA
½ TEASPOON SALT
5 TABLESPOONS UNSALTED BUTTER, AT ROOM TEMPERATURE
½ CUP PLUS 2½ TEASPOONS GRANULATED SUGAR
1 LARGE EGG, AT ROOM TEMPERATURE
½ CUP BUTTERMILK
½ CUP SORGHUM

FOR THE DRIED APPLE FILLING
1½ POUNDS HOME-DRIED OR ORGANIC DRIED APPLES
1 CUP (PACKED) LIGHT BROWN SUGAR
1 TEASPOON GROUND GINGER
1 TEASPOON GROUND CINNAMON
½ TEASPOON GROUND ALLSPICE
½ TEASPOON GROUND NUTMEG

1   Preheat the oven to 400°F. Grease and flour five 9-inch cake pans and set them aside.

2   To make the cake layers, in a large bowl, whisk together the flour, baking powder, baking soda, and salt and set it aside. In another large bowl, beat the butter and ½ cup of the sugar with an electric mixer for 5 to 7 minutes, until creamy. Add the egg and beat until the yellow disappears.

3   In a small bowl, stir together the buttermilk and sorghum. Add the flour mixture to the egg mixture in three additions, alternating with the buttermilk mixture, beating well after each addition.

4   Divide the dough into 5 equal parts. Use your fingers to press each piece evenly and firmly into the bottom of a prepared cake pan. Prick the dough evenly with a fork and then sprinkle each layer with ½ teaspoon of the remaining sugar.

5   Bake for 8 to 10 minutes, until the layers are firm when lightly touched. Cool the layers in the pans for 5 minutes, turn them out onto wire racks, and cool to room temperature.

6   To make the filling, in a large saucepan, stir together the apples, 6 cups water, and the brown sugar. Bring to a simmer over medium heat and cook, stirring occasionally, for about 30 minutes, until the apples are soft and most of the water has cooked away. Stir in the ginger, cinnamon, allspice, and nutmeg and cook, stirring occasionally, until the remaining water cooks away. Set aside to cool to room temperature.

7   To complete the cake, place a layer on a serving plate or cake stand. Cover with one fourth of the filling. Stack a second layer over the filling and top with one fourth of the filling. Repeat the stacking and filling to make two more layers, finishing with a bare cake layer on top.

8   Cover the cake with plastic wrap and let sit at room temperature for at least 1 day and up to 3 days before slicing.

At Blackberry Farm, there are six varieties of heirloom apple trees, including Chesney, Doctor Matthews, Nickajack, Winter Jon, Winter Sweet, and Wolf River. Using a combination of tart and sweet apples to make cider provides complexity to the drink. It takes many harvests' worth of experience to hand-select the right apples for pressing. The best cider comes from apples that are consistent in shape and free of bruising or marks.

CORN BREAD 〜

CORN BREAD IS ONE OF THE CORNERSTONES OF APPALACHIAN COOKING. LIKE MOST OF THIS CUISINE, IT WAS PROBABLY DEVELOPED IN RESPONSE TO THE AREA'S TRADITIONAL ISOLATION AND DEPRIVATION, WHICH RENDERED WHEAT RARE. ANY LACK WAS USUALLY COMPENSATED FOR BY THE CREATIVITY OF THE REGION'S COOKS, HOWEVER.

The progression of bread-like dishes made from cornmeal demonstrates a brief history of the mountain south. In the region's wilderness days, corn pone, a mush that was made of cornmeal, salt, and water, was probably the earliest corn bread batter. If cooked on a flat, hot rock, this became hoecakes; if baked or boiled, it was called corn bread dodgers. As the region became cleared, settled, and farmed, cooks had bacon grease and cracklings, which they added to the mixture; they also had the cast-iron skillet that accompanied most settlers on their journey from the East. Pouring the enriched batter into a

skillet and baking it created corn bread as we know it today. This paved the way for the muffins and corn sticks that can be baked in specially forged pans and the lacy thin cakes that can be made on top of the stove. The availability of lard and bear fat was most likely the mother of hush puppies. Spoonbread, which consists of cornmeal mixed with butter, eggs, and milk baked to a soufflé-like puff, bespeaks the time when mountain life had become well enough established that chicken and dairy were a part of the Appalachian farm.

Like most iconic dishes of our region, corn bread is an art form that continues to evolve, continues to spark individual renditions, continues to inspire poetry and prose. Cooks add chilies, bacon, aromatics, and a wide range of vegetables and meat to the basic pan. We are purists and stand by our family recipes—one for skillet corn bread, the other for the thin, lacy version—but we are tolerant except for one issue: the addition of sugar. We agree with Ronni Lundy, author of *Shuck Beans, Stack Cakes and Honest Fried Chicken,* who wrote, "If God had meant for corn bread to have sugar in it, he'd have called it cake."

There are three elements to fine corn bread: the corn, the mill, and the cook. We get our meal from our friend Glenn Roberts of Anson Mills in Columbia, South Carolina. He is committed to saving the traditional corns of the region, kernel by kernel, and we work with him, planting some of the endangered, antique varieties in our garden simply to preserve the seeds. His corn is dried and then stone-ground, creating a meal that has a lot of texture and a lot of flavor. If the cook has this high-quality meal, the rest is a matter of practice. In *Southern Food: At Home, on the Road, in History,* John Egerton writes

A properly prepared dish of spoonbread can be taken as testimony to the perfectibility of humankind; a crisp corn bread dodger or hoecake, on the other hand, demonstrates another kind of perfection, an enduring strength that has not been improved upon in four centuries of service to hungry people.

SKILLET CORN BREAD

SERVES 8

This is the most traditional form of corn bread, the one that we use for eating with butter, sopping soup, or making stuffing. It is important to get the cast-iron skillet very hot before pouring in the batter.

2 TABLESPOONS LARD, BACON FAT, OR VEGETABLE OIL
3 CUPS STONE-GROUND YELLOW CORNMEAL
1¼ TEASPOONS BAKING POWDER
1¼ TEASPOONS BAKING SODA
2½ TEASPOONS KOSHER SALT
2 LARGE EGGS, LIGHTLY BEATEN
3 CUPS BUTTERMILK

1   Preheat the oven to 400°F. Place the lard in a 10-inch cast-iron skillet and put it into the oven to heat up. Pull it out just before it starts to smoke.

2   In a medium bowl, whisk together the cornmeal, baking powder, baking soda, and salt. Add the eggs and buttermilk and whisk just until combined. Immediately remove the hot skillet from the oven and gently swirl it to coat the bottom with the hot lard. Pour the cornmeal batter into the skillet; the hot lard will sizzle around the edges of the batter.

3   Bake the corn bread for 15 minutes. Reduce the oven temperature to 325°F and continue to bake the corn bread for another 15 minutes, or until the top is golden brown and a toothpick inserted into the center comes out clean. Turn the corn bread out of the skillet, cut into wedges, and serve hot or at room temperature.

LACY CORN BREAD

MAKES ABOUT THIRTY-TWO 2-INCH ROUNDS

These thin, delicate pancakes are wonderful topped with a ragout, rolled around caviar, or eaten by themselves.

¾ CUP STONE-GROUND YELLOW CORNMEAL
1 TABLESPOON KOSHER SALT
⅛ TEASPOON FRESHLY GROUND BLACK PEPPER
¾ CUP BUTTERMILK
2 TABLESPOONS UNSALTED BUTTER, MELTED
½ CUP VEGETABLE OIL

1   In a medium bowl, stir together the cornmeal, salt, and pepper. In a small bowl, stir together the buttermilk and ⅓ cup water. Pour the buttermilk mixture into the cornmeal mixture and stir to combine. Stir in the melted butter and set aside.

2   In a medium skillet, heat 1 tablespoon of the oil over medium-high heat until it shimmers. Working in small batches, drop rounded tablespoons of batter into the hot oil, then fry for 1½ to 2 minutes, until the edges are crispy, lacy, and browned and the centers are golden. Flip the rounds with a spatula and cook for 1½ to 2 minutes more, until set and golden brown. Repeat with the remaining batter, adding about 2 teaspoons of oil to the skillet between batches.

3   Drain the corn bread on paper towels and serve hot.

ABOVE LEFT: The October Pea is grown for fall harvest and planted among the corn so that the stalks can serve as a natural support to the pea vine.

ABOVE RIGHT: Autumn brings the peak of seed-saving season, where seeds are first allowed to dry and mature on the plant, then harvested, shelled, and packaged so they can be used for winter cooking or saved for the next year's planting.

FATHERS FRYING TURKEYS WITH SONS

My father believes that whatever comes next will always be better. He never stops imagining, inventing, improving, moving forward. This quality has served him well in business but it created something of a challenge when it came to settling down and calling one place our family home.

For all this motion and change throughout the years, however, we always returned to Blackberry Farm at Thanksgiving. And we always had two kinds of turkey, three kinds of dressing, and enough side dishes to feed Blount County. Unless there is a foot of snow on the ground, we see Thanksgiving as summer's last cry and we can't help ourselves—we have to cook everything and taste every little bit of the autumn bounty. Every year, we convince ourselves that another twelve months could pass before we have the chance to taste pork belly or turkey, onions or squash, cornmeal, peanuts, corn bread, or pecans. In fact, most of these ingredients are the mainstays of cold-weather cooking in the foothills, foods that we will eat every day until spring. But in late November they are shiny and special and new.

My mother always roasted turkey in the kitchen, and my father always deep-fried turkey outside on the deck. Long before frying turkey was fashionable, a friend from Louisiana taught my father how to fix the dish when they were staying at a hunting camp. Since then, every Thanksgiving Day just after noon, my father has set one of those huge, straight-sided pots that you use for a shrimp boil on a big portable gas burner, added peanut oil, and let it get hot enough to sizzle the bird. It's an art— knowing how much oil will cover the bird but not spill out of the pot, knowing how to insert a three-pronged metal rod through the cavity of the turkey to use as a handle, knowing when to slide the bird into the oil, when to remove it.

It takes about an hour and a half to fry a Thanksgiving-size turkey. Every year, as my father minded the bird, the men (and their sons) all stood around the pot, staring. For most, watching a turkey fry is like watching a sunset.

The appetizers and side dishes on my family's Thanksgiving menu change every year. In fact, the ideas and recipes often change as we cook them. But the "fixin's" always end up telling the history of our family's lifelong journey around the American South and back to Tennessee. No matter where we are, Thanksgiving is our homecoming, our ritual.

A few years ago, I noticed that when my parents began the annual discussions about traveling someplace else for Thanksgiving, one of them said, "Well, Sam won't leave here, so why bother discussing it." Though I didn't consciously set out to, I guess I've become guardian of that tradition both for our family and for the guests who return to Blackberry Farm the third Thursday of November, year after year.

Come midday, we start deep-frying turkeys on the patio or at the Yallerhammer. We serve the meat on angel biscuits with other snacks while the rest of the turkeys roast and pies bake and the entire culinary team fixes side dishes. There is something to be said for the familiar, for the thing you do from the heart and without thinking. For this reason, the only thing that changes at Blackberry Farm on Thanksgiving is the weather.

ON WINE *We are always on the lookout for versatile wines that not only pair well with all the different flavors of the winter holiday table but also deliver a feeling of celebration. We want crisp, elegant, dry white wines, and those made from Austria's Grüner Veltliner grape are just the ticket: tart, powerful, and with a hint of radish-like spiciness that complements the spice and balances the richness of the holiday table. It's fun to start the meal with young, sassy versions and progress to the more rounded, aromatic and cellar-aged ones.*

PEANUT SOUP

SERVES 8

Tennessee red (or Valencia) peanuts are small, firm nuts that ripen, two to each pod, more quickly than the Virginia varieties. The raw peanut makes a fine soup, inextricably linked to the final harvest of the year, and it is a constant feature at our Thanksgiving table. If the organic Tennessee variety is not available, any small red peanut can be substituted.

4 TABLESPOONS (½ STICK) UNSALTED BUTTER

1 CUP DICED CELERY

¼ CUP CHOPPED LEEK, WHITE PART ONLY

2 TABLESPOONS CHOPPED SHALLOT

2 TABLESPOONS ALL-PURPOSE FLOUR

¾ CUP CREAMY (ORGANIC, NATURAL-STYLE) PEANUT BUTTER

½ CUP CHOPPED, LIGHTLY TOASTED TENNESSEE RED PEANUTS

6 CUPS CHICKEN STOCK (PAGE 268) OR VEGETABLE STOCK (PAGE 268), OR LOW-SODIUM CHICKEN OR VEGETABLE BROTH

2 CUPS HEAVY CREAM

½ TEASPOON FINE SEA SALT, PLUS MORE TO TASTE

1   In a large saucepan set over medium heat, melt the butter. Add the celery, leek, and shallot and cook, stirring, for 5 minutes, or until soft. Stir in the flour, peanut butter, and peanuts. Cook, stirring frequently, for 5 minutes. Stir in the stock, adjust the heat, and simmer, uncovered, for 30 minutes.

2   Whisk in the cream and ½ teaspoon of the salt and heat through. Taste the soup and add more salt if desired.

DEEP-FRIED TURKEY

SERVES 10 TO 12

It is safest and easiest to deep-fry turkey outside. There are now outdoor fryers made specifically for turkeys, but we still use a gas ring and a very large straight-sided heavy pot. Three secrets ensure a perfect fried turkey. To keep the bird basting itself, use a large syringe to inject the marinade two days ahead of cooking. To make deep, significant injections (we make about fifty, evenly spaced, all over the bird), you need a large syringe. The bird must be brought to room temperature prior to frying to prevent splattering. And if you are not using a fryer with a basket designed to hold a turkey, you must fashion a very secure metal handle to allow you to move the bird around. We wrap the legs in heavy coat hangers as described below. We have also used a heavy metal rod with three prongs on the end to essentially skewer the bird. The prongs keep the rod in place. Use a deep-fry thermometer to gauge the temperature of the oil, and lower the bird very gently into the fryer. We allow about three minutes per pound of frying time.

FOR THE TURKEY AND MARINADE

1 CUP CHAMPAGNE VINEGAR

1 CUP EXTRA-VIRGIN OLIVE OIL

8 TABLESPOONS (1 STICK) UNSALTED BUTTER, MELTED

¼ CUP WORCESTERSHIRE SAUCE

1 TABLESPOON FRESH LEMON JUICE

1 TABLESPOON HOT SAUCE

¼ CUP CHOPPED SHALLOT

10 SPRIGS OF FRESH THYME

1 TEASPOON FINE SEA SALT

1 TEASPOON FRESHLY GROUND BLACK PEPPER

¼ TEASPOON CAYENNE PEPPER

1 12- TO 14-POUND TURKEY

1½ GALLONS (24 CUPS) PEANUT OIL, OR ENOUGH TO FULLY IMMERSE THE TURKEY IN

FOR THE RUB

2 TABLESPOONS BARBECUE SAUCE

2 TABLESPOONS CHILI POWDER

1 TABLESPOON GROUND CUMIN

1 TABLESPOON GROUND CORIANDER

1 TABLESPOON LEMON PEPPER

1 TEASPOON FRESHLY GROUND BLACK PEPPER

1 To make the turkey and marinade, the day before cooking, combine all the ingredients except the turkey and the peanut oil in a medium bowl, add ¼ cup water, and stir until combined. Let this mixture stand for 1 hour, then strain it through a fine-mesh strainer and discard the solids. Using a marinade injector, inject the liquid into all parts of the turkey.

2 To make the rub, combine the barbecue sauce, chili powder, cumin, coriander, lemon pepper, and black pepper in a small bowl and mix to form a smooth paste. Using your hands, massage the paste all over the skin and inside the cavity of the turkey, leaving no clumps of paste. Wrap the turkey tightly with plastic wrap and refrigerate it overnight.

3 At least 1 hour before cooking, bring the turkey to room temperature. When ready to cook, tie the legs of the turkey together with butcher's twine. Heat the peanut oil in a turkey fryer or very large, heavy pot until a deep-fry thermometer registers 350°F. Wrap a wire coat hanger or heavy wire around the legs of the turkey to use as a handle (make sure it's very secure) or use a special metal turkey lifter if you have one.

4 Immerse the turkey in the oil so that it is completely covered. Adjust the temperature so that the oil maintains an even 350°F. Cook the turkey for about 45 minutes (3½ minutes per pound of turkey); the turkey is done when the legs move freely at the joints and the juices run clear when the thigh is pierced at the thickest point, or an instant-read thermometer inserted into the thickest part of the thigh reads 170°F.

5 Very gently remove the turkey from the oil; use a large spatula or tongs to support the underside of the turkey as you lift it. Transfer the turkey to a rack set over a baking sheet and let rest for 30 minutes before carving.

ROAST TURKEY WITH CORN BREAD STUFFING AND GRAVY

SERVES 12 TO 14

The traditional inspiration for this recipe was leftovers— leftover giblets and dry leftover corn bread. Our corn bread, however, tends to disappear, so we "stale" it ourselves.

FOR THE STUFFING

6 CUPS DICED CORN BREAD (SEE SKILLET CORN BREAD, PAGE 125)

8 TABLESPOONS (1 STICK) UNSALTED BUTTER

1 SMALL ONION, DICED

1 GREEN BELL PEPPER, CORED, SEEDED, AND DICED

1 RED BELL PEPPER, CORED, SEEDED, AND DICED

3 STALKS OF CELERY, DICED

8 TO 10 OUNCES TURKEY GIBLETS, CHOPPED

4 OUNCES SMOKED BREAKFAST SAUSAGE (EITHER LOOSE OR LINKS, CASINGS REMOVED)

1½ CUPS FRESH BREAD CRUMBS, TOASTED

4 LARGE EGGS

1½ TABLESPOONS CHOPPED FRESH SAGE LEAVES

2 TEASPOONS KOSHER SALT

1 TEASPOON FRESHLY GROUND BLACK PEPPER

2 TO 2½ CUPS CHICKEN STOCK (PAGE 268) OR CHICKEN BROTH

FOR THE TURKEY

8 TABLESPOONS UNSALTED BUTTER, AT ROOM TEMPERATURE

1 TABLESPOON CHOPPED FRESH ROSEMARY LEAVES

1 TABLESPOON CHOPPED FRESH THYME LEAVES

1 TABLESPOON CHOPPED FRESH CHIVES

1 TABLESPOON CHOPPED FRESH FLAT-LEAF PARSLEY LEAVES

ONE 13- TO 15-POUND TURKEY, RINSED AND PATTED DRY

3 TEASPOONS KOSHER SALT

1½ TEASPOONS FRESHLY GROUND BLACK PEPPER

3 MEDIUM CARROTS, PEELED AND DICED

2 MEDIUM VIDALIA ONIONS, PEELED AND QUARTERED

3 STALKS OF CELERY, DICED

2 TABLESPOONS VEGETABLE OIL

FOR THE GRAVY

4 TABLESPOONS UNSALTED BUTTER

½ CUP ALL-PURPOSE FLOUR

3½ CUPS CHICKEN STOCK (PAGE 268) OR CHICKEN BROTH

1 TEASPOON KOSHER SALT

¼ TEASPOON FRESHLY GROUND BLACK PEPPER

1   To make the stuffing, spread the corn bread on a rimmed baking sheet and let it dry either by leaving it on the counter overnight or by placing it in a 300°F oven for 10 to 15 minutes, until just crisped but not browned. Set aside.

2   In a large skillet, melt 4 tablespoons of the butter over medium heat. Stir in the onion, green pepper, red pepper, and celery and cook, stirring frequently, for about 6 minutes, until the vegetables are soft but not browned. Transfer the onion mixture to a large bowl; set aside.

3   Melt the remaining 4 tablespoons butter in the same skillet, add the giblets, and cook, stirring often, for 8 to 10 minutes, until they are cooked through; scrape into the bowl with the onion mixture. Add the sausage to the same skillet and cook for 10 minutes, or until browned, breaking up the meat with the side of a spoon. Use a slotted spoon to transfer the sausage to the onion mixture, leaving the fat behind.

4   Add the corn bread, bread crumbs, eggs, sage, salt, and pepper to the onion mixture and mix well. Stir in 2 cups of the chicken stock. The stuffing should be moist; add the remaining ½ cup of stock if needed. Cover the bowl and refrigerate the stuffing until completely cool.

5   To make the turkey, preheat the oven to 350°F. In a small bowl, stir together the butter, rosemary, thyme, chives, and parsley; set aside. Use your fingers to gently loosen the skin over the breast and thighs. Spread the butter mixture under the loosened skin, smooth the skin back into place, and gently massage the skin to distribute the butter evenly. Season the inside of the turkey with 2 teaspoons of the salt and 1 teaspoon of the pepper.

6   Fill the cavity of the turkey loosely with the cooled stuffing (do not pack it; if you have leftover stuffing, bake it in a small casserole dish along with the turkey until browned). Tie the drumsticks together with kitchen string and tuck the wings under the body.

7   In a large roasting pan, toss the carrots, onions, and celery with 1 tablespoon of the oil. Place the turkey on top of the vegetables, brush the skin with the remaining 1 tablespoon oil, and sprinkle with the remaining 1 teaspoon salt and ½ teaspoon pepper.

8   Roast for 3½ to 4 hours; the turkey is done when an instant-read thermometer inserted into the stuffing registers 165°F, and into the fleshy part of the turkey thigh (but not touching bone) registers 170°F, or when the juices run clear when the tip of a paring knife is inserted into the thickest part of the thigh. Transfer the turkey to a cutting board and let it rest, uncovered, for 30 minutes before carving.

9   While the turkey rests, make the gravy. Lift out and discard the vegetables, leaving any juices in the bottom of the pan. Use a spatula to scrape up the browned bits from the bottom, then pour the liquid into a degreasing cup or glass measuring cup. Let the fat rise to the top, discard the fat, and place ¼ cup of the defatted drippings into a large saucepan.

10 Add the butter and cook over medium-low heat, stirring, until melted. Sprinkle in the flour and cook, whisking constantly, for 7 minutes, or until the mixture turns light brown. Slowly whisk in the stock a little at a time. Increase the heat to medium, switch to a spoon, and cook, stirring almost constantly, for 7 to 8 minutes, until the gravy is thick enough to coat the back of the spoon. Stir in the salt and pepper, transfer to a gravy boat or pitcher, and serve along with the turkey.

STEWED SPICED APPLES

Very crisp tart apples are essential for this recipe. Sweeter or soft apples will become mushy. The apples can be made the day before, stored in the refrigerator, and gently warmed or simply brought to room temperature before serving.

- 1 2-INCH PIECE OF FRESH GINGER, PEELED AND THINLY SLICED
- 2 CINNAMON STICKS
- 8 WHOLE CLOVES
- 1 TABLESPOON WHOLE ALLSPICE BERRIES
- 6 CUPS APPLE CIDER
- 8 LARGE GRANNY SMITH OR OTHER LARGE, VERY CRISP APPLES, PEELED, CORED, AND CUT INTO 1-INCH PIECES

1   Tie the ginger, cinnamon, cloves, and allspice in a square of cheesecloth. Place it in a large saucepan, add the cider, and bring to a boil over high heat. Add the apples, return the liquid to a boil, and reduce the heat to medium-low. Simmer the apples for 10 minutes, or until they are just tender.

2   Remove and discard the spice bag. Strain the apples and discard the cooking liquid or save it for another use. Serve the apples warm, or cover and refrigerate for up to 1 day and reheat just before serving.

DRIED CHERRY AND CRANBERRY SAUCE

MAKES ABOUT 4 CUPS

Dried fruit of any sort adds a foothills note to cranberry sauce. We've used apples and even dried peaches, but cherries keep the sauce vividly red and oh so delicious.

- 4 CUPS FRESH CRANBERRIES
- 2 CUPS DRIED CHERRIES
- ¼ CUP CANE SYRUP (AVAILABLE IN SPECIALTY FOOD MARKETS AND HEALTH FOOD STORES)
- FINELY GRATED ZEST OF 1 ORANGE
- ¾ CUP ORANGE JUICE
- ½ CUP RED WINE
- 2½ TEASPOONS FRESHLY GRATED PEELED GINGER

In a medium saucepan, stir together the cranberries, cherries, cane syrup, zest, juice, wine, and ginger. Bring to a simmer over medium heat and cook, stirring frequently, for about 10 minutes, until some of the cranberries pop and the mixture thickens. Serve warm or at room temperature.

BEALL FAMILY OYSTER DRESSING

SERVES 8

Freshly shucked oysters make the best dressing, but it can be difficult to protect them from snackers. We've found it wise to have an extra pint of freshly shucked oysters on hand as a backup.

1-POUND LOAF OF COUNTRY WHITE BREAD, CUT INTO
 ¼-INCH CUBES (ABOUT 10 CUPS)
4 TABLESPOONS (½ STICK) UNSALTED BUTTER
1 MEDIUM ONION, DICED
2 STALKS OF CELERY, DICED
¾ TEASPOON KOSHER SALT
½ TEASPOON FRESHLY GRATED BLACK PEPPER
¼ TEASPOON GRATED NUTMEG
⅛ TEASPOON GROUND CLOVES
1 PINT SHUCKED OYSTERS WITH THEIR LIQUOR
2 LARGE EGGS
¼ CUP MINCED FRESH FLAT-LEAF PARSLEY LEAVES
1 TABLESPOON MINCED FRESH SAGE LEAVES

1   Preheat the oven to 350°F. Butter an 8 × 8-inch baking dish and set aside.

2   Spread the bread cubes on a rimmed baking sheet and bake for 25 minutes, or until golden brown. Transfer the bread to a large bowl and set aside.

3   In a medium skillet, melt the butter over medium heat. Add the onion and celery and cook, stirring frequently, for about 6 minutes, until the vegetables are soft but not browned. Add the salt, pepper, nutmeg, and cloves and mix well. Pour the onion mixture into the bowl with the bread.

4   Add the oysters with their liquor and the eggs to the bowl and mix well to moisten the bread. Stir in the parsley and sage. Transfer the dressing to the prepared baking dish. Bake for 35 minutes, or until golden brown. Serve warm.

SAM'S CARROT SOUFFLÉ

SERVES 8

This simple soufflé is tasty and durable, and it brings a warm spot of color to the table, making it a constant at our fall feasts. Thanksgiving, in fact, marks the annual debut of this homey family favorite. Use the sweetest carrots you can find.

2 POUNDS CARROTS, PEELED AND CUT INTO ¼-INCH-THICK ROUNDS

1 CUP WHOLE MILK

1 CUP SALTINE CRACKER CRUMBS

¾ CUP GRATED SHARP CHEDDAR CHEESE

⅓ CUP MINCED ONION

1 TABLESPOON UNSALTED BUTTER, AT ROOM TEMPERATURE

1 TEASPOON KOSHER SALT

⅛ TEASPOON CAYENNE PEPPER

¼ TEASPOON FRESHLY GROUND BLACK PEPPER

3 LARGE EGGS

1   Preheat the oven to 350°F. Butter a 2-quart soufflé dish or baking dish and set it aside.

2   Put the carrots into a large pot and cover with about an inch of salted water. Bring to a boil over high heat, reduce the heat, and simmer the carrots for about 10 minutes, until tender when pierced with the tip of a sharp knife.

3   Strain the carrots, purée in a food processor, and transfer to a large bowl. Stir in the milk, cracker crumbs, cheese, onion, butter, salt, cayenne, and black pepper.

4   In a large bowl, use an electric mixer or wire whisk to beat the eggs until they are foamy, and then whisk them into the carrot mixture.

5   Transfer the carrot mixture into the prepared soufflé dish and bake for 40 to 45 minutes, until puffed and light golden brown on top. Serve warm.

WHIPPED MASHED POTATOES

SERVES 8

For a big festive meal, we love potatoes whipped with milk and butter. The result is a fluffy mass that looks (deceptively) airy and light.

3 POUNDS RUSSET POTATOES, PEELED AND CUT INTO 2-INCH CHUNKS

4 TABLESPOONS (½ STICK) UNSALTED BUTTER, AT ROOM TEMPERATURE

¾ CUP MILK

2½ TEASPOONS KOSHER SALT, OR TO TASTE

½ TEASPOON FRESHLY GROUND WHITE PEPPER

1   Place the potatoes in a large pot and cover with about an inch of cold salted water. Bring to a boil over high heat, reduce the heat, and simmer for about 25 minutes, until the potatoes are tender when pierced with the tip of a sharp knife.

2   Strain the potatoes, transfer them to a large bowl, and add the butter, milk, salt, and pepper. Use an electric mixer to whip the potatoes into a smooth, fluffy purée and serve warm.

SWEET POTATO PIE

SERVES 8

For this recipe, we use a little lemon to balance the sweetness of the brown sugar and sweet potatoes. It also gives a fresh note to the warm spices in this classic Southern pie.

½ RECIPE BASIC PASTRY (PAGE 270)

½ CUP (PACKED) LIGHT BROWN SUGAR

2 LARGE EGGS, LIGHTLY BEATEN

2 TEASPOONS VANILLA EXTRACT

2 TEASPOONS FRESH LEMON JUICE

½ TEASPOON FINE SEA SALT

½ TEASPOON GROUND CINNAMON

½ TEASPOON GROUND ALLSPICE

¼ TEASPOON FRESHLY GRATED NUTMEG

3 MEDIUM SWEET POTATOES (ABOUT 1½ POUNDS)

½ CUP HEAVY CREAM

1 TABLESPOON DEMERARA SUGAR, OR REGULAR WHITE SUGAR

1   Preheat the oven to 350°F.

2   On a lightly floured surface, roll the pastry out into a circle about 10 inches in diameter. Fold the dough over your rolling pin and unroll it over a 9-inch pie pan. Ease the dough into the bottom and up the sides of the pan, turn excess dough under, and crimp the edges all around with your fingers to make an even edge.

3   Line the pastry shell with parchment paper or aluminum foil and fill it with pie weights or dry beans. Bake the pastry for 10 minutes, or until the edges of the crust are firm but not browned. Remove the weights and parchment paper. If the bottom of the pastry looks moist, return the pie pan to the oven for about 5 more minutes, until the dough looks firm and dried but not browned. Place the pan on a wire rack to cool to room temperature.

4   In a medium bowl, whisk together the brown sugar, eggs, vanilla, lemon juice, salt, cinnamon, allspice, and nutmeg and set aside.

5   Peel the sweet potatoes and use a mandoline or very sharp heavy knife to cut them into ⅛-inch-thick slices. In a large saucepan, bring the potato slices and cream to a simmer over medium-high heat. Reduce the heat to medium, cover the pan, and gently cook the potatoes for about 8 minutes, until they are tender but not falling apart.

6   Use a slotted spoon to transfer the potatoes to the pie shell. Whisk the cream left in the saucepan into the brown sugar mixture. Pour the brown sugar mixture over the sweet potatoes until the liquid comes just to the rim of the pie shell; there might be a little left over. Sprinkle the Demerara sugar evenly over the top.

7   Place the pie on a baking sheet lined with aluminum foil (this will catch any drips and make cleanup easy) and bake for about 40 minutes, until the filling is set and a knife inserted into the center comes out almost clean. Place the pan on a wire rack to cool to room temperature before serving.

PECAN TART WITH SORGHUM

SERVES 8 TO 10

John and Emma Guenther, a Mennonite couple from Saskatchewan, Canada, moved to Tennesssee's Cumberland Plateau forty years ago. They'd never heard of sorghum, the dense, reed-shaped grass that produces a sweet juice; nor did they know that sorghum juice could be cooked to a thick, brown elixir that is often mistaken for molasses (much to the horror of sorghum connoisseurs). But they bought a farm and learned how to hand-thresh the sorghum grass, extract its juice, and boil it over fire to create sorghum syrup. When they deliver jugs of their sorghum, the Guenthers' children often take the time to talk about cooking with sorghum; they are the inspiration for what has become one of our favorite pies.

½ RECIPE BASIC PASTRY (PAGE 270)

6 TABLESPOONS (¾ STICK) UNSALTED BUTTER, AT ROOM TEMPERATURE

¾ CUP (PACKED) LIGHT BROWN SUGAR

2 LARGE EGGS, LIGHTLY BEATEN

¼ CUP SORGHUM

1 TEASPOON PURE VANILLA EXTRACT

¼ CUP ALL-PURPOSE FLOUR

¾ TEASPOON GROUND CINNAMON

¼ TEASPOON FINE SEA SALT

2 CUPS TOASTED PECAN HALVES

1   Preheat the oven to 350°F.

2   On a lightly floured surface, roll the pastry dough out to a circle 11 inches in diameter. Fold the dough over your rolling pin and unroll it over a 10-inch tart pan with a removable bottom. Ease the dough into the bottom and up the sides of the pan. Run your rolling pin over the top to trim off any excess dough and refrigerate the tart shell.

3   In the bowl of an electric mixer, beat the butter and brown sugar together until light and fluffy. Add the eggs, sorghum, and vanilla and beat until combined. Stir in the flour, cinnamon, and salt. Fold in the pecans.

4   Pour the mixture into the tart shell and bake for about 30 minutes, until the crust is golden brown and the filling is set. Cool to room temperature before slicing and serving.

ABOVE LEFT: Connie Clabo is a mountain man, adept at every Appalachian craft imaginable, from farming to basket- and cane-making, as well as knowledgeable about each and every trail and mountain slope in the Smokies. He comes down every fall to share his skills with guests at our fall harvest festivals in October and November.

ABOVE RIGHT: Fly-fishing tie strings.

OPPOSITE: Traditional white oak baskets.

WINTER ❧ Smoke and Fire, Sausage and Ham

Ham's substantial, ham is fat
Ham is firm and sound.
Ham's what God was getting at
When he made pigs so round. —ROY BLOUNT JR.

There are more folkloric ways of forecasting winter in the mountainous south than there are centimeters of snowfall in the course of winter. The watching and counting begins as early as May. First, there is grass to study: "The darker green the grass is, the harder winter will be." Next, there is produce to measure and weigh: when blackberry blooms are especially heavy, when carrots grow deeper or onions grow more layers or corn shucks grow tighter around the ear, winter will be hard. Insects and animals are also studied closely. Anybody can tell you that a bad winter is brewing when ants build their hills higher or butterflies gather in bunches, when beaver lodges have more logs than usual or squirrels grow bushier tails.

Each method takes for granted that the natural world is in close and constant contact with Old Man Winter (and that Old Man Winter has a long-term plan). Humans, on the

other hand, can do nothing but watch. Gauging the green-ness of grass or the height of an anthill will, at the very least, make one aware of impermanence, the constant, incremental shifts that eventually amount to a serious change. Fall is a surprise in the foothills. Winter, on the other hand, seems to have been here long before it actually arrives.

What, if not thoughts of the cold months, fuels the frenzy to preserve the summer garden? In fact, for each prediction of snow, wind, and hail, there is the solace—and excitement—of gatherings that the cooler months promise. After cooperating to husk and mill and can and pickle, neighbors in Appalachia traditionally moved from farm to farm on the "hog killin' days" that occurred in November, after nights of hard frost turned the days as cold as a walk-in refrigerator. Only then could hogs be safely slaughtered

and hung; only when conditions were cold enough to inhibit bacteria and rot could every scrap of the pork safely be turned into hams and sausage, bacon and scrapple and other forms of "keepin' meat."

Dispatching the hogs was a communal ritual long before Abraham Lincoln declared Thanksgiving a national holiday. The smoking and early incubation of hams and sausages traditionally continued well into December, com-pleting the twelve-month arc that began with pale green shoots and wobbly-legged newborns and ended with matu-rity, harvest, and putting-by. Each successive crop asks a little more of those who would preserve and keep it—more time, more skill, more stomach for the grittier demands of husbanding life from earth to table.

Michael Sullivan, who reigns over sausage, bacon, and ham at the farm, shepherds the year's final harvest—pork

ear Chutney

— from the East Indian —

a sweet and spicy sauce used as

pork, chicken and fish

vinegar, raisins, mango, lemon,

hot pepper

ABBY FARM

meat—into the preserved, dried, and smoked meat that, in days of yore, was often the only protein available during the cold months.

He is a tall man who doesn't dash as much as he lurches between sides of meat, grinders, and the spice shelf in his butcher shop. In his excitement, his skin flushes, his eyes burn, his knife never stops moving. His enthusiasm peaks during the shank of the year. Others light candles and count shopping days. Mr. Sullivan, who grew up in Alabama, studied theology, and was called to charcuterie while serving as a church pastor, counts scraps and ounces of meat and makes lists of the preserved meats he's known and those he would like to know.

His curing room is regularly stocked with at least fifteen types of cured meat, fifteen varieties of sausages and five sorts of hams drawn from traditional sausage making

ghum, and spice berries; and his Christmas sausage contains persimmon cider as well as the spices used in local mulled cider.

"I'm always coming up with something," he says, brandishing his long, curved blade. "I am the mad scientist of charcuterie."

He learned about the importance of passion from his father, a baker who was overjoyed to wake before dawn and never lost his excitement for how each day's yeast was different from the previous day's. Mr. Sullivan assumed that the joy he took in preaching and caretaking meant that he was born to minister. It wasn't, however, until he was in his early thirties that he understood that these qualities were destined, instead, for a belly pulpit. He left the church, moved his family to upstate New York so that he could attend the Culinary Institute of America while continuing to work full time in restaurants, and then apprenticed himself to sausage makers who, like he, experienced their work as pork art, as well as a form of living history.

"I am all about heritage, tradition; I go back in time rather than forward to learn," he says, his eyes like black lakes under the blaze of a winter sun.

He handles meat with a deep reverence. "I butcher every ounce that I use. It is my responsibility. I hand tie my sausages with hemp in the old Italian way; it grips the casing better. I mix my meats with my hands in order to put a little of myself in it. I want people to taste the human touch, not some cold, stainless-steel machine," he says.

He is zealous in his evocations. "I talk about sausage like fine wine. I tell people, 'put it in your mouth, taste the succulent sweetness of the pork first, then the spices, then the back bite and, oh, here comes an echo of wine!'"

And on the rare occasion that a hog contains the slab of four-inch-thick fatback that is necessary to make the creamy Italian "lardo," Mr. Sullivan's ecstasy causes him to

around the world: guanciale, prosciutto, dried lamb bellies, salami, soppressata, toscano, chorizo, coppa, lomo, as well as boar salami, venison salami, pepperoni, brasciole, tecatorini, mohama, andouille, kielbasa and smoked sausages, hot dogs, brats, mettwurst, bockwurst, merguez, summer sausage, and boudin.

He also creates sausages from foothills ingredients. His foothills salami deploys local muscadine wine, sor-

move and sway and wiggle. "I have a lardo dance," he admits. "It is gratitude in motion."

By the winter solstice, the darkest day of the year, there are no more hogs to butcher and there is no more room in Mr. Sullivan's smokers and curing rooms. It is, for all those who spend the year husbanding the earth's offerings to the table, a time of reckoning. How did they fare against the weather and the unknown? Is there enough food to carry over until it is time to suit up for another life cycle?

The cold nights in these rare moments between the end of one year and the beginning of another create a particular hunger. Like our guests, we reach for rich, robust food—and usually too much of it—along with large, deep wine. Once we are warmed and sated, our thoughts turn to the fireplace, a hearth-side seat, the cocoon of a bed. Mr. Sullivan has his particular variation on this winter-night theme.

"I want to bring a blanket and curl up under my sausages," he says. "I want to breathe them, just like I smelled the heads of my children when they were little, inhaling who they were, exhaling my prayer for who they would become."

THE TRUFFLE MAN OF EAST TENNESSEE ⌒ TOM MICHAELS IS A PLANT PATHOLOGIST, A PIANIST, A SCRABBLE TOURNAMENT COMPETITOR AND JIGSAW-PUZZLE AFICIONADO. HE LIVES IN A MODEST, SUBURBAN-STYLE HOME THAT IS PERCHED ON A HILL IN CHUCKEY, TENNESSEE, OVERLOOKING DAVY CROCKETT'S BIRTHPLACE ABOUT

forty-five minutes away from Blackberry Farm. Dr. Michaels is also the man who got highly aromatic, black Périgord truffles to grow in his backyard.

It was not an accident. Dr. Michaels grew up on a mushroom farm outside of Chicago and wrote his thesis on the difficulty of the in vitro cultivation and growth of *Tuber melanosporum,* the famed black truffle. He is fifty-nine years old, has researched and experimented with *T. melanosporum* for more than thirty years and is well aware of the fortunes that have been lost in the attempt to cultivate truffles in the United States. Dr. Michaels had, in fact, worked on several white truffle efforts in the Pacific Northwest before moving to one of the few areas of the country where he thought truffles might be able to grow.

Michaels continued innoculating the roots of infant trees (both hazelnut and oak) with the truffle spores, in a rudimentary greenhouse and lab that he built onto his garage in Tennessee. He planted the seedlings in orchards and, like a winemaker aging a fine Bordeaux, he waited. If it grows at all, *T. melanosporum* takes seven to ten years to produce the dense, deeply aromatic subterranean fungus that is the "black diamond" of the epicurean world.

Dr. Michaels taught occasionally and consulted even less, but he resisted dreams of a truffle bonanza as assiduously as he limed his soil and trimmed his trees. He played the piano, studied the Scrabble dictionary, and spoiled his cat. And then shortly after the winter holidays during his orchard's sixth year, Dr. Michaels looked up from the jigsaw puzzle he was working and noticed patches of the tawny Tennessee soil bubbling up like blistered asphalt in his orchard just outside his living room window. A closer inspection revealed black diamonds—many of them—and most well over one thousand carats in size.

"I was jumping around yelling 'Eureka!' " he said. Only a small percentage of truffles break the ground; most grow too deep and need to be located and dug up. Slowly it dawned on Dr. Michaels that up to 150 pounds of world-class truffles could be ripening in his backyard and that he had neither dog nor pig to sniff them out before they withered and disappeared. He did not blame himself for being unprepared. Growing truffles, he said, is not like growing tomatoes. "You don't just plant them one day and know that a certain number of days later they will bear fruit." It was possible to buy a trained and ready truffle dog, but the process took years and was not cheap.

"Besides," Dr. Michaels told the chefs at Blackberry Farm when he arrived with a brown paper bag of his black diamonds, "I'm a cat person. I can't keep a dog."

Along with some of the nation's top chefs, Sam Beall was besotted by the mere aroma of Dr. Michaels's black truffles. He listened intently as the truffle man talked about how, in his expert opinion, the land and the climate of eastern Tennessee are perfect for cultivating truffles. After some moments of silence, Sam Beall quietly posed a question: "If we get you some dogs and keep them here on the farm, will you help us try to grow some truffles?"

Tom and Lussi, two bouncing Lagotto (or truffle) dogs, arrived from Italy not long after. Tom (no relation to Dr. Michaels) was a trained and experienced truffler. Lussi, his young girlfriend, was just learning to sniff, yap, and dig. So far, the couple has shown no interest in our baby truffle orchard. After working Dr. Michaels's second harvest, they took some months off to start a family in their well-appointed quarters in the far corner of the riding barn.

It may have been painful for them to take time away from being adored all day every day by anyone who meets them, but a Lagotto knows that growing a big family is a smart move when you are looking at 175 hazelnut trees in eastern Tennessee.

A COZY COMPANY MEAL FOR WINTER

Again, we turn to the Southerners' eternal dilemmas: Tradition or innovation? Pie or tart? Fried or grilled? Pulled pork or sushi? Often, we rely on the time of year or the occasion to resolve those deep divides. In the short days of winter between the holidays and the return of steady blue skies, the urge for tradition is matched only by the need to stop napping away the weekends by the fire. As always, our solution is to honor the forefathers and then sack the decorum and let our imaginations run wild. Often, we make a meal of charcuterie: a big platter of prosciutto, salami, spicy toscano sausage, and venison salami, along with chowchow and Haesel's other pickles, bread, and our nutty, creamy blue cheese. We might begin with a winter soup or something soft and gentle, like a savory flan. We might find that even after all the rich preserved meat, we want some spicy, sweet dessert. But it is the pork that we crave, in embarrassing profusion. Others, of course, may prefer one perfect specimen of pork art, the wafer of perfect country ham enveloping a snowy white piece of sturgeon, for instance; and in this menu, we offer that choice.

In this menu for a small sit-down dinner, we use local ingredients to create dishes of something old and something new. The flan combines our staff of life—corn—with the intense black truffles that were, until recently, the sole province of the Périgord region in France but that are now, miraculously, being cultivated in Tennessee. The next course plays to our weakness for the flavor of ham and the weight of beans but contrasts both with the dense, snowy meat of sturgeon. Pineapple upside-down cake brooks no innovation. There is nothing better, especially when the cake is served warm on a winter night.

ON WINE 〜 *With their pronounced acidity and light fruitiness, the Chianti wines of Tuscany are beautifully suited to tomato and ham. We've found that the wine also works well with the delicate flavors in the sturgeon.*

TENNESSEE CORN AND TRUFFLE FLAN

SERVES 8

Of the many dishes that our chefs imagined to welcome the remarkable black Tennessee truffles, this silky flan is the one we dream about from mid-January (when Tennessee truffles are finished) until mid-December (when the tubers begin to bloom). To intensify the truffle flavor, use truffle oil or truffle butter in place of butter to prepare the ramekins.

¼ CUP ALL-PURPOSE FLOUR

½ CUP FRESHLY MILLED FINE CORNMEAL

1 TABLESPOON SUGAR

¼ TEASPOON BAKING SODA

⅛ TEASPOON SEA SALT

2 CUPS FRESH OR FROZEN CORN KERNELS

8 TABLESPOONS (1 STICK) UNSALTED BUTTER, MELTED

2 LARGE EGGS, BEATEN WELL

DASH OF CAYENNE PEPPER

2 CUPS SOUR CREAM

1 CUP GRATED PARMESAN CHEESE

1 OUNCE FINELY SHAVED FRESH BLACK TENNESSEE TRUFFLE

1   Preheat the oven to 325°F.

2   Combine the flour, cornmeal, sugar, baking soda, and salt and set aside. If using frozen corn, make sure it is well defrosted and drained. Warm a nonstick skillet over high heat and toss the corn to dry and toast slightly. Combine the cooked corn, 7 tablespoons of the butter, eggs, cayenne, and sour cream. Using a few swift strokes, add the dry ingredients to the corn mixture. Stir in the cheese and the shaved truffle, reserving just enough truffle to garnish the flan before serving.

3   Use the remaining 1 tablespoon butter to grease eight 8-ounce ramekins. Spoon the mixture into the ramekins, cover each with foil, and place in a baking pan. Add boiling water to the pan until it reaches halfway up the ramekins.

4   Bake for 25 minutes. Remove from the oven and allow to rest, covered, for 10 minutes before serving. The flan can be served, garnished with additional truffle slices, in the ramekin or loosened and turned out on a plate.

COUNTRY HAM-WRAPPED STURGEON WITH FENNEL AND SUN-DRIED TOMATO WHITE BEAN RAGOUT

SERVES 4

Tennessee was one of the first states to farm-raise sturgeons. The enterprise was started in order to restock rivers and lakes with the big fish that was once king, but it became clear that at least one out of ten of the farmed sturgeon should be sold, especially now that landing wild sturgeon is illegal in most states. Those who do not have the good fortune to live within cooking distance of country ham and very fresh (and legal) sturgeon could use prosciutto and grouper instead. The beans can be made well in advance of dinner; in fact, they improve with several days' rest. Just keep in mind that they need to be soaked overnight.

FOR THE RAGOUT
½ CUP DRY NAVY BEANS

1 TABLESPOON VEGETABLE OIL

½ WHITE ONION, DICED

1 CARROT, PEELED AND DICED

1 SMALL FENNEL BULB, SLICED VERY THIN

3 CUPS VEGETABLE STOCK (PAGE 268) OR WATER

½ CUP SUN-DRIED TOMATO HALVES, CUT INTO THIN STRIPS

1½ TEASPOONS KOSHER SALT

½ TEASPOON FRESHLY GROUND BLACK PEPPER

FOR THE STURGEON
4 4-OUNCE SKINLESS STURGEON FILLETS

1 TEASPOON KOSHER SALT

1 TEASPOON FRESHLY GROUND BLACK PEPPER

4 PAPER-THIN SLICES OF COUNTRY HAM

1 TABLESPOON VEGETABLE OIL

1   Soak the beans overnight in water to cover.

2   Drain the beans, place them in a medium saucepan with 4 cups cold water, and bring to a boil. Lower the heat and simmer the beans, uncovered, for 40 to 45 minutes, until tender. Strain and set aside.

3   To make the ragout, in a large skillet, heat the oil over medium heat and add the onion. Cook, stirring frequently, for 6 to 7 minutes, until the onion is translucent. Stir in the carrot and fennel and continue to cook for about 15 minutes, until all the vegetables are tender. Add the beans and the stock to the skillet and cook for 5 minutes. Stir in the tomatoes and cook for another 10 minutes to allow all the flavors to meld. Season with the salt and pepper.

4   To make the sturgeon, preheat the oven to 400°F. Sprinkle the fish with the salt and pepper, then wrap each piece of fish in a slice of country ham, leaving the ends exposed.

5   In a large ovenproof skillet, heat the oil over medium-high heat until hot. Add the fish and cook on all sides until the ham is golden brown. Transfer the skillet to the oven and continue to cook for another 4 to 5 minutes; the fish is done when it feels firm to the touch. Serve the fish on top of the ragout.

ROASTED PINEAPPLE UPSIDE-DOWN CAKE

SERVES 8

A native of the West Indies, the pineapple was the colonial symbol of hospitality. The pineapple symbol is used throughout the South, and, fortunately, so is the sweet fruit. In the winter, we add cinnamon and vanilla bean to our pineapple upside-down cake. The cake may be made ahead of time, but it is extraordinary when served warm.

FOR THE PINEAPPLE

I PINEAPPLE, PEELED

4 TABLESPOONS (½ STICK) UNSALTED BUTTER, MELTED

½ CUP GRANULATED SUGAR

I TEASPOON GROUND CINNAMON

¼ TEASPOON GROUND CLOVES

⅛ TEASPOON FINE SEA SALT

6 TABLESPOONS (¾ STICK) UNSALTED BUTTER

¾ CUP (PACKED) LIGHT BROWN SUGAR

FOR THE CAKE

1½ CUPS ALL-PURPOSE FLOUR

2 TEASPOONS BAKING POWDER

I TEASPOON GROUND CINNAMON

¼ TEASPOON FINE SEA SALT

6 TABLESPOONS (¾ STICK) UNSALTED BUTTER, AT ROOM
TEMPERATURE

I VANILLA BEAN, SPLIT AND SEEDS SCRAPED OUT WITH THE
TIP OF A KNIFE

I CUP GRANULATED SUGAR

2 LARGE EGGS, AT ROOM TEMPERATURE

½ CUP HEAVY CREAM

1   Preheat the oven to 350°F. Position a rack in the center of the oven.

2   To make the topping, cut the pineapple in quarters lengthwise and cut out the core. Cut each quarter into ½-inch-thick wedges. Pour the melted butter into a small bowl. In another small bowl, stir together the granulated sugar, cinnamon, cloves, and salt. Dip both sides of each pineapple wedge in the melted butter, then lightly coat in the sugar mixture.

3   Arrange the pineapple wedges in the bottom of a 10-inch cast-iron skillet, positioning them very close together to cover the bottom of the skillet, overlapping the wedges if necessary.

4   Roast in the oven for 20 minutes, until the pineapple begins to brown on the edges. Combine the butter and brown sugar in a small saucepan; cook over medium heat until the butter melts and the mixture becomes smooth. Pour the warm butter mixture over the roasted pineapple and set it aside.

5   To make the cake, in a medium bowl, whisk together the flour, baking powder, cinnamon, and salt. In the bowl of an electric mixer, beat the butter until creamy.

6   Add the vanilla seeds and granulated sugar and beat until fluffy. Add the eggs one at a time, beating well and scraping down the sides of the bowl between additions. Beat in the flour mixture in three additions, alternating with additions of the cream. Spread the batter over the pineapple topping and smooth with a spatula.

7   Bake for 35 to 40 minutes, until a toothpick inserted into the center of the cake comes out clean. Let the cake cool in the skillet on a rack for 10 minutes.

8   Place a large dinner plate or round platter a little bigger than the skillet upside down over the skillet. Protecting your hands with oven mitts, grasp the skillet and plate on both sides and, in one swift motion, invert it and place it on the counter. Carefully lift the skillet off the plate; if any of the pineapple wedges stick to the bottom of the skillet, just use a spatula to loosen them and then replace them on the cake. Let the cake cool for a few more minutes, just until the topping firms a bit, then slice and serve warm or at room temperature.

SOUTHERN MOUNTAIN CAVIAR ⌒ THE MOST SIGNIFICANT DISTINCTION BETWEEN OUR LATE FALL HOLIDAY MENUS AND OUR WINTER HOLIDAY SPREADS IS CAVIAR AND CHAMPAGNE. IT IS NOT POSSIBLE TO STAND IN FRONT OF A FIRE, SURROUNDED BY THE SCENT OF BALSAM AND THE AROMA OF HOLIDAY SWEETS, WITHOUT THINKING OF THE

quickly approaching year's end and the arrival of a new set of seasons. We've always served imported beluga, sevruga, and osetra caviar, but in recent years, we've been thrilled to add cured golden trout eggs from North Carolina and luminous, sevruga-like pearls of cured hackleback fish roe to our winter celebrations along with the American white sturgeon caviar and paddlefish roe that we like so well. American caviar is a salute to a luxury that had been lost.

When the Europeans arrived in North America, no fish was more plentiful than the various sorts of sturgeon that lived in the lakes, streams, and rivers from upstate New York to the Great Lakes and the Pacific Northwest, and in the entire length of the Mississippi River. By the nineteenth century, the United States produced 90 percent of the world's caviar, and within a few decades the fish were nearly harvested to extinction and American caviar became a thing of the past. Over the past several decades, Tennessee, Kentucky, and North Carolina have led the nation in restocking rivers and lakes with the hackleback sturgeon and paddlefish that once teemed in these waters. And although we have no proof that the roe from these fish was salted and cured in earlier eras, there is no doubt that the fish farmers who have been rearing the high-grade hackleback, paddlefish, and trout for river restocking have found an exciting sideline in caviar.

Caviar making was a logical extension of the Jennings family's Sunburst Trout Company, a fifty-year-old business built on land in North Carolina that the family has owned since the 1880s. We've long been fans of their firm, sweet, clean-tasting trout and, despite our bias for sturgeon egg, we were eager to see what the Jenningses would make of trout eggs. What they've made is a delicious, subtle, and far less cured fish egg with a buttery finish that is reminiscent of osetra-grade caviar.

Shuckman's Fish Company and Smokery in Louisville, Kentucky, did not have a history of curing fish eggs. The company grew from a grocery and meat store that Issa Shuckman opened in 1919 and as the generations passed, the family began smoking meat and fish to sell in the store. Lewis Shuckman, the grandson of the founder, now runs the family business and in recent decades, as the public appetite veered from meat to fish, he began smoking more varieties of fish, including Kentucky paddlefish. Paddlefish roe can make good caviar, and Mr. Shuckman began experimenting with various formulas. His cured paddlefish roe has a deep sheen and a silky flavor that our guests have compared to the sevruga grade.

Whether the caviar is domestic or imported, we like to serve it with our farm-fresh scrambled eggs, on small crackers, stuffed into small potatoes, or on blini.

CORN BLINI

MAKES ABOUT 24 BLINI

We make both buckwheat and corn blini, but the corn version seems best suited to our regional caviar.

1 TABLESPOON ACTIVE DRY YEAST
¾ CUP LUKEWARM WATER, PLUS MORE IF NEEDED
2 LARGE EGGS, SEPARATED
2 TABLESPOONS CRÈME FRAÎCHE
1 TABLESPOON SORGHUM
¾ CUP STONE-GROUND CORNMEAL
¼ CUP ALL-PURPOSE FLOUR
½ TEASPOON SALT
2 TABLESPOONS UNSALTED BUTTER, MELTED

1   In a mixing bowl, stir the yeast and lukewarm water until well combined and let sit for 5 minutes, until it becomes foamy. Stir in the egg yolks, crème fraîche, and sorghum. In a separate mixing bowl combine the cornmeal, flour, and salt. Fold the egg yolk mixture into the cornmeal mixture a little at a time and then add the melted butter.

2   In another bowl, beat the egg whites until they form stiff peaks. Using a rubber spatula, fold the egg whites into the cornmeal and egg mixture.

3   Heat a medium nonstick skillet or a griddle over medium heat. Drop tablespoon-size spoonfuls of the mixture into the pan spaced 1-inch apart and cook until golden brown on both sides. Remove, repeat with the remaining batter, and serve.

Cornmeal blinis with crème fraîche, chives, and American caviars:
Steelhead, Paddlefish, and Golden Char Roe.

MIDWINTER DINNER

Our garden rises remarkably early in the year and goes to bed for the winter quite late. In the coldest months our lettuce comes from the hothouse. You know you are spoiled by a farm when vegetables from the greenhouse feel special. This impressive meal for company pairs a salad of toothsome butter lettuce with a succulent wintery pork dish. Most of the fixin's for this menu can be done ahead of time.

ON WINE ⤳ *A rich, robust pork belly asks for a wine that is both deeply aromatic and not overly rich. Roussanne wines achieve these traits, and one we particularly like is Alban Roussanne from the Edna Valley, near San Luis Obispo, California—proof that a world-class wine can be made in areas of our country that are off the beaten path.*

BUTTER LETTUCE WITH SHEEP'S MILK DRESSING

SERVES 4 TO 6

This simple dressing is one of our most requested. It is best on mild greens. A slab of fresh cheese or a grate of aged sheep's cheese makes it even finer.

¼ CUP SHEEP'S MILK YOGURT

¼ CUP MAYONNAISE

I TEASPOON FRESH LEMON JUICE

¼ TEASPOON KOSHER SALT

⅛ TEASPOON FRESHLY GROUND BLACK PEPPER

I HEAD OF BUTTER LETTUCE, SEPARATED INTO LEAVES

In a small bowl, whisk together the yogurt, mayonnaise, lemon juice, salt, and pepper. Divide the lettuce among serving plates and drizzle with the dressing.

BOURBON-BRAISED PORK BELLY ON GRITS WITH CARAMELIZED ONIONS

SERVES 4 TO 6

With a little notice, most butchers can get pork belly, which is basically just fresh bacon. Pork cheeks can also be seared and braised this way. Kimchee Collards (see page 103) make a tasty accompaniment. Low and slow heat is the key to this recipe.

FOR THE BELLY

2½-POUND SLAB OF PORK BELLY

½ CUP KOSHER SALT

½ CUP SUGAR

I TABLESPOON VEGETABLE OIL

1½ CUPS BOURBON

1½ CUPS VEGETABLE STOCK (PAGE 268) OR LOW-SODIUM VEGETABLE BROTH

FOR THE GRITS

2 CUPS MILK

2 CUPS WATER

2 TEASPOONS KOSHER SALT

½ CUP WHITE STONE-GROUND GRITS

2 TEASPOONS UNSALTED BUTTER

I TEASPOON FRESHLY GROUND BLACK PEPPER

FOR THE ONIONS

I TEASPOON VEGETABLE OIL

2 LARGE VIDALIA OR OTHER SWEET ONIONS (ABOUT 12 OUNCES EACH), HALVED AND SLICED PAPER-THIN

¼ TEASPOON KOSHER SALT

¼ TEASPOON FRESHLY GROUND BLACK PEPPER

½ TEASPOON APPLE CIDER VINEGAR

1   To make the belly, sprinkle it all over with the salt and sugar, place on a rimmed baking sheet, and cover with plastic wrap. Refrigerate for at least 12 hours and up to 1 day.

2   When ready to cook the belly, preheat the oven to 325°F. Rinse the belly briefly under cold water to remove the excess salt and sugar and then pat it dry. In a large skillet, heat the oil over high heat and cook the belly for 6 to 8 minutes, turning it once, until browned on both sides.

3   Transfer the belly to a large casserole dish and add the bourbon and stock. Cover with foil and bake for 4 to 4½ hours, or until the belly is so tender a fork can be inserted into the center and turned with ease. Remove the belly from the cooking liquid and let it sit on a cutting board for 5 minutes before slicing and serving.

4   About 1 hour before the pork is done, make the grits. In a large saucepan, bring the milk, 2 cups water, and 1 teaspoon of the salt just to a boil over medium-high heat. Whisking constantly, very slowly whisk the grits into the milk mixture. Switch to a wooden spoon and stir the grits until the liquid returns to a boil. Reduce the heat to low, cover the pan, and cook, stirring occasionally to prevent the grits from scorching and sticking, for 45 to 60 minutes, until the grits have thickened to the consistency of thick oatmeal. Stir in the butter, pepper, and remaining 1 teaspoon salt. Keep the grits warm until serving.

5   Meanwhile, to make the onions, in a medium skillet, heat the oil over medium heat. Add the onions, salt, and pepper and cook, stirring every few minutes, for 20 to 25 minutes, until golden brown. Stir in the vinegar and cook for 1 more minute.

6   To serve, place a scoop of warm grits in the center of each plate and put a serving of the belly on top of the grits with some onions on the side.

COCONUT CAKE

MAKES ONE 9-INCH LAYER CAKE

Lane cake, caramel cake, hummingbird cake—Southerners have a special place in their hearts and a special aptitude for baking layer cakes, and coconut cake reigns. Like most icons, coconut cake has many recipes vying for best of show. Only one thing is non-negotiable: coconut cake has got to be good.

FOR THE CAKE

1½ CUPS MILK

2 STICKS PLUS 2 TABLESPOONS UNSALTED BUTTER

3 CUPS ALL-PURPOSE FLOUR

4 TEASPOONS BAKING POWDER

¾ TEASPOON FINE SEA SALT

6 LARGE EGGS, AT ROOM TEMPERATURE

3 CUPS SUGAR

1½ TEASPOONS PURE VANILLA EXTRACT

FOR THE FROSTING AND FILLING

3 STICKS UNSALTED BUTTER, AT ROOM TEMPERATURE

1½ TEASPOONS PURE VANILLA EXTRACT

6 CUPS (1½ POUNDS) CONFECTIONERS' SUGAR, SIFTED

3 TO 5 TABLESPOONS HEAVY CREAM

2 CUPS UNSWEETENED SHREDDED COCONUT

2 6-OUNCE BAGS OF UNSWEETENED FRESH FROZEN FLAKED COCONUT, THAWED (AVAILABLE IN ASIAN MARKETS AND HEALTH FOOD STORES; CONVENTIONAL UNSWEETENED [FRESH OR DRIED] COCONUT CAN ALSO BE USED)

1   Preheat the oven to 325°F. Grease and flour three 9-inch cake pans and set them aside.

2   To make the cake, in a small saucepan, heat the milk and butter over low heat, stirring, until the butter melts. Remove the milk mixture from the heat and set it aside to cool to room temperature.

3   In a medium bowl, combine the flour, baking powder, and salt and set aside. In the bowl of an electric mixer, beat the eggs and sugar, scraping down the sides of the bowl often, until the mixture is thick and pale yellow in color. Using a spatula, stir the flour mixture into the egg mixture, stirring just until combined. Add the cooled milk mixture and the vanilla and stir until smooth.

4   Divide the batter evenly among the prepared cake pans. Bake for 25 to 30 minutes, until the tops of the cakes are golden and spring back when touched lightly in the center, and the sides of the cake begin to pull away from the pan. Cool in the pans for 10 minutes. Turn the cakes out onto wire racks to cool to room temperature.

5   To make the frosting and filling, combine the butter and vanilla in a large bowl and beat until smooth. Gradually beat in the confectioners' sugar, scraping down the sides of the bowl often. The frosting will be very stiff; beat in enough cream, 1 tablespoon at a time, until it is creamy and spreadable. Set aside 1 cup of the frosting in a medium bowl to use in the filling. Cover the rest of the frosting with plastic wrap and set it aside.

6   Preheat the oven to 350°F. Spread the shredded coconut evenly on a rimmed baking sheet. Bake the coconut for 5 to 6 minutes, until it is golden brown. Transfer the coconut to a bowl and set aside to cool to room temperature.

7   Stir the thawed flaked coconut into the reserved cup of frosting.

8   To assemble the cake, place one of the cake layers on a cake stand or large plate and spread the top with half of the flaked coconut and frosting mixture. Cover with another cake layer, top side down, and spread with the rest of the coconut mixture. Cover with the last cake layer, then spread the top and sides of the cake with the remaining frosting. Using your hands, press the toasted coconut gently onto the sides of the cake.

9   Cover the cake loosely with plastic wrap and let sit at room temperature for at least 4 hours and up to 1 day before serving.

SUNDAY SUPPER

Sunday dinner is served midday in our neck of the woods. It was designed as an after-church event and, lest the preacher happen by, the meal was home cooking at its best. Sunday supper is different. It is an evening meal usually for immediate family and very close friends; it is quieter and not bound to the same fried-chicken convention as Sunday dinner. Sunday evening is one of our favorite times to spend a little longer at the table. We try to set a cozy mood through the dishes we serve.

ON WINE ⁓ *This menu is a study in juxtaposition—the lemony flavors of the chicken marry with the robust, almost oaky tones of the butternut squash purée—and this makes us think of a wine with light hints of fruit and stronger, exotic spice notes, especially in the winter. With their affinity for birds of all kinds, Pinot Noirs, especially those with a ginger-like spice, make a wonderful match. We love the classic Russian River–style Pinot Noir, particularly those crafted by Williams Selyem Winery.*

RAW WINTER VEGETABLE SALAD

SERVES 4

The dense vegetables of the cold months seem ever destined for the long cooking that creates a soft, comforting texture. If shaved fine, however, these same vegetables are lively and crunchy and surprising enough to make one sit up and take notice: Raw winter squash? Who would have thought it could taste so good? A vegetable peeler, the long grate on a hand grater, a mandoline, or a very sharp knife and a culinary degree can be used to create the thin slices that are essential to this dish. To ensure peak crispness, let the vegetables sit in ice water for a few minutes prior to cutting them.

I BUTTERNUT SQUASH, BULB ONLY, PEELED, SPLIT IN HALF, AND SEEDED

I CELERY ROOT, PEELED

I LARGE CARROT WITH GREENS ATTACHED, PEELED AND TRIMMED, GREENS RESERVED SEPARATELY

5 VERY SMALL STRIPED BEETS, TRIMMED AND PEELED

I POMEGRANATE

2 TABLESPOONS CELERY LEAVES, THE SMALL YELLOW ONES FROM THE HEART

I TEASPOON BANYULS VINEGAR

1½ TABLESPOONS GRAPESEED OIL

½ TEASPOON KOSHER SALT

¼ TEASPOON FRESHLY GROUND BLACK PEPPER

1   Shave the butternut squash into paper-thin strips and place the strips in a bowl of ice water to keep crisp. Next, square off the edges of the celery root, then cut the root into 4 or 5 slices and shave paper-thin strips off the thin sides of the slices. Finally, shave slices off the carrot and cover with the ice water.

2   To prepare the beets, shave them into paper-thin slices; place them in a second bowl of ice water. Finally, cut the pomegranate in half and, using a spoon, knock all of the seeds into a bowl and remove any bits of white membrane.

3   To assemble the salads, drain the vegetables from the ice water and dry them by either spinning them in a salad spinner or patting them dry with paper towels. Place all the vegetables in a large bowl and toss with the celery leaves. Add the vinegar, oil, salt, and pepper and toss again. Divide among 4 serving plates, sprinkle with pomegranate seeds, and top each with a few feathery pieces of carrot top.

OPPOSITE: Outside and fireside at the holidays.

POUSSIN ROASTED WITH SUMAC-GINGER BUTTER

SERVES 4

While many farmers are now raising and selling small, tender chickens, the little French poussin is perhaps even more widely available. Fresh or dried sumac, which is native to Tennessee, can easily be found elsewhere in the country in Middle Eastern grocers as well as in specialty food stores. The zest of one lemon, or a teaspoon of lemon juice, can be used instead.

2 MEDIUM VIDALIA OR OTHER SWEET ONIONS

I TABLESPOON VEGETABLE OIL

8 TABLESPOONS (I STICK) UNSALTED BUTTER, AT ROOM TEMPERATURE

I TABLESPOON GROUND SUMAC

I TABLESPOON FRESHLY GRATED PEELED GINGER

I½ TEASPOONS KOSHER SALT

4 I½-POUND POUSSINS, WING TIPS REMOVED

1   Preheat the oven to 475°F.

2   Cut two ½-inch-thick slices from the center of each onion. Place the slices in a roasting pan, brush them with the oil, and set the pan aside. (Save the rest of the onions for another use.)

3   In a small bowl, stir together the butter, sumac, ginger, and ½ teaspoon of the salt; set aside.

4   Rinse the poussins inside and out under cold running water and pat them dry with paper towels. Sprinkle them inside and out with the remaining I teaspoon salt. Use your fingers to gently loosen the skin over the breasts of the poussins, being careful not to puncture the skin. Push a quarter of the butter mixture under the skin and over the breast meat of each bird, then gently smooth the skin back into place. Massage the skin to evenly distribute the butter.

5   Cut a small slit in the skin above the legs on each poussin. Crisscross the legs and tuck the ends through the slits on the opposite leg to hold them together. Place a poussin on top of each onion slice in the roasting pan.

6   Roast the poussin for 30 minutes, or until they begin to brown. Reduce the oven temperature to 350°F and roast for 10 minutes more, or until an instant-read thermometer inserted into the thickest part of the thigh (but not touching bone) registers 170°F, or when the juices run clear when the thigh is pierced with the tip of a sharp knife.

7   Let the poussins rest at room temperature for 5 minutes, then serve one per person. If you'd like to serve the birds halved rather than whole, use kitchen shears to split each poussin down the breast bone and then cut along both sides of the back bone.

WINTER SQUASH PURÉE

SERVES 8

A variety of spices can be added to the squash, but we think it's sublime au naturel. Served alongside roasted chicken and meats, the purée soaks up excess juices well.

5 POUNDS WINTER SQUASH, SUCH AS BUTTERNUT, ACORN, HUBBARD, AND/OR KABOCHA

¼ CUP VEGETABLE OIL

1 TEASPOON KOSHER SALT, PLUS MORE TO TASTE

½ CUP HEAVY CREAM, OR AS NEEDED

2 TABLESPOONS UNSALTED BUTTER

¼ TEASPOON GROUND WHITE PEPPER

1   Preheat the oven to 400°F.

2   Cut the squashes in half and scrape out and discard the seeds and strings from each. Brush the cut sides with oil and sprinkle with 1 teaspoon of the salt. Place the squashes cut side down on one or more rimmed baking sheets and roast for 1 hour to 1¼ hours, until they are very tender when pierced with the tip of a paring knife. Remove from the oven and let sit at room temperature until the squashes are cool enough to handle.

3   Scoop the tender flesh out of each squash with a spoon and transfer it to a food processor (work in batches if necessary). Pulse the squash, then begin adding cream and processing until the mixture is very smooth and about as thick as mashed potatoes.

4   Reheat the purée if necessary in a large saucepan, and stir in the butter and pepper; add more cream if the mixture has become too stiff. Taste the purée and add more salt if desired. Serve warm.

BAKED BUTTERSCOTCH PUDDING

SERVES 6

Scotch amplifies the butterscotch flavor in our version of a Southern classic. The pudding can be made a day before serving and served cold or brought to room temperature.

8 LARGE EGG YOLKS

¼ CUP (PACKED) LIGHT BROWN SUGAR

½ TEASPOON FINE SEA SALT

2½ TABLESPOONS SCOTCH

2 CUPS HEAVY CREAM

1 CUP MILK

¾ CUP GRANULATED SUGAR

1   Preheat the oven to 325°F. Arrange six 6-ounce ramekins in the bottom of a baking dish and set aside. In a large bowl, whisk together the yolks, brown sugar, salt, and Scotch and set aside. In a medium saucepan, bring the cream and milk just to a boil over medium heat and set aside.

2   In a small heavy saucepan, heat the granulated sugar over medium heat until it melts, swirling the pan to make sure all the sugar dissolves. Continue cooking until the sugar turns a deep amber. Whisking constantly, very slowly add half of the warm cream mixture to the melted sugar; be careful as the mixture will bubble and steam vigorously. Continue whisking until the mixture is smooth, then whisk it back into the saucepan with the remaining warm cream mixture. Whisking constantly, whisk the cream and sugar mixture into the egg mixture in a slow, steady stream, then strain through a fine-mesh sieve into a large bowl or pitcher with a pouring spout.

3   Divide the egg mixture among the ramekins. Pour enough hot water into the baking dish to come halfway up the sides of the ramekins and cover the baking dish with aluminum foil. Bake the puddings for 35 to 40 minutes, until a thin knife inserted into the centers comes out clean. Let the ramekins sit in the water bath until the puddings cool to room temperature. Remove the ramekins from the water, cover with plastic wrap, and refrigerate until chilled.

SAM'S CASSOULET

SERVES 6

In this recipe, the best flavor comes from using one spicy, garlicky sausage and another that is sweeter and more herbaceous. The beans require six hours of soaking, but the dish can be cooked up to three days before serving. Bring the cassoulet to room temperature several hours before dinner and reheat it slowly in a very low oven.

12 OUNCES (2 CUPS) CANNELLINI BEANS

4 CUPS CHICKEN STOCK (PAGE 268) OR LOW-SODIUM CHICKEN BROTH

1 WHITE ONION, HALVED

6 SPRIGS OF FRESH THYME

7 SPRIGS OF FRESH FLAT-LEAF PARSLEY

2 BAY LEAVES

3½ TEASPOONS KOSHER SALT

1¾ TEASPOONS FRESHLY GROUND BLACK PEPPER

¼ POUND PORK SAUSAGE, CHOPPED

¼ POUND VENISON SAUSAGE, CHOPPED

¼ POUND THICK-CUT BACON, DICED

1 MEDIUM CARROT, PEELED AND FINELY DICED

6 CLOVES OF GARLIC, MINCED

½ CUP WHITE WINE

2 TABLESPOONS TOMATO PASTE

3 CUPS DRIED BREAD CRUMBS

3 TABLESPOONS DUCK FAT OR OLIVE OIL

1 TABLESPOON CHOPPED FRESH FLAT-LEAF PARSLEY

4 CONFIT DUCK LEGS (SEE RESOURCES)

1 TABLESPOON SHERRY VINEGAR

1   In a large bowl, soak the beans in 6 cups water for 8 hours or overnight.

2   Drain the beans and place them in a large saucepan along with the stock, half of the onion, 3 sprigs of the thyme, 4 sprigs of the parsley, and 1 bay leaf. Bring the mixture to a boil over high heat, then simmer, uncovered, for about 1 hour, until the beans are tender.

3   Strain the beans over a bowl and reserve the liquid. Discard the herb sprigs and bay leaf. Stir 2 teaspoons of the salt and 1 teaspoon of the pepper into the beans and set them aside.

4   Preheat the oven to 350°F. Place a medium skillet over medium heat and add the pork and venison sausages. Cook, stirring occasionally, about 10 minutes, until the sausage is lightly browned. Using a slotted spoon, remove the sausage from the skillet and set it aside, leaving the fat in the skillet.

5   Return the skillet to medium heat and add the bacon. Cook for 7 to 8 minutes. Meanwhile, dice the remaining onion and add it to the skillet along with the carrot. When the bacon is crisp, remove it from the pan using a slotted spoon and set aside. Continue cooking the carrots and onions for 6 to 7 minutes or until tender. Add 1 of the minced garlic cloves and cook for 2 more minutes. Add the white wine and cook 2 minutes more. Add the other bay leaf, remaining sprigs of thyme and parsley and cook for 1 minute. Stir in the tomato paste, 1 teaspoon of the salt, ½ teaspoon of the pepper. Cook another 3 minutes; remove the skillet from the heat and set aside.

6   In a small bowl, toss together the bread crumbs, remaining minced garlic clove, duck fat, parsley, and remaining ½ teaspoon salt and ¼ teaspoon pepper.

7   To assemble the cassoulet, spread half of the vegetable mixture over the bottom of a 9 x 13-inch baking or casserole dish. Spread half of the beans evenly on top, then nestle the duck legs into the beans and sprinkle with the sausage. Top with the remaining vegetable mixture, the remaining beans, and sprinkle with the bacon. Pour in enough of the reserved bean liquid to come just to the top of the beans; if you don't have enough, use a little more stock. Sprinkle the bread crumbs over the top and bake for 30 minutes.

8   Remove the dish from the oven. Using a table knife, pierce the top of the casserole 5 or 6 times to allow the juices to bubble up onto the surface; this will help a really good crust to form. Return the dish to the oven and continue baking another 30 to 40 minutes, until the bread crumbs are golden brown and the filling is bubbling. Serve hot.

DINNER IN DEER SEASON

Most venison that is served in restaurants (or in the homes of those who do not hunt) is farm-raised. Nevertheless, the sharp edge of the air on a late fall evening can make even the nonhunter feel as if he has returned from a long tramp through the woods in pursuit and is ready to tuck into a venison meal.

ON WINE *Venison's lean, peppery character is beautifully complemented by a Syrah. We particularly like the Syrahs from a town in the northern Rhone called Côte Rôtie. This region is a colder region for Syrah and produces more elegant and floral wine with a hint of black pepper that makes a fine counterpoint—and echo—for the venison. Most producers in this region make a fairly small amount of wine and are family owned. Bernard Burgaud and his family offer a beautiful version of this wine.*

SUNCHOKE SOUP

SERVES 8

Also called sunroot, Jerusalem artichoke, and earth apple, the sunchoke grows from Maine to the Eastern mountain states; however, Sir Walter Raleigh found one growing in the state now called Virginia, so Southerners tend to claim the gnarly little root. It is in the sunflower family and we love its potato-like texture and sweet, nutty taste.

1½ POUNDS JERUSALEM ARTICHOKES, PEELED AND CHOPPED

2 TEASPOONS PLUS 1 TABLESPOON EXTRA-VIRGIN OLIVE OIL

½ TEASPOON KOSHER SALT, PLUS MORE AS NEEDED

¼ TEASPOON FRESHLY GROUND BLACK PEPPER

2 STALKS OF CELERY, DICED

1 VIDALIA OR OTHER SWEET ONION, DICED

1 LEEK, WHITE PART ONLY, THINLY SLICED

1 MEDIUM RUSSET POTATO, PEELED AND DICED

2 TABLESPOONS MADEIRA OR SHERRY

1 TABLESPOON FRESH THYME LEAVES

1 BAY LEAF

4 CUPS VEGETABLE STOCK (PAGE 268) OR LOW-SODIUM VEGETABLE BROTH, PLUS MORE AS NEEDED

1 Preheat the oven to 375°F.

2 Toss the Jerusalem artichokes with 2 teaspoons of the olive oil and the salt and pepper. Place on a rimmed baking sheet and roast for 25 to 30 minutes, until tender, stirring once or twice. Set aside.

3 Meanwhile, in a large saucepan over medium heat, heat the remaining tablespoon of oil. Add the celery, onion, leek, and potato. Cover and cook for 7 to 8 minutes, until the vegetables are just tender, then stir in the roasted artichokes along with the Madeira, thyme, and bay leaf. Cook for 2 to 3 minutes, then add the stock and bring to a simmer. Cover the pan and reduce the heat to medium low. Cook for 25 to 30 minutes, until all the vegetables are very tender. Discard the bay leaf.

4 Working in small batches, purée the soup in a blender or food processor and pass the soup through a strainer to remove any fibers. Return the soup to the pot, and stir in more vegetable stock if you need to for a nice velvety consistency to your soup. Taste it and season with more salt if you wish. Reheat the soup and serve.

CIDER-BASTED VENISON

SERVES 4

Using cider brings out the sweet tones in venison and also amplifies the autumn mood of the meat. Here, we seal in some juices by browning the loin in a hot pan prior to putting it in the oven. Even so the roast needs to be watched carefully. Venison is lean and even a few minutes of overcooking will result in a tough piece of meat.

3 CUPS APPLE CIDER

ZEST OF ½ ORANGE, REMOVED IN STRIPS WITH A VEGETABLE PEELER

1 CINNAMON STICK

4 6-OUNCE BONELESS VENISON LOIN STEAKS

1½ TEASPOONS KOSHER SALT

½ TEASPOON FRESHLY GROUND BLACK PEPPER

1 TABLESPOON VEGETABLE OIL

2 TEASPOONS UNSALTED BUTTER

1   In a medium saucepan, combine the cider, zest, and cinnamon stick and bring to a boil over high heat. Lower the heat to medium and boil until the mixture is reduced to ½ cup, about 25 minutes. Remove from the heat, discard the cinnamon and orange zest, and set the reduced cider aside.

2   Sprinkle the venison with the salt and pepper. In a medium skillet, heat the oil over medium-high heat. When very hot, add the venison and cook, turning once, until well browned, about 2 minutes per side. Add the butter and half the cider reduction to the pan. Continue cooking the meat for 5 minutes, spooning the sauce in the pan over it every minute or so. Check the meat; it should be medium-rare, still vibrant red (but not raw) at the center if you cut into a piece with a paring knife. (An instant-read thermometer inserted into the center of a piece should register 130°F.)

3   Transfer the venison to a cutting board and let rest for 5 minutes. Slice the steaks in half long ways, if you like, to show their bright-red centers. Place the steaks on plates and drizzle with the pan juices and the remaining cider reduction.

SKILLET SLAW

SERVES 4

This simple cabbage sauté is a winter favorite. It flatters almost any roast—chicken, pork, venison, or veal—and makes a nice companion to sliced sausages and hams, as well.

2 OUNCES BACON, DICED

2 TEASPOONS VEGETABLE OIL

½ SMALL HEAD OF WHITE CABBAGE, CORED AND VERY THINLY SLICED

½ SMALL HEAD OF RED CABBAGE, CORED AND VERY THINLY SLICED

3 TABLESPOONS APPLE CIDER VINEGAR

1 TEASPOON CARAWAY SEEDS

1 TEASPOON KOSHER SALT

½ TEASPOON FRESHLY GROUND BLACK PEPPER

1   In a large skillet, cook the bacon over medium-high heat for 10 minutes, until crispy. Transfer the bacon to paper towels with a slotted spoon and set it aside.

2   Reduce the heat to medium. Add 1 teaspoon of the oil and the white cabbage to the skillet. Toss the cabbage with tongs until it is lightly coated with fat. Cover the skillet and cook, stirring often, for about 8 minutes, until the cabbage is just tender. Transfer the cabbage into a bowl and set aside. Add the remaining 1 teaspoon of oil and the red cabbage to the skillet. Toss the cabbage with tongs until it is lightly coated with fat. Cover the skillet and cook, stirring often, for about 8 minutes, until the red cabbage is just tender. Add the cooked red cabbage to the white cabbage.

3   Pour 2 tablespoons of the vinegar into the skillet and stir to scrape up the browned glaze from the bottom of the pan. Pour this hot vinegar over the cabbage and toss to coat. Add the remaining 1 tablespoon of vinegar, the caraway seeds, salt, and pepper to the slaw; toss to combine. Sprinkle the reserved bacon over the slaw and serve warm.

ROAST PARSNIPS

SERVES 4

This simple method brings out the parsnip's natural sweetness and gives a thin, caramelized crust. Roast parsnips are delicious with game, pork, or chicken. Roast parsnips, carrots, and potatoes make a satisfying winter supper as well.

2½ POUNDS (ABOUT 12 MEDIUM) PARSNIPS, PEELED AND SLICED ½ INCH THICK

2 TABLESPOONS VEGETABLE OIL

¾ TEASPOON KOSHER SALT

¼ TEASPOON FRESHLY GROUND BLACK PEPPER

Preheat the oven to 350°F. In a large bowl, toss the sliced parsnips with the oil, salt, and pepper. Transfer them to a rimmed baking sheet and roast for 30 to 40 minutes, stirring once or twice, until tender and browned. Remove from the oven and serve warm.

FIG TART

SERVES 8

Fig jam intensifies the fruit flavor in this tart. We make our own jam, but high-quality commercial versions work nicely as well. We like the free-form shape and rustic feel of the tart and have shaped them smaller to make individual tarts and larger to feed a crowd. Whipped cream, slightly sweetened, is a nice addition.

½ RECIPE BASIC PASTRY (PAGE 270)
¼ CUP FIG JAM
1 POUND FRESH FIGS, STEMMED AND HALVED LENGTHWISE
⅓ CUP PLUS 1 TEASPOON SUGAR
¼ CUP HEAVY CREAM
1 TABLESPOON UNSALTED BUTTER
1 LARGE EGG
2 TABLESPOONS MILK

1   Preheat the oven to 400°F. Lightly butter a baking sheet and set it aside.

2   Divide the pastry in half. On a lightly floured surface, roll each piece of dough into a 9-inch circle. Place the pastry on the prepared baking sheet; overlapping the two circles a little on one side is okay as the edges will be folded in later. Spread 2 tablespoons of jam evenly over each piece of pastry, leaving a 1½-inch border. Arrange the figs over the jam. Cover the tarts with plastic wrap and set them aside.

3   In a small saucepan, cook ⅓ cup of the sugar over medium-high heat without stirring until it melts and turns amber in color. Remove the pan from the heat and carefully stir in the cream and butter, stirring until the mixture is smooth. Brush the tops of the figs with the caramel mixture. Fold the edge of the pastry over the outer edge of the figs, pleating the dough to hold it in place.

4   In a small bowl, whisk together the egg and milk. Brush the edges of the pastry with the egg mixture and then sprinkle with the remaining 1 teaspoon of sugar. Bake for about 25 minutes, until the pastry is golden brown and the figs are just tender. Serve warm or at room temperature, cut into generous wedges.

ABOVE LEFT: The game plan for an evening meal.

ABOVE RIGHT: Built in the 1930s, the Main House, which includes the Laurel Dining Room (foreground) and Dogwood Bar, captures the elegant, clubby feel and slower-paced days of an older South.

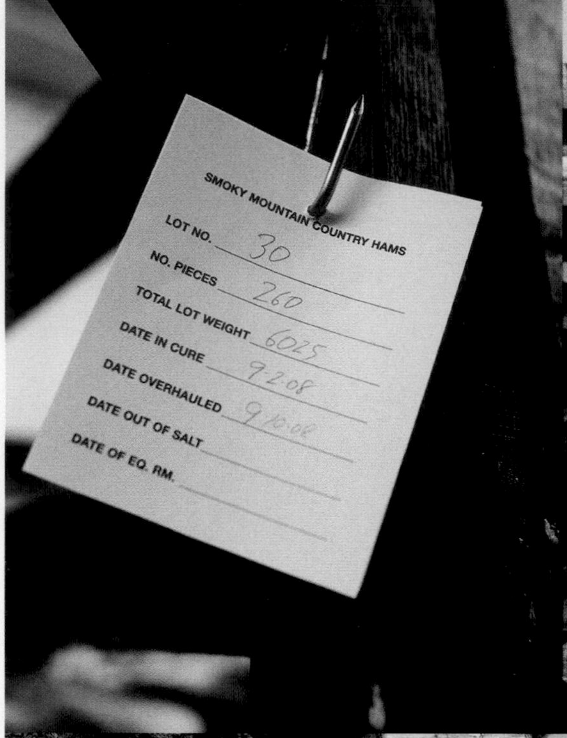
SMOKY MOUNTAIN COUNTRY HAMS
LOT NO. 30
NO. PIECES 260
TOTAL LOT WEIGHT 6025
DATE IN CURE 9-2-08
DATE OVERHAULED 9-10-08
DATE OUT OF SALT
DATE OF EQ. RM.

Bentons

THE DEAN OF AMERICAN BACON ∾ PIGS FLY NOT FAR FROM BLACKBERRY FARM. ABOUT FIFTY MILES SOUTH IN MADISONVILLE, A FEW SELECT BERKSHIRE HOGS LEAVE THE ORDINARY LIFE OF HOOF-AND-FLY TO THE HIGHER REALM OF POETRY. THEIR CHUBBY HAUNCHES BECOME COUNTRY HAM. THEIR FAT-STREAKED BELLIES BECOME

country bacon. Benton's Smoky Mountain County Hams, a low-slung concrete block building on the side of the Highway 411, is the way station, the place where, each year, fewer than ten thousand pigs are anointed into the exclusive order of divine bacon.

In this incarnation—cured in salt and brown sugar, dried and then smoked over hickory and apple wood—pig can live forever, if not in reality, then in the memory of its taste. Critics and food savants are unanimous in their opinion: Benton Bacon is the best bacon in the world. Anything touched by it—the Mississippi sturgeon that is wrapped and roasted in it at Blackberry Farm or the dish of cockles stewed in ham broth that David Chang serves at Momofuku in Manhattan or the froth of bacon sabayon that is served with braised sweetbreads at Craft Restaurant—gains an aspect of hardscrabble mountain life. Intense smoke, the interplay of the sweet and the salty, and the flavor of pork: the taste of Benton Bacon is a Tennessee tattoo.

Allan Benton, the man who shepherds the meat of heirloom hogs into another realm, is fifty-nine years old, compact and lean, with an unflinching blue eyed gaze and a smile that recalls Jimmy Carter's. He grew up butchering hogs at Thanksgiving on his grandparents' farm. He did not, however, grow up imagining a future in pork. Benton was, instead, a high school guidance counselor with a master's degree

when, in 1973, he stopped to think long and hard about his salary and came to the conclusion that he had to make bacon. By chance, a local dairy farmer who had long made custom bacons and hams in his backyard was ready to retire just when Mr. Benton decided to try something new.

The first several decades were sleepless. But gradually, there was more demand for his ham and bacon than Mr. Benton could fill. At the same time, he realized the satisfaction of doing one thing really, really well.

WE CURE 'EM reads the words painted on his smokehouse, a cinder-block building that stands behind his shop that resembles a single-car garage. The building has a concrete floor and a small and cast-iron wood stove that he bought forty years ago from a cousin for fifty dollars. After curing the pork bellies in brown sugar and salt, hanging them and aging them, he rolls racks of the meat into the building, loads the stove with apple and hickory, fires it up, and forgets about it for a few days.

Mr. Benton mentors the bacon-makers at Blackberry Farm. He sees himself as a person who has learned to be patient. In bacon, as in wine, he says, "you have to trust time."

OPPOSITE: A humble concrete block building on the side of Highway 411 is home to Allan Benton's famed bacon and ham. Mr. Benton, a former high school guidance counselor, is still befuddled by the recognition accorded to him, his bacon, and his ham. There is, he says, nothing complicated about doing a job right. Hams are tagged for aging, slabs of bacon are cured and then smoked in the former garage behind his shop. In addition to creating his own cured pork, Mr. Benton has mentored Blackberry Farm's butcher, as well.

SHORT RIBS FOR A LONG WINTER NIGHT

The cooks of the southern mountains took pride in making something from nothing—or at least from bits of meat, such as short ribs, that were considered to be "low on the cow" (or hog). The slow cooking afforded by traditional wood-fired stoves was ideal for such cuts of meat. Over time, the meat could be tenderized by the liquid in which it was braised, and the liquid, in turn, could be enriched by the meat. The result was fall-off-the-bone-tender meat and succulent juices. We love to make braised short ribs for company on cold nights. We like to eat the meal slowly, savoring the afterglow.

ON WINE ∼ *With a leaner and simple cut of meat we often offer up a lighter wine, but with an aged rib eye or short ribs we love a California Cabernet. The structured and lower-throttle style from producers like Philip Togni, Lail, or Ridge Monte Bello is an especially good choice for this rich meal.*

BRAISED SHORT RIBS

SERVES 4

Ample time, as well as a good heavy roasting pan, are the keys to the success of this dish. The ribs are cooked the day before serving and sit overnight. Any high-quality red wine will make good magic with this rich cut of beef.

3 PIECES OF BEEF SHORT RIB, EACH ABOUT 2 POUNDS

¼ CUP KOSHER SALT

1 TABLESPOON VEGETABLE OIL

1 WHITE ONION, PEELED AND ROUGHLY CHOPPED

1 LARGE CARROT, PEELED AND ROUGHLY CHOPPED

1 STALK OF CELERY, ROUGHLY CHOPPED

2 CUPS CABERNET SAUVIGNON OR OTHER HEAVY RED WINE

1 QUART BEEF STOCK (PAGE 269) OR VEGETABLE STOCK (PAGE 268), OR LOW-SODIUM VEGETABLE BROTH

7 SPRIGS OF FRESH THYME

1 BAY LEAF

4 SPRIGS OF FRESH FLAT-LEAF PARSLEY

1   Sprinkle the beef with the salt and let sit at room temperature for 1 hour; this will help season the meat all the way through.

2   Preheat the oven to 325°F.

3   Place the oil in a large skillet set over high heat. When very hot, add the ribs to the skillet and sear until golden brown on all sides. Remove the short ribs from the pan and reduce the heat to medium.

4   Add the onion, carrot, and celery and cook for 7 to 8 minutes, until soft. Pour in the wine and cook until the liquid has evaporated and become syrupy, about 15 minutes. Pour the wine mixture into a small roasting pan and add the ribs, stock, and herbs. Cover the roasting pan with foil and place in the oven. Roast for 4 to 5 hours, or until the bones easily slide out of the meat.

5   Remove the pan from the oven and let the ribs sit in the liquid at room temperature until cool. Cover and refrigerate for 8 hours or overnight.

6   Just before serving, preheat the oven to 325°F and bake the ribs, uncovered, for 20 to 25 minutes, or until they are hot in the center. Cut the rib meat into serving pieces and serve over generous mounds of celery root and potato purée.

CELERY ROOT AND POTATO PURÉE

SERVES 4 WITH LEFTOVERS

Since the celery root and potatoes are both starchy without being sticky, they whip into a perfectly fluffy purée that nicely balances the velvety richness of the short ribs.

3 POUNDS YUKON GOLD OR RUSSET POTATOES, PEELED AND CUT INTO 2-INCH CHUNKS

1 POUND CELERY ROOT, PEELED AND CUT INTO ½-INCH CHUNKS

4 TABLESPOONS (½ STICK) UNSALTED BUTTER

½ CUP WHOLE MILK

2 TEASPOONS KOSHER SALT, OR TO TASTE

¼ TEASPOON FRESHLY GROUND WHITE PEPPER

1   Place the potatoes and celery root in a large saucepan and cover with about an inch of cold salted water. Bring to a boil over high heat, reduce the heat, and simmer for about 25 minutes, until the vegetables are tender when pierced with the tip of a sharp knife.

2   Strain the potatoes and celery root, transfer them to a large bowl, and add the butter, milk, salt, and pepper. Use an electric mixer to quickly whip the potatoes and celery root into a smooth, fluffy purée. Reheat if necessary and serve hot.

CITRUS CARPACCIO WITH CHOCOLATE-COVERED CLEMENTINES

SERVES 4

There are two secrets to this simple dessert: a sharp knife and high-quality chocolate. The chocolate-covered clementines can be made the day before serving, covered carefully, and stored in a cool, but not cold, place.

2 BLOOD ORANGES

2 NAVEL ORANGES

1 PINK GRAPEFRUIT

2 TABLESPOONS SUGAR

2 CLEMENTINES

4½ OUNCES BITTERSWEET CHOCOLATE, CHOPPED, PLUS ANOTHER LARGE CHUNK OF CHOCOLATE FOR MAKING SHAVINGS

1   Using a citrus zester, remove the zest in fine strips from one blood orange, one navel orange, and the grapefruit and place in a small bowl. Stir in 1 tablespoon of the sugar, cover, and set aside.

2   Segment all the blood oranges, oranges, and the grapefruit: Working with one fruit at a time, first slice off the top and the bottom. Place one of the flat sides down on the cutting board and, using a sharp knife, slice off the skin and pith, following the curve of the fruit to remove all the skin and pith but leaving as much of the flesh as possible. Place the fruit in your hand and, using a small paring knife, cut down on either side of each segment, releasing them from the membrane. Place all of the fruit segments in a bowl and sprinkle with the remaining sugar. Toss gently and set aside.

3   Peel the clementines, removing as much of the pithy threads that adhere to the outside of the fruit as possible. Pull the fruits into individual segments.

4   Place the chocolate in a microwave-safe bowl and heat on high, stopping to stir every 10 seconds, until melted.

5   Carefully dip the clementine segments in the chocolate and place on a baking sheet lined with wax paper. Refrigerate until the chocolate has hardened.

6   To assemble, place the fruit segments in a circular pattern, alternating the different fruits, on 4 plates. Garnish with a few of the chocolate-dipped clementines. Run a sharp vegetable peeler over the side of the block of chocolate to make a few tablespoons of thin chocolate shavings and sprinkle them around the plates. Serve cool or at room temperature.

SPRING ⤳ An Appalachian Spring

A body needed a good mess of greens to purify the blood and give vim and vigor for spring planting. —FRANNY BROKC OF KENTUCKY,

as quoted by Joseph Dabney in *Smokehouse Ham, Spoonbread and Scuppernong Wine: The Folklore and Art of Appalachian Cooking*

Were she to be flown around the world blindfolded and dropped in this spot, Ila Hatter would know the month, the day, the time, and exactly where she stood. Mrs. Hatter, a descendant of Pocahontas, is an herbalist, a healer, a writer, and a forager. She teaches wild cookery and plant lore at the University of Tennessee and the Great Smoky Mountain National Park. She has been walking the creases and ridges of western North Carolina and eastern Tennessee for most of her life. Pat Sandler and Jeff Ross, gardeners who also forage for the kitchens at Blackberry Farm, say that ambling through the fields and woods with Mrs. Hatter is like learning to race from a Nascar driver. The chefs compare her to Escoffier. She is the forager's forager, the chef's wild-foods chef.

Mrs. Hatter sees and hears and smells and feels entire worlds that most hikers, birders, fly fishers, and hunters do not know exist. To her, the woods are a symphony, and she recognizes each instrument and every note. More importantly, she knows what all the sensory notes combine to say.

Hundreds of yards away, the smell of the four bears who occupy our valley identifies the land that rolls down from Chilowee Mountain as decisively as a picture postcard might for someone else. After her visits, another wild thing makes its way onto the table at Blackberry Farm, and without knowing it at the time, those who walk with her have absorbed another bit of wisdom.

Walking between Mr. Ross and Ms. Sandler just after dawn one early April morning, Mrs. Hatter smiles and nods as her protégés "read" the air—the scent of white trillium, painted trillium, and yellow trillium, dogwood, rue anemone, and the wild ginger flower; the feel and smell of the earth, loosening and sweet underfoot; the particular sound of spring's snowmelt: a consistent stream of water over rocks in Hesse Creek.

"The trout are running," she says matter-of-factly, as if anybody could tell that a quarter mile from the Hesse Creek. Inhaling as she nears the stream, she points to a green patch, lush as a miniature Ireland on the brown creek bank—cress, tiny-leafed, tender cress!—and promises a grocery list that also includes the tart poke and crow's-feet "salat" as well as morels, chanterelles, and chicken-of-the-woods mushrooms. Farther up Trunk Branch Valley, she assures her protégés, they will find serviceberries and the first raspberries of spring.

In the 1800s, a writer for the *Atlantic Monthly* called the Appalachian people "our contemporary ancestors." The regional response to wild food suggests that little has changed. For locals, there is nothing as fine as pokeweed picked when it is no more than three inches tall, boiled twice, and tossed with bacon fat; nothing more toothsome

than crow's-feet, young dandelion greens, lamb's-quarter, and wood sorrel. Nothing better than creek cress, raw, to scrub away the lingering taste of winter's game and cured meats. Ramps, the wild, garlicky leek whose leaves resemble lily of the valley, are the pride of Appalachian spring, and they are all but a fetish in the region where they are celebrated in festivals. The one in nearby Cosby lasts a week: the vegetable is boiled and sautéed and stewed and baked; turned into omelets and frites; stuffed into chicken, trout,

and sturgeon; wrapped around pork; barbecued and deep-fried; but still, no one ever feels they've had enough.

On this spring morning, the foraging party crosses the creek and continues on toward the mountain. Each of the three carries a white oak basket over the wrist, and the baskets swing in unison with the delicate, step-by-step squish of Mrs. Hatter's walking stick poking and rising from the ground like a metronome. The taste for the wild things of spring was, she says, an early expression of health food.

In addition to managing the garden at Blackberry Farm, Mr. Ross is also a cook. He is more interested in flavor than in folk medicine. The first tart greens of the season brighten the taste of the chicken, trout, and lamb that the farm produces. Young greens are a perfect counterpoint to the richness of suckling pigs and the fatty flesh of grouper. Wild mushrooms—the morels that pop up like gnome hats from the spongy, damp earth, the honey-colored chanterelles that cluster in abandoned orchards, the huge chicken-of-the-woods that grow on the shady side of oak trees—can supply the meaty texture and earthy taste that can otherwise be missing from spring.

Foraged food is a great luxury in the modern world, but when Mr. Ross carries his morning's take up to the kitchen and begins sorting the pickings and imagining dishes with the chefs, he feels that he is tapping into an unbroken stream of making more from less. Every day is a surprise.

Spring, after all, is a fragile and intermittent victory in the foothills. It is impossible to predict. It can appear in one patch of ground and, several feet away, spring can turn into winter. It is difficult to predict when the wild greens and mushrooms will suddenly sprout. And it is not much easier to predict how the spring garden will grow. "The key for farmers, and the planters of flowers and fruit trees," said the writer Peter Jenkins of his home state, "is to figure out when all the little winters that interrupt our spring will be done."

Soon, the buds on the great poplar, the black birch, and the beech will explode and conceal the view. But in the early spring it is still possible to see the tidy patchwork of Blackberry Farm from deep inside the forested hills that surround it. Framed by the trunks of the trees, the fields of sheep and cattle and poultry, the barns and farmstead, and the raised beds of the gardens all appear like the dream of civilization. In the gusty chill of an April morning, it's a hungry-making sight.

The peppery greens and the garlicky greens are a tonic. The local craving to inhale them, preferably stewed in bacon fat, is like spring cleaning for the soul. There is something atavistic and deeply human about this particular appetite.

As her mentor describes the folkloric remedies she has gathered in reading old household diaries and interviewing Cherokee elders as well as the handful of centurions who continue to keep house up in the mountains, Ms. Sandler listens intently.

SPRING PICKIN'S

In early April, morels begin to sprout on the mountains. Mushroom foragers begin to sneak off. They are paranoid about losing the singular knowledge (and ability to pick the fruits) of a prime morel patch. The dome-shaped cap with its honeycombed surface just happens to grow very well in our area, especially in spring. The morel even has a local name: "dry-land fish." According to Fred Sauceman in his book, *The Place Setting*, "It's a delicacy that rewards the instinctual human desire to forage in the forest. And it illustrates one of nature's many ironies, that out of dampness and decay, among the dying root systems of trees, sustenance emerges each spring."

ON WINE *The sweet earthiness of the mushroom bisque and the fresh and pungent flavors of the trout call for a fresh wine with a solid character. A clean young Chablis that has not seen the inside of an aging barrel comes to mind. One version we like is Jean-Marc Brocard, which not only cuts through the richness of the bisque but also cleanses the palate of the ramps' youthful intensity.*

WILD MUSHROOM SOUP

SERVES 4

This bisque allows us to use as many or few wild mushrooms as we have. Although we usually have an abundance of morels, we like to combine them with at least one other variety of mushroom for the greatest depth of flavor.

2 POUNDS WILD SPRING MUSHROOMS (MOREL,
  CHANTERELLE, SHIITAKE, OYSTER, PORCINI)
5 CUPS WATER
1 SPRIG OF FRESH ROSEMARY
8 TABLESPOONS (1 STICK) UNSALTED BUTTER, MELTED
2 TEASPOONS KOSHER SALT, OR TO TASTE
1 TABLESPOON EXTRA-VIRGIN OLIVE OIL
2 SMALL SHALLOTS, CHOPPED
1 TABLESPOON TOMATO PASTE
½ CUP SHERRY
1 CUP HEAVY CREAM

1   Preheat the oven to 350°F.

2   Trim the stems off the mushrooms and place them in a saucepan with the water. Bring to a boil, then cover the pan, reduce the heat, and simmer for 30 minutes. Remove from the heat and strain, reserving the liquid; discard the stems.

3   Brush any dirt off the mushroom caps and chop them if they are large. Place them on a rimmed baking sheet along with the rosemary, drizzle with the butter and 1 teaspoon of the salt, and toss. Roast until the mushrooms are tender, about 20 minutes. Remove from the oven, discard the rosemary, and set the mushrooms aside.

4   In a large saucepan, heat the oil over medium-low heat and add the shallots. Cook for about 10 minutes, stirring occasionally, until the shallots are translucent. Add the tomato paste and continue to cook for another 4 to 5 minutes, until the color becomes brick red. Stir in the sherry and cook for another 3 minutes. Add the roasted mushrooms, reserved mushroom broth, and cream. Cover the pan and simmer for 30 minutes. Season with the remaining teaspoon of salt and serve.

OVEN-BAKED TROUT WITH RAMPS AND MORELS

SERVES 4

We catch trout in our creek and purchase it from our farming friends at Sunburst Trout Company, over the mountain in North Carolina. In the spring and fall, we have more and better trout than seems fair. Here, the firm, sweet fish becomes a study in the season.

2 TABLESPOONS VEGETABLE OIL
1 POUND WHOLE RAMPS PLUS ½ CUP CHOPPED RAMP BULBS
3 CUPS (6 OUNCES) FRESH MORELS, CUT INTO ¼-INCH-
  THICK ROUNDS
1¼ TEASPOONS KOSHER SALT
6 OUNCES COOKED, SHELLED CRAWFISH TAILS
4 8-OUNCE TROUT FILLETS
¼ TEASPOON FRESHLY GROUND BLACK PEPPER

1   Preheat the oven to 325°F.

2   In a large skillet, heat 1 tablespoon of the oil over medium heat. Add the chopped ramp bulbs and cook, stirring often, for about 5 minutes, until they soften. Add the morels and ¼ teaspoon of the salt. Cook, stirring often, for about 6 minutes, until the morels are tender. Fold in the crawfish and set aside.

3   Spread the whole ramps on a rimmed baking sheet and drizzle them with the remaining tablespoon of oil. Arrange the trout fillets over the ramps and sprinkle them with the remaining teaspoon of salt and the pepper. Bake for 8 to 10 minutes, until the fish is cooked through.

4   Meanwhile, reheat the morel mixture over low heat. Top each fillet with an equal portion of the morel mixture and serve warm.

RHUBARB TART WITH WILD RASPBERRY CREAM

SERVES 8

Dock, the green leaves of the rhubarb plant, is one of the first signs of spring. The leaves are edible when very young, but become toxic as the season progresses. Shortly after the leaves emerge, the red stems begin to appear. Sour and sturdy, rhubarb makes a delectable tart. Here we add another hallmark of spring—wild raspberries—for a sweet, flowery note.

½ RECIPE BASIC PASTRY (PAGE 270)

6 CUPS SLICED RHUBARB (ABOUT 6 MEDIUM STALKS)

¾ CUP GRANULATED SUGAR

I TABLESPOON ARROWROOT OR CORNSTARCH

JUICE OF I ORANGE (ABOUT ⅓ CUP)

2 CUPS WILD OR REGULAR RASPBERRIES

I CUP HEAVY CREAM

I TABLESPOON CONFECTIONERS' SUGAR

1   Preheat the oven to 350°F.

2   On a lightly floured surface, roll the pastry dough out to a circle about 11 inches in diameter. Fold the dough over your rolling pin and unfold over a 10-inch tart pan with a removable bottom. Ease the dough into the bottom and up the sides of the pan. Roll your pin over the top to trim off any excess dough.

3   Line the pastry with parchment paper and then fill with pie weights or dried beans. Place the pan on a baking sheet and bake for about 10 minutes, until the dough is firm around the edges and looks dry but not browned. Remove from the oven, remove the parchment and weights, and cool the tart shell.

4   In a medium saucepan, combine 3 cups of the rhubarb, the granulated sugar, arrowroot, and orange juice. Cook over medium heat, stirring occasionally, for 6 to 7 minutes, until thickened. Remove from the heat and fold in the remaining 3 cups of rhubarb.

5   Pour the rhubarb mixture into the tart shell and bake for 25 to 30 minutes, until bubbling in the center. Remove from the oven and let cool to room temperature on a wire rack.

6   Just before serving, in a medium bowl, crush the raspberries with the side of a spoon; set aside. In another medium bowl, use an electric mixer to whip the cream and confectioners' sugar together until it forms soft peaks. Fold in the crushed raspberries. Serve the tart with a dollop of the raspberry cream on top.

OPPOSITE: Scenes of spring: Kreis Beall and her mother, Jane Bailey. Kreis Beall with a newborn goat.

SPRING GREENS 〜

A Georgia man recalled the urgency, but couldn't remember the specific dire results if spring greens were not devoured. "It was a must that we eat at least one mess of poke sallet or else we were sure to have pneumonia, or maybe it was typhoid fever," he said.

"Creasy greens" are a mountain cousin of watercress and are usually the first spring green to appear. They are sharper-tasting and more peppery than watercress and are usually braised with fatback, sautéed, or boiled.

Pokeweed, locally known as poke salat, starts popping up in ditches and fence rows next. Young, tender leaves, three to four inches tall, are mild, almost spinach-like, and can be parboiled and then fried in bacon grease or olive oil. Poke is a member of the deadly nightshade family and should always be parboiled several times before being used. After the plant has grown tall and leafy, the greens are bitter and the plants' berries and roots are poisonous. Poke leaves and poke stems also can be dipped in a light batter of flour and salt and fried up like fish, according to one account.

While poke is still beginning to grow, dandelion greens begin to appear. The smallest ones are tart, almost sorrel-like, and are wonderful in salads. As they mature and become thicker and more bitter, they need to be sautéed or boiled. Lamb's-quarter and dock (rhubarb greens) are best parboiled and fried. Crow's-feet, a mustard green, is great plunged into hot grease and served with vinegar on top. Spring greens are the best for "wilting"—preparing as a salad and then cooking in hot bacon fat along with vinegar, chopped eggs, sugar, and salt. In East Tennessee, we don't talk "wilted salad," though. We call it "kilt lettuce."

Well before the wild greens have become tough and bitter, the cultivated greens begin to pop up in the garden. Baby kale, beet greens, turnip greens, collards, and chard are tender and far milder early on than when they mature. They need little heat or seasoning. For those whose interests run more toward the hedonistic than toward spring vitamin loading, blood purifying, and detoxifying, a little heat, and a splash of the heaviest cream you can find, does these mild little greens just fine. (Spinach can be substituted for these greens.)

DANDELION GREENS

SERVES 4

When the dandelion greens come up, we know it's spring. Traditionally, young dandelion greens were eaten to "clean the blood" after a winter of fatty preserved meats and beans. Thought to be a "liver tonic," the greens were also dried to use after someone had a "few too many." They also made a fine wine, a good soup, and, as in the recipe below, a wonderful counterpoint to spring dishes. Praised for their assertive, almost peppery flavor, dandelions are often eaten raw in salads (think: mesclun). But we find that a short time in a hot pan mellows them just enough to mitigate their bitterness, while still showcasing their lively flavor.

2 TEASPOONS VEGETABLE OIL

4 RAMPS OR SPRING ONIONS, DARK GREEN TOPS TRIMMED OFF AND DISCARDED, WHITE PARTS SLICED

8 CUPS DANDELION GREENS

½ TEASPOON SALT, OR TO TASTE

Heat the oil in a large skillet over low heat. Add the sliced ramps and cook for 5 to 6 minutes, until tender. Stir in the dandelion greens, sprinkle with salt, and cook for 30 seconds more. Immediately remove the greens from the pan and serve.

WILTED GARLICKY GREENS

SERVES 4

The mustard greens we grow down south have curled leaves and a sharp, spicy flavor. As a counterpoint to spring lamb and goat, the young mustard greens of spring can be quickly sautéed or even braised. We also like to temper the assertiveness of the greens by combining them with a sweet, buttery spinach as in the recipe below. The same combination of garlicky and mellow flavors can be used to make a puréed spring soup, as well.

1 TABLESPOON EXTRA-VIRGIN OLIVE OIL

1 CLOVE OF GARLIC, MINCED

1 POUND YOUNG MUSTARD GREENS (ABOUT 5 WELL-PACKED CUPS), RINSED, TOUGH STEMS DISCARDED

1 5-OUNCE BAG SPINACH LEAVES (ABOUT 5 WELL-PACKED CUPS), RINSED, TOUGH STEMS DISCARDED

½ TEASPOON SALT, OR TO TASTE

Heat the oil in a large skillet over medium heat. Add the garlic and cook, stirring, for 2 minutes, until lightly browned. Add the greens a few cups at a time, tossing and letting them cook down until all of them fit in the skillet. Cook just until wilted. Remove from the heat and stir in the salt.

WILD CRESS WITH WARM HAM VINAIGRETTE

SERVES 4

Cress is a name given to a variety of small-leafed greens with big flavor. Watercress seems to get all the attention (and we love it, too!), but there are other types—garden cress, winter cress, Indian cress, land cress, and arugula—that are worthy of cooking and eating.

2 OUNCES COUNTRY HAM OR PROSCIUTTO, CUT INTO
   ¼-INCH DICE
2 CUPS VEGETABLE STOCK (PAGE 268) OR LOW-SODIUM
   VEGETABLE BROTH
¼ CUP EXTRA-VIRGIN OLIVE OIL
I TABLESPOON APPLE CIDER VINEGAR
3 CUPS WATERCRESS LEAVES AND TENDER SPRIGS
3 CUPS LAND CRESS, SUCH AS CREASY GREENS (ARUGULA
   CAN BE SUBSTITUTED)

1   In a medium cast-iron skillet set over medium heat, cook the ham, stirring frequently, for 8 to 9 minutes, until crispy. Remove half of the ham and set aside. Add the stock to the skillet and increase the heat to medium high. Boil the mixture until it is reduced to ½ cup, about 10 minutes.

2   Remove the skillet from the heat and whisk in the oil and vinegar. Place the watercress and land cress in a large bowl, toss with the warm dressing, and sprinkle the reserved ham on top. Serve immediately.

CREAMED CHARD

SERVES 4

This recipe is our take on the classic steakhouse side dish. The earthy sweetness of the chard is the perfect complement to the rich, creamy sauce and nutty Parmesan. Of course spinach can be substituted, but it will cook more quickly. The chard stems can be saved and pickled, sautéed, or braised.

2 TABLESPOONS EXTRA-VIRGIN OLIVE OIL
½ CUP MINCED ONION
4 CLOVES OF GARLIC, MINCED
2 POUNDS CHARD, STEMS REMOVED, LEAVES CUT INTO
   ½-INCH STRIPS
½ TEASPOON KOSHER SALT, OR TO TASTE
⅔ CUP HEAVY CREAM
½ CUP FINELY GRATED PARMESAN
WHITE PEPPER, IF DESIRED

1   In a large skillet, heat the oil over medium heat. Add the onion and cook, stirring often, for about 5 minutes, until it softens. Stir in the garlic and cook for 1 minute more. Add the chard and salt and toss with tongs until it begins to wilt.

2   Stir in the cream, increase the heat to medium high, and cook for about 5 minutes, until the cream thickens enough to coat the back of a spoon. Stir in the cheese, taste and adjust seasoning with additional salt and white pepper if desired, and serve warm.

There is a garden for every season. Our temperate climate keeps the fall and winter gardens giving well into the spring. Fall brings collard greens, purple-top turnips, and late-season radishes. These vegetables are often overlooked, but they are so versatile and delicious that we count them as some of the most important parts of cooler nights. Slow cooking banishes the sulfurous aspect of the root vegetable and turns it sweet. These offerings from the autumn garden keep well in cool cellars.

AN EXPRESSION OF PLACE

If we seem to celebrate certain ingredients over and over again, it is because they are what grows well in our mountain valley and what local people have had several centuries of practice cooking. Our spot is not your spot. Often, rather than buying an ingredient that has no place on the landscape, it is better to stop, inhale, and imagine how something from that land might work in a particular recipe. Be not shy! Just have some good books with accurate cooking times on hand, accommodate for the changes you are making, and cook away. This is the way we've made some of our most memorable meals.

ON WINE — *With its acidic and peppery notes, Côte-Rôtie is an excellent match for this full-flavored, slightly spicy lamb. The wine's light violet aromas also complement the fresh earthiness of the morels. Look to a traditional producer of Côte-Rôtie, such as René Rostaing or Bernard Burgaud.*

TEN-HOUR BRAISED LAMB NECK WITH WILTED CREASY GREENS AND CRISP-ROASTED MORELS

SERVES 4

Lamb neck is available with some notice at good butchers. Arugula or watercress can be used instead of East Tennessee creasy greens, but there is nothing quite like a fresh morel.

FOR THE LAMB
2 LARGE CARROTS, PEELED AND CHOPPED
1 LARGE WHITE ONION, CHOPPED
2 STALKS OF CELERY, CHOPPED
1 LAMB NECK, ABOUT 1½ POUNDS
2½ TEASPOONS KOSHER SALT
1 TEASPOON FRESHLY GROUND BLACK PEPPER
3 CUPS PINOT NOIR OR OTHER LIGHT RED WINE
3 CUPS VEGETABLE STOCK (PAGE 268) OR LOW-SODIUM VEGETABLE BROTH

FOR THE MORELS
5 OUNCES (ABOUT 3 CUPS) MOREL MUSHROOMS, CLEANED
1 TABLESPOON OLIVE OIL
1½ TEASPOONS KOSHER SALT
½ TEASPOON FRESHLY GROUND BLACK PEPPER

FOR THE GREENS
1 TABLESPOON VEGETABLE OIL
6 CUPS CREASY GREENS OR TENDER ARUGULA
1 TEASPOON KOSHER SALT
½ TEASPOON FRESHLY GROUND BLACK PEPPER

1 Preheat the oven to 250°F.

2 To make the lamb, combine the carrots, onion, and celery and use the mixture as a bed in the bottom of a roasting pan. Sprinkle the lamb neck with 2 teaspoons of salt and the black pepper and place on top of the vegetables. Put it in the oven, uncovered, and roast for 6 hours. About 30 minutes before the lamb is done, pour the Pinot Noir into a medium saucepan and simmer over medium-high heat until reduced to 1½ cups.

3 Remove the pan from the oven and pour the reduced wine into the pan. Heat the stock in a saucepan to just under boiling, then add it to the pan along with the remaining ½ teaspoon of salt. Cover with foil and put back in the oven for another 4 hours, until the meat is almost falling off the bone. Remove from the oven; if you're not serving the lamb immediately, cool it in the liquid, cover, and refrigerate. When ready to serve, place the pan, uncovered, in a 325°F oven for about 30 minutes, until the lamb is heated through.

4 To make the morels, turn the oven up to 425°F. Toss the morels with the oil, salt, and pepper on a rimmed baking sheet. Roast for 15 to 20 minutes, until crispy on the outside and tender on the inside. Remove from the oven and set aside.

5 To make the greens, heat the oil in a large skillet over high heat. When very hot, add the greens, salt, and pepper and cook, tossing, for about 1 minute, until the greens are just hot. Toss in the morels.

6 To serve, remove the neck from the braising liquid and use a fork to scrape the meat away from the bones (you should have about 3 cups of meat). Divide the meat among 4 plates, along with the mushrooms and greens.

HERBED SPOONBREAD

SERVES 4 TO 6

Spoonbread is a cross between a pudding, a bread, and a soufflé. Be sure to serve it soon after it comes out of the oven, as it will quickly deflate.

2¼ CUPS WHOLE MILK

1 CUP PLUS 1 TABLESPOON CORNMEAL

6 TABLESPOONS (¾ STICK) UNSALTED BUTTER

3 LARGE EGGS, SEPARATED

1½ TEASPOONS CHOPPED FRESH FLAT-LEAF PARSLEY
    LEAVES

1 TABLESPOON CHOPPED FRESH THYME LEAVES

1½ TEASPOONS CHOPPED FRESH CHIVES

1 TEASPOON KOSHER SALT

¼ TEASPOON FRESHLY GROUND BLACK PEPPER

1½ TEASPOONS BAKING POWDER

1   Preheat the oven to 375°F. Grease a 9 × 5 × 3-inch loaf pan and set aside.

2   Bring 1½ cups of the milk to a boil in a medium saucepan. Whisk in the cornmeal and butter and cook, stirring constantly with a wooden spoon, for 3 minutes. Remove from the heat and let cool until lukewarm.

3   In a separate bowl, beat the egg yolks with the herbs, salt, and pepper. Once the cornmeal has cooled, stir the yolk mixture into it until just combined. Stir the baking powder into the remaining ¾ cup milk and then stir it into the cornmeal mixture as well.

4   In a clean bowl, beat the egg whites until they hold soft peaks, then gently fold them into the cornmeal mixture. Scrape the mixture into the prepared loaf pan and bake for 35 to 40 minutes, until a toothpick inserted into the center comes out clean. Serve warm.

BUTTERMILK PANNA COTTA WITH WILD STRAWBERRIES

SERVES 6

Buttermilk adds a welcome tang and Southern flair to this classic Italian dessert. If wild strawberries are unavailable, use what you can find—just be sure to taste them and adjust the amount of sugar accordingly. If you are lucky enough to have small, sweet wild ones, you may find them to be all the garnish this needs.

1 PACKET (¼ OUNCE) POWDERED GELATIN

1½ CUPS HALF-AND-HALF

¾ CUP PLUS 3 TO 4 TABLESPOONS SUGAR

2 VANILLA BEANS, SPLIT LENGTHWISE

2¼ CUPS BUTTERMILK

2 CUPS WILD STRAWBERRIES, HULLED AND HALVED

1   Combine the gelatin and ¼ cup of the half-and-half and microwave on high, stopping every 10 seconds to stir, until the gelatin is dissolved. Set aside.

2   In a medium saucepan, combine the remaining 1¼ cups of half-and-half, ¾ cup of the sugar, and the vanilla beans. Place over medium heat and bring to a boil. Immediately turn off the heat and add the gelatin mixture, stirring until it has completely melted. Pour through a strainer into a 1-quart container with a pouring spout; discard the vanilla beans.

3   Place the bottom of the container in a bowl of ice water and stir until the mixture is no longer warm. Whisk in the buttermilk. Divide the mixture among six 6-ounce ramekins, cover the top of each with plastic wrap, and refrigerate for at least 3 hours, until firm.

4   In a medium bowl, toss together the strawberries and 3 tablespoons of the remaining sugar. Taste the berries and add another tablespoon of sugar if they're not sweet enough.

5   Serve the panna cotta with the berries on the side.

THE OTHER "TENNESSEE TRUFFLE": RAMPS ⟿ RAMPS, THE WILD MOUNTAIN LEEKS THAT TASTE MORE LIKE GARLIC THAN LEEKS, ARE ANOTHER POINT OF LOCAL PRIDE, AS WELL AS A BAEDEKER OF SPRING. THEIR GRACEFUL LEAVES LOOK LIKE LILY OF THE VALLEY, BUT RAMPS ARE PRIZED FOR THEIR SMALL WHITE BULBS THAT MUST BE DUG—AND

that *are* dug with great excitement and speed throughout the region. The wild leek grows in fertile, shady spots above three thousand feet. East Tennessee is the geographic heart of the Appalachian ramp belt that stretches from West Virginia to mountainous spots in northern Georgia.

Every spring, in nearby Cosby, Tennessee, the ramp festival crowns its new ramp queen. Once within a few miles of Cosby, you need no map to locate the festival. Ramps, wrote John Parris in *Mountain Cooking*, "are the stinkenest [sic] vegetable known to man." But that does not stop the race to find them and cook them. Ramps are pickled, fried, boiled, sautéed, jellied, and eaten raw. The preferred dish in eastern Tennessee is ramps scrambled with eggs. Home-style potatoes and ramps run a close second. The strong bulb makes a fine spring-green soup. While ramp salad is also enticing, it dramatically reduces the chances for kissing, unless, of course, a fellow ramp lover is the object of one's affection.

The "stinkenest" wild leek was not well known outside the region until the past twenty years, when a generation of young chefs began turning away from France and looking more closely at the native ingredients and foodways of the United States. Ramps were all but a poster child for this cause. By 1996, a group of backcountry rangers registered their concern that the ramp was being over-harvested and threatened with extinction. Studies were commissioned and conservation efforts were recommended, but they have not yet been enforced.

The wild leeks look like lily-of-the-valley and tend to abound in shady spots deep in the woods. The earliest ones are the most delicate and prized, so dedicated diggers pack their spades after the thaw. A circle is dug around the ramp and then it is tugged from the earth. Cleaning ramps is nearly as arduous as digging them, as each must be cleaned by hand and soaked in a few changes of water to rid the leaves of grit.

Because of their powerful aroma, we like to cook ramps slowly in olive oil until they are soft and caramelized. At that point, ramps are sweet like roasted garlic and are delicious on pizza, served with meat or fish, or added to pasta, rice, or spoonbread. Before black Périgord truffles had been successfully cultivated in eastern Tennessee, ramps were known as Tennessee truffles. Oddly, the dishes we like best from our spring ramp menus, like the recipe for risotto with Jack Daniel's that appears on page 230, could, in fact, be made with truffles. Big aromatics seem to share certain affinities.

IN PRAISE OF THE RAMP

Someone said that garlic is a sissy compared to an Appalachian ramp. Because of the wild leek's huge flavor, we tend to build up to it in a menu. Here, we serve the main-course trout first, in order to exercise the palate a bit before ramps have their way. The rapid-fire appearance of spring ingredients makes us dizzy, so the nip of good whiskey in several of the courses that follow sends a sensible, calming message to the heart of this frenzy.

ON WINE *The clean, fresh notes of a vibrant wine made from Sauvignon Blanc grapes play off the young, verdant flavors that are alive in this menu. Sancerres, particularly those crafted by Domaine Thomas, work well with the acidity of the pickled fennel while also refreshing the palate for another bite of the pungent ramp risotto.*

RYE WHISKEY-CURED TROUT WITH FRESH AND PICKLED FENNEL

SERVES 4

In addition to the predictable smoking, trout is wonderful cured with aromatics; just be aware that this process takes five hours. Here, whiskey and rye seeds work a tasty bit of magic on one of the staples of our spring pantry.

FOR THE TROUT

1 CUP KOSHER SALT

1 CUP (LIGHTLY PACKED) LIGHT BROWN SUGAR

½ CUP RYE WHISKEY, SUCH AS WILD TURKEY

1 TEASPOON RYE SEEDS OR CARAWAY SEEDS

3 DASHES OF BITTERS

GRATED ZEST OF 1 ORANGE

2 5-OUNCE (SKIN ON) TROUT FILLETS

FOR THE FENNEL SALAD

1½ CUPS RICE VINEGAR

6 TABLESPOONS GRANULATED SUGAR

⅛ TEASPOON CRUMBLED SAFFRON THREADS

1 STAR ANISE POD

2½ TEASPOONS KOSHER SALT

3 FENNEL BULBS, VERY THINLY SLICED

1½ TABLESPOONS EXTRA-VIRGIN OLIVE OIL

¾ TEASPOON FRESHLY GROUND BLACK PEPPER

1   To make the trout, in a small bowl, combine the salt, sugar, whiskey, rye seeds, bitters, and zest. Using your hands, smear the mixture over both sides of the trout fillets. Put the trout on a rimmed baking sheet, and place a layer of parchment paper or wax paper on top of the fillets. Place another baking sheet on top, weight it down with some heavy food cans, and refrigerate the whole thing for 5 hours.

2   After 5 hours, remove the fillets from the pans and rinse the fillets under cold water to remove the salt mixture. Pat them dry with paper towels. If you're not serving the fillets immediately, they can be rewrapped and refrigerated for up to 4 days. When ready to serve, use a very sharp knife to thinly slice the trout, holding your knife at an angle and slicing along (not through) the skin.

3   To make the fennel salad, combine the vinegar, sugar, saffron, star anise, and 2 teaspoons of the salt in a medium saucepan. Bring to a boil, add half of the sliced fennel, and bring the mixture just back to a simmer. Remove the pan from the heat and let the mixture cool to room temperature. Once it is cool, discard the star anise, drain the fennel, and coarsely chop it. Transfer it to a medium bowl and toss it with the fresh fennel slices, olive oil, pepper, and remaining ½ teaspoon of salt. Place the trout slices on plates and place a mound of the fennel salad on top.

SMOKY MOUNTAIN RAMP RISOTTO WITH JACK DANIEL'S

SERVES 4

Loyal as we are, it takes a lot to make us choose medium-grained Arborio rice from Italy over the Carolina gold rice from the other side of the mountain from our farm. Ramps are a lot. Cooking the sturdy Arborio rice in its traditional way, using the slow risotto method, gives the wild mountain leeks time to relax and offer a little of their sweetness along with their pungent taste. Whole scallions, along with some garlic cloves, can be used in place of the ramps.

FOR THE WHISKEY BUTTER

1 RAMP BULB, MINCED

4 TEASPOONS JACK DANIEL'S TENNESSEE WHISKEY OR BOURBON

2 TEASPOONS MINCED RAMP LEAVES

4 TABLESPOONS (½ STICK) UNSALTED BUTTER, AT ROOM TEMPERATURE

⅛ TEASPOON WORCESTERSHIRE SAUCE

⅛ TEASPOON DIJON MUSTARD

¼ TEASPOON KOSHER SALT

FOR THE RISOTTO

8 CUPS CHICKEN STOCK (PAGE 268) OR LOW-SODIUM CHICKEN BROTH

½ POUND RAMPS

1½ TABLESPOONS UNSALTED BUTTER, AT ROOM TEMPERATURE

¼ CUP OLIVE OIL

2 CUPS ARBORIO RICE

⅓ CUP JACK DANIEL'S TENNESSEE WHISKEY OR BOURBON

1 CUP FINELY GRATED PARMESAN CHEESE

2 TEASPOONS KOSHER SALT, OR TO TASTE

1 TEASPOON FRESHLY GROUND BLACK PEPPER

1. To make the whiskey butter, in a small bowl, stir together the ramp bulb and whiskey and set aside for 15 minutes. Add the ramp leaves, butter, Worcestershire, mustard, and salt and mix well. Cover the bowl and refrigerate for at least 1 hour and up to 1 day before serving.

2. To make the risotto, pour the broth into a large saucepan, place over high heat, and bring to a boil. Turn off the heat, cover the pan, and let it sit at the back of the stove while you prepare the rice.

3. With a paring knife, separate the ramp greens from the bulbs. Place 5 of the ramp greens on a cutting board and discard the remaining greens. Finely chop the reserved greens and place them in a small bowl with the butter. Using the back of a spoon, mash the butter and ramps together. Set aside.

4. Slice the ramp bulbs about ¼ inch thick. In a large skillet, heat the olive oil over medium-low heat and cook the ramp bulbs, stirring, for 3 to 4 minutes, until tender. Add the rice and cook, stirring often, for about 4 minutes, until the rice grains turn a pearly color.

5. Raise the heat to medium-high and add the whiskey. Cook, stirring constantly, until the pan is nearly dry. Using a 6-ounce (¾-cup) ladle, add one ladle of the hot chicken stock to the risotto and cook, still stirring constantly. When all the liquid has been absorbed, add another ladle of stock. Continue this process for about 25 to 30 minutes, all the while stirring constantly, until the rice is soft and creamy but still has a bit of bite.

6. Remove the risotto from the heat and stir in the ramp and butter mixture, the cheese, and the salt and pepper. Divide the risotto among 4 serving plates or bowls and garnish each serving with a dollop of the whiskey butter.

OPPOSITE, LEFT: Smoky Mountain Ramp Risotto

BOURBON ZABAGLIONE

SERVES 4

Lest the Italian rice feel lonely, we offer an Italian dessert, a Bluegrass variation on the classic. Some of the recipe can be made ahead of time, but the glory of this dish is its immediacy.

1½ CUPS HEAVY CREAM

2 TABLESPOONS JACK DANIEL'S TENNESSEE WHISKEY
   OR BOURBON

6 LARGE EGG YOLKS

½ CUP SUGAR

1   In the bowl of an electric mixer, beat the cream until it forms soft peaks. Cover and refrigerate.

2   In the top of a double boiler or in a medium metal bowl, whisk together the whiskey, yolks, and sugar. Place the bowl over a pan of simmering water, making sure the bowl does not touch the water. Whisk the mixture constantly for 6 or 7 minutes, until it is very light and airy and has almost tripled in volume. Remove from the heat and chill over a bowl of ice water, whisking frequently. (The zabaglione can be made up to this point, covered, and refrigerated several hours ahead.)

3   Set aside about a quarter of the whipped cream for garnish, and use a large rubber spatula to fold the remaining whipped cream into the zabaglione. Divide the mixture among 4 martini glasses or small bowls and place a dollop of the reserved whipped cream on top. Serve cold.

SPRING CHICKEN

Until we had our own, we thought the term *spring chicken* was a fanciful thing, or perhaps a way to romanticize a chicken that was on the small size. We quickly realized that different varieties of birds mature at different times. Spring chickens are small, juicy, mildly flavored birds that would be no fun to fry or stew. The spring chicken loves to be moistened. The bird's flesh is tender and seems to absorb the perfume of herbs more quickly than do birds of, well, other feathers. It's tough to beat the traditional spring accompaniments—smashed new potatoes and steamed spring peas—but fiddlehead ferns sautéed in butter, or spring greens (see page 217), are also lovely with this herbaceous little bird. Given their small size, spring chickens need a substantial first course. Still, a chicken dinner is a chicken dinner, a fine thing for family or close friends.

ON WINE 〜 *The salty country ham and asparagus in this menu is best suited to a floral muscat from Alsace. We like Domaine Ehrhart medium-bodied versions. The fresh herbaceousness of the chicken is well served by a wine from southern France such as a light Minervois, which gestures deftly toward the Provençal-like herbs used in the dish.*

ASPARAGUS AND COUNTRY HAM SALAD WITH MUSCADINE VINAIGRETTE

SERVES 4

This salad, inspired by a similar idea sampled in the hills around Parma, Italy, is substantial, but not heavy. By increasing the amount of ingredients, and adding some boiled and chilled new potatoes, we transform this salad into one of our favorite spring lunches, as well.

I CUP MUSCADINE WINE OR RIESLING

1½ TEASPOONS LEMON JUICE

I TEASPOON PLUS 3 TABLESPOONS KOSHER SALT

½ TEASPOON DIJON MUSTARD

½ TEASPOON CRACKED BLACK PEPPER

¼ CUP GRAPESEED OIL

I BUNCH (I POUND) THICK ASPARAGUS, BOTTOM 2 INCHES OF EACH SPEAR TRIMMED OFF AND DISCARDED

6 CUPS BABY LETTUCES

2 OUNCES COUNTRY HAM OR PROSCIUTTO, THINLY SLICED AND JULIENNED

1   Place the wine in a small saucepan and bring to a boil over high heat. Lower the heat and simmer until the wine is reduced to ½ cup. Cool to room temperature, and then whisk in the lemon juice, I teaspoon of the salt, the mustard, and the pepper. Whisk in the oil and set aside.

2   Fill a large saucepan two-thirds full of water, add the remaining 3 tablespoons of salt, and bring to a boil over high heat. Add the asparagus and cook for 3 to 4 minutes, until bright green and just tender. Drain the asparagus and cool under cold running water. Once cooled, pat dry and split each spear in half lengthwise.

3   In a large bowl, toss together the asparagus, lettuces, and ham. Drizzle with the vinaigrette, toss again, and serve.

HERB-ROASTED SPRING CHICKEN

SERVES 4

Roasting in high heat crisps the skin of the little chickens and helps preserve their juices. The chickens need to be marinated a day in advance.

2 SPRING CHICKENS OR POUSSINS, EACH ABOUT 1 POUND

2 TABLESPOONS CHOPPED FRESH FLAT-LEAF PARSLEY LEAVES

1 TABLESPOON CHOPPED FRESH ROSEMARY LEAVES

1 TABLESPOON CHOPPED FRESH THYME LEAVES

1 TABLESPOON KOSHER SALT

1½ TEASPOONS FRESHLY GROUND BLACK PEPPER

¼ CUP EXTRA-VIRGIN OLIVE OIL

1   The day before serving, rinse the chickens inside and out and pat dry. In a small bowl, whisk together the parsley, rosemary, thyme, salt, pepper, and olive oil. Place each chicken in a quart-size resealable plastic bag and pour half the olive oil mixture into each bag. Seal the bags and rub the outside of the bags to work the herb mixture into the chickens, coating them entirely. Refrigerate overnight to allow the herb flavor to penetrate the chickens.

2   The next day, preheat the oven to 425°F.

3   Remove the chickens from the bags and place them on a rack in a roasting pan; allow to come to room temperature. Roast the chickens for about 30 minutes, until the juices run clear when the birds are poked in the thickest part of the thigh, or an instant-read thermometer inserted into the thickest part of the thigh (but not touching bone) reads 170°F. Remove from the oven and let rest in the pan on the counter for 10 minutes.

4   To serve, using a very sharp knife, split the birds in half, lengthwise, using the breast bone as a guide; use a towel to protect your hand from the heat. Cut around both sides of the back bone and remove and discard it. Place half a bird on each plate and serve immediately.

WARM CAFÉ-AU-LAIT SABAYON WITH CREOLE KISSES

SERVES 4

The kisses can be made several days in advance, covered tightly, and stored in a cool place. The sabayon is best made just before serving.

FOR THE KISSES

1 LARGE EGG WHITE

¾ CUP CONFECTIONERS' SUGAR

¼ TEASPOON PURE VANILLA EXTRACT

2 TABLESPOONS CHOPPED PECANS

FOR THE SABAYON

6 LARGE EGG YOLKS

½ CUP GRANULATED SUGAR

2 CUPS HEAVY CREAM

1 TABLESPOON GROUND ESPRESSO OR OTHER FINELY GROUND DARK-ROAST COFFEE

1   To make the kisses, preheat the oven to 250°F. Line a baking sheet with parchment paper.

2   Place the egg white in the bowl of an electric mixer and beat until it holds soft peaks. Slowly beat in the confectioners' sugar about a tablespoon at a time, making sure all is incorporated before adding more. Beat in the vanilla. Using a rubber spatula, fold in the pecans.

3   Using a teaspoon, scoop the batter onto the parchment-lined baking sheet (you should have about 16 cookies). Bake for 12 to 15 minutes, until the cookies are crisp on top and slightly puffed. Allow to cool completely before removing from the paper.

4   To make the sabayon, in the top of a double boiler or in a medium metal bowl, whisk together the egg yolks and granulated sugar until the sugar dissolves; set aside. In a medium saucepan, bring the cream and espresso just to a simmer, remove the pan from the heat, cover, and let sit for 2 to 3 minutes.

5   Strain out and discard the coffee grounds. Slowly whisk the hot cream into the yolk mixture, then place the whole thing over (not in) a pan of simmering water. Cook, whisking constantly, for 6 to 7 minutes, until slightly thickened and frothy. Divide the mixture among coffee cups and serve with the kisses on the side.

OPPOSITE: Equipped with a state-of-the-art Viking teaching kitchen, the Gambrel Dining Room is where guest chefs and authors give cooking demonstrations in the mornings. Later in the day, the room, which overlooks the dairy barn, is the spot for local cheese tastings and early evening cocktails.

CHEESE OF PLACE, TIME, AND DAY ∕ JUST BEFORE THE PALE NEW GREEN BEGINS TO CREEP

THROUGH THE PASTURES, THE SHEEP START TALKING. MOST HAVE ALREADY LAMBED; THE EWES STILL TO LAMB ARE IN THE

PADDOCK ADJOINING THE DAIRY BARN, AND THEY ALSO HAVE A LOT TO SAY ABOUT THEIR CONDITION. THOSE NOT

scheduled for a maternal event are heading to the pasture, and they have become chatty—and a little testy—about the menu. After a few months of hay and corn, the ladies—who have names like Mavis, Liberace, Pipi, Skippy, Miss Kicks, and Loretta—are eager to tuck into the first shoots of clover fescue grass, Indian grass, broad leaf, and dandelion greens in their forty acres of pasture. At this time of year, their torsos rounded with the added thickness of winter's unshorn white curls, the ladies' midsections seem even larger and more preposterous, their dainty ankles even slimmer. They are the ewe equivalent of ladies who lunch. The gentlemen are elsewhere. The sexes rarely mingle.

Baaah, the ladies say. *Baaah, baaah*, and, just to make their point, *Baaaah*.

"I hear you," says Kristian Holbrook. The cheese maker has walked down the hill from the larder and is heading toward the white dairy barn.

Until recently, Mr. Holbrook single-handedly made cheese and managed the East Friesian sheep. But that was when the herd was a chorus of twelve and, pound for pound, Mr. Holbrook's cheese production was not much greater. Now, however, there are 160 East Friesian ladies and gentlemen, and they have six humans, four water dogs named Marshal, Dharma, Queenie Lilly, and Rebecca, and a llama named George serving as their butlers and security staff. Mr. Holbrook has a shiny new cheese-making studio and a cheese-aging room. Last year, he began to win awards for the four cheeses that are sold and served on the farm.

Violet, the first cheese of the year, is soft-ripened, aged for only several weeks. A fresh, tart cheese with a bloomy rind, it was traditionally made by the shepherds in Avignon, France, for their own use, not to sell. He makes Trefoil, "a cheese that is reminiscent of Reblo-

chon," in the late spring. The cheese is aged for thirty to sixty days and he uses linen and the farm's hard cider to wash its rind every day. "That's what gives the cheese that characteristic blush and aroma of spring," says Mr. Holbrook. From June to early August, Mr. Holbrook makes Blackberry Blue, a mountain-style, mildly blue cheese with strong earth and mineral tones that resembles Bleu de Termignon and is aged for three to four months. From August until the sheep stop producing milk, Mr. Holbrook makes Singing Brook cheese, ten-pound wheels that are aged for at least four months. Young Singing Brook smells of autumn grass and hazelnuts, and as it ages the cheese has an aroma of hazelnuts and caramel.

Mr. Holbrook, who is thirty-six years old and a former chef, makes other cheeses, but he says that so far, only these four have captured a particular moment in the ladies' lives and the seasonal cycle of the farm. "That's what it's about. If a cheese doesn't taste of its place, it's not cheese. It's . . . compressed dairy product."

The cheese-making kitchen at Blackberry Farm is quiet and sterile, like a laboratory. When he makes cheese, he wears an immaculate white jacket and apron and scours his hands like a surgeon; he could just as easily be readying himself to deliver babies. But when he walks down to visit the sheep on a morning in early March, his barn jacket flapping, his hair blown helter-skelter, and his face quickly burning in the wind, Mr. Holbrook looks just like who he once was: between cooking at the famed Magnolia Grill in Durham, North Carolina, and becoming the cheese maker at Blackberry Farm, he was a cook at Outward Bound in Greenville, Maine.

Like an artisanal cheese, a person's career requires a certain amount of experimenting and calibrating, he says. Restaurant kitchens showed him that he needed to be outdoors; working in an outdoor program showed him that he needed to flex his culinary muscle more than campfire cookery allowed. "By then, I had a very clear vision of my style of cooking," he says. "I understood that for me, the reason to make food is to express a place. The job of the cheese maker, the cook, the baker is to respond with intelligence and sensitivity to what the ground and the water and the air and the weather give up. It's not about high style or superstardom, it's about shepherding ingredients

to the plate. There aren't many opportunities to do that, though."

Ten years ago, when he visited Sweetgrass Dairy in Georgia, Mr. Holbrook understood that making cheese is one way to express the essence of a place.

"As soon as I walked in the dairy, I knew that I had to learn how to do what they were doing," Mr. Holbrook says. He had left the campfire and taken a job as a private chef in Atlanta by then, and on his days off, Mr. Holbrook began to learn about cheese at the dairy—and to practice at home. "I was what they call a weck-canner around here, an obsessive, weekend-cheese-making warrior. I had a five-gallon stockpot, a mentor at Sweetgrass, some books, an idea of what was possible—and I was on fire."

After several years, Mr. Holbrook decided to tour the artisanal cheese shrines in Europe and perhaps apprentice himself to several master cheese makers. By then, he knew enough about basic cheese making to understand the masters' techniques for imbuing a cheese with, say, a whiff of spring, or of the fallen leaves, ripe apples, and grapes of an autumn day. Having long since moved from making simple, fresh cheese, Mr. Holbrook began to learn how to use time as an ingredient, how to anticipate what a flavor will become and how any sort of intervention might change it. He also understood that a particular cheese, a real Brie, for instance, can only happen in one place. The Brie style can be made in other climates, but the true cheese has to have the elements and temperature and trace bacteria that exist only in one spot.

Mr. Holbrook felt most at home in the South and, while traveling, he'd discovered that he favored mountain-style cheeses. When Sam Beall contacted him after he returned to the United States, Mr. Holbrook didn't hesitate.

"He wanted to build a herd and make some of the best cheese in the world," he said.

And that's what they did.

Mr. Holbrook made small batches of cheese every day, tracking the character and underlying flavors of each and then matching these subtle attributes to influences such as the weather, the variety of grass that was dominant that week, and the mood of the herd. Were a photographer commissioned to document Blackberry Farm, she would be charged with capturing the essence of the place at various times of day and in different seasons. She would be looking for the single shadow that says "summer evening," and for the play of lemon-colored light on the creek bed that trumpets "spring."

Mr. Holbrook approaches cheese making in much the same way. There is a certain style of cheese that feels like early spring in the mouth, a creamy, soft, mold-ripened cheese with a bloomy rind. If he can produce the precise balance of floral and herbal tones that exist on such a day in that style of cheese, he has, Mr. Holbrook says, made something worth eating. Capturing these moments that express the whole, he believes, "is about biology and paying attention."

"You are either attentive or you are not," he says, adding, "I am not naturally attentive; I had to learn how to be attentive."

He describes the cheese-making moments when he has to be focused on minute details, how his paddle moves through the milk as it warms and coagulates in his fifty-gallon pot, how his harp-like curd knife cuts through the mass, and then the weight of an individual cheese as it begins to form, soft and round in his hands.

"It's easy to feel maternal about cheese," says Mr. Holbrook. The ladies have by now moved from a remote corner to the piece of pasture that parallels the cheese maker's path.

Baaah, they exclaim. *Baaah, baaah, baaah.*

East Friesian sheep originally came from Friesland on the North Sea. The breed is not well known in the United States, but East Friesians are hearty and produce prodigious quantities of milk; each makes about a gallon a day. Mr. Holbrook says that East Friesians are also smart. "Studies have shown that they remember people," he observes, as the herd presses closer to the fence standing between them and the cheese maker.

"They have a lot of personality and they are usually well behaved. CUT IT OUT, LORETTA," he says, stepping back and out of range of the ewe who has pushed her head through the fence and begun to nibble the pocket of his jacket.

Baa (a short, insulted snort).

"They're not usually like this," says the cheese maker, apologetically. "They're excited."

Do the ladies remember him? Oh, yeah. Are they excited to see him? Probably.

"But that's not what's going on," he explains. "They're smelling the violets. I saw a few this morning. By next week the pasture will be purple. These ladies will move through there like machines; they love violets. And when they're mowing down acres of violets? That week? That's the only time of the year, the only time they make milk that smells like violets, the only time I get to make violet cheese."

THE PIG IN SPRING

Poets and philosophers, novelists, song writers, social historians—who hasn't written about the position of pig in the South? In areas other than the mountains, there is no explanation for the Southern preference for pork. Up country, there is a skein of logic. Cattle were also not naturally inclined to flourish in rock and brambles. Pigs, on the other hand, did just fine. Beef was a once-a-year event. Pork is more versatile. Finally, at any stage of its life, pork can be cooked into something good. In spring, pork tends to be more about parts—loins, fresh hams, and chops. And while pigs of almost any other season want a rough-and-ready and rustic preparation, spring pork seems to ask for more fuss and style and daintiness. We oblige. You just don't say no to a pig if you are from these hills. The pork roulade in this menu is pretty enough for company and looks more complicated than it is to fix. A wild cress salad with a warm ham vinaigrette (see page 219) supplies a nice bit of porcine foreshadowing. If it's too early for berries and a big skillet of berry crisp, chess pie is a most excellent choice. The pie would offer a certain synchronicity, a luxurious smooth feel, if the pashminas and sweaters have come out by that time, as well.

ON WINE ⟩ *In the face of a big, rich, spicy dish, the first instinct is always to reach for a big, spicy red wine. We resist this urge and temper this pork with a slightly off-dry version of German Riesling. Robert Weil's Rieslings are some of our favorites.*

BRAISED RABBIT WITH DANDELION GREEN SALAD

SERVES 4

Dandelion greens, with their sharp, peppery bite, are the best to use in this dish, but milder arugula or frisée can be substituted. We love the delicate flavor of rabbit, but preparing chicken, guinea hen, or game hen legs using the same method creates an equally delicious dish.

4 CUPS CHICKEN STOCK (PAGE 268) OR LOW-SODIUM CHICKEN BROTH

4 CUPS WATER

½ STALK OF CELERY, HALVED

½ CARROT, PEELED AND HALVED

¼ VIDALIA OR OTHER SWEET ONION, PEELED

2 TEASPOONS VEGETABLE OIL

4 8-OUNCE RABBIT LEG QUARTERS, OR 1 3-POUND RABBIT, QUARTERED

2 TEASPOONS FINE SEA SALT, PLUS MORE TO TASTE

½ TEASPOON FRESHLY GROUND BLACK PEPPER, PLUS MORE TO TASTE

3 TABLESPOONS GRAPESEED OIL

1½ TEASPOONS FRESH LEMON JUICE

LEAVES AND TENDER STEMS FROM 2 POUNDS DANDELION GREENS

1 Preheat the oven to 350°F.

2 In a large Dutch oven or heavy pot with a tight-fitting lid, bring the stock, water, celery, carrot, and onion to a boil.

3 In a large skillet, heat the vegetable oil over medium-high heat. Sprinkle the rabbit legs with the 2 teaspoons salt and ½ teaspoon pepper, place in the skillet, and cook until golden brown, about 2 minutes per side. Add the browned legs to the pot, cover, and place in the oven. Cook for about 2 hours, until the meat begins to fall off the bone.

4 In a small bowl, whisk together the grapeseed oil, lemon juice, and salt and pepper to taste. Toss the greens in this mixture and divide among 4 plates. Remove the rabbit legs from the braising liquid (they should still be warm) and place one atop each mound of greens.

STUFFED PORK ROULADE

SERVES 4

The greatest liability with modern, defatted pork is dry meat. We do not use modern pork, but many of our friends do, and in this recipe, the layer of fennel adds a touch of anise and, along with the sausage, keeps the meat succulent. The initial searing is another help: it seems to seal in the pork's natural juices. If nothing else, it reduces the time the roulade requires in the oven.

2 LARGE FENNEL BULBS, TRIMMED AND FINELY DICED (ABOUT 4 CUPS)

16 LARGE CLOVES OF GARLIC (ABOUT 1 CUP)

1 TABLESPOON EXTRA-VIRGIN OLIVE OIL

ZEST OF 1 LEMON

JUICE OF ½ LEMON

ZEST OF ½ ORANGE

1½ TEASPOONS KOSHER SALT

4 OUNCES SMOKED COUNTRY BREAKFAST SAUSAGE, CASINGS REMOVED

1 1½-POUND BONELESS PORK LOIN

1 Preheat the oven to 350°F.

2 In a medium ovenproof skillet, combine the fennel, garlic, and oil. Roast, stirring occasionally, for 1 hour, until the garlic is very soft but not browned. Transfer the fennel mixture to a food processor and process until smooth. Transfer the purée to a small bowl and stir in the lemon zest, lemon juice, orange zest, and 1 teaspoon of the salt. Set aside to cool to room temperature.

3 In a large ovenproof skillet, cook the sausage over low heat for 20 minutes, or until it renders its fat and is just cooked through, breaking the sausage into small clumps with the side of a spoon. Use a slotted spoon to transfer the sausage to a small bowl and set it aside to cool to room temperature. Pour off all but 2 tablespoons of the drippings. If there is less than 2 tablespoons, make up the difference with olive oil. Set the skillet aside.

4 Butterfly the pork loin by cutting it almost in half through one long side, stopping about ½ inch from the edge. Open the loin as you would a book and then place it between two sheets of plastic wrap. Pound it with a meat mallet or heavy rolling pin to a uniform ½-inch thickness. Season the inside of the roast with the remaining ½ teaspoon salt.

5 Turn the pork loin so that one long side faces you. Spread the fennel purée evenly over the bottom half of the meat. Scatter the sausage over the purée. Starting with the bottom edge, roll up the meat like a jelly roll. Tie the meat with kitchen twine at 1½-inch intervals.

6 Place the reserved skillet over high heat. When the sausage drippings are very hot, brown the pork on all sides. Transfer the skillet to the oven and roast for 35 minutes, or until an instant-read thermometer inserted into the center registers 145°F. Remove the meat from the oven and let rest for 10 minutes before removing the strings and slicing.

LEMON CHESS PIE WITH OPAL BASIL SYRUP

SERVES 8 TO 10

No one knows how chess pie got its name. A similar dessert used to be called transparent pie. Then, sometime in the 1950s, any pie with a filling made from eggs, sugar, and butter was "Chess pie." Here, opal basil steeped in a simple syrup give this everyday pie a stylish twist.

FOR THE SYRUP

1 CUP WATER

1 CUP OPAL BASIL LEAVES

½ CUP SUGAR

FOR THE PIE

½ RECIPE BASIC PASTRY (PAGE 270)

4 LARGE EGGS

1½ CUPS SUGAR

8 TABLESPOONS (1 STICK) UNSALTED BUTTER, MELTED
   AND SLIGHTLY COOLED

⅓ CUP CORNMEAL

3 TABLESPOONS FRESH LEMON JUICE

ZEST OF 2 LEMONS

PINCH OF SALT

1   To make the syrup, in a small saucepan, bring the water to a boil. Turn off the heat and add the basil leaves. Let sit for 15 minutes, then strain out and discard the leaves. Return the water to the pan and add the sugar. Bring back to a boil, reduce the heat, and allow the syrup to simmer gently, uncovered, for 10 to 12 minutes, until reduced by half.

2   To make the pie, place the dough on a well-floured surface and use a rolling pin to roll it out to a circle 11 inches in diameter and about ⅛ inch thick. Fold the dough over your rolling pin and unroll over a 9-inch pie pan. Ease the dough into the bottom and up the sides of the pan. Trim the dough if needed, leaving a 1-inch apron all around. Fold excess dough over and use your fingers to crimp the edges. Refrigerate.

3   Preheat the oven to 325°F. In a medium bowl, whisk the eggs until frothy. Whisk in the sugar, butter, cornmeal, lemon juice, zest, and salt. Pour this mixture into the chilled pie shell. Place the pie on a baking sheet and bake for 25 to 30 minutes, until a knife inserted into the filling comes out clean.

4   Allow the pie to cool to room temperature, then refrigerate until ready to serve, at least 1½ to 2 hours. Slice and serve drizzled with the syrup.

A COMPANY DINNER FOR A VERNAL EVENING

Just about the time we've gotten used to the wild pace of the forest and garden in the spring, the explosion settles into a steady rhythm. Cooking from the earth will never be perfectly predictable, but during patches, such as late spring and early summer, a pattern asserts itself. We can plan to make something slightly more labor-intensive, like corn pudding, and be assured that there will still be hen-of-the-woods mushrooms, with their sweet earthy taste and fine toasty tones. If not, the pudding could be served with shiitake mushrooms or even flash-boiled shrimp. The rabbit has a delicate flavor in contrast to the assertive mustard in the traditional cream sauce. Wilted dandelion greens (see page 218) are a nice accompaniment. There is an old-fashioned feel to this menu. Sorbet, be it buttermilk, chocolate, or both, provides the perfect finish to the meal.

ON WINE ⤳ *The golden flavors of the mustard cream and the corn pudding in this menu allow us to showcase older white Burgundies with their buttery notes. As the wines develop, the sweetness inherent to ripe Chardonnay grapes delicately emerges, dispelling any notion that white wines cannot age. Maison Leroy's are among those we favor because of the winery's well-established aging program.*

ROASTED HEN-OF-THE-WOODS WITH CORN PUDDING

SERVES 4

The pudding can be made in individual ramekins for a tonier presentation; adjust the heating time. Larger mushroom pieces lend a more dramatic presence, and they heighten the chances that the mushroom can caramelize and take on a toasty flavor.

FOR THE CORN PUDDING

6 TABLESPOONS (¾ STICK) UNSALTED BUTTER, MELTED

¾ CUP YELLOW CORNMEAL

1 CUP WARM WATER

3 LARGE EGGS

2 CUPS MILK

2 TEASPOONS BAKING POWDER

1 TEASPOON KOSHER SALT

½ TEASPOON FRESHLY GROUND BLACK PEPPER

1 CUP FRESH OR THAWED FROZEN SWEET CORN KERNELS

FOR THE MUSHROOMS

1 POUND HEN-OF-THE-WOODS OR OYSTER MUSHROOMS, BRUSHED TO REMOVE ANY DIRT

1 TABLESPOON VEGETABLE OIL

1½ TEASPOONS KOSHER SALT

½ TEASPOON FRESHLY GROUND BLACK PEPPER

1   To make the corn pudding, preheat the oven to 375°F. Grease a 9 × 9-inch casserole or glass baking dish with 2 tablespoons of the melted butter and set it aside.

2   In a large bowl, whisk together the cornmeal and warm water. Whisk in the remaining 4 tablespoons melted butter. Whisk in the eggs, milk, baking powder, salt, and pepper. Fold in the corn kernels. Scrape the batter into the buttered casserole dish, cover the dish with foil, and bake for about 35 minutes, until the center is slightly puffed. Remove the foil and continue to bake for about 10 minutes more, until the top is golden brown. Remove from the oven and let cool for a few minutes before serving.

3   Meanwhile, to make the mushrooms, heat a large cast-iron skillet over medium-high heat. Add the mushrooms, oil, salt, and pepper and toss to coat. Cook, tossing frequently, for 6 to 7 minutes, until the mushrooms are lightly browned. Remove the skillet from the heat and place it in the oven along with the corn pudding. Roast the mushrooms for about 12 minutes, until they are very tender.

4   To serve, place a scoop of the pudding on each serving plate and rest the mushrooms on top.

OPPOSITE, LEFT: Sam Beall and Bill Harlan, guest vintner.

FRICASSEE OF RABBIT IN MUSTARD CREAM

SERVES 4

This updated old-fashioned dish can be made ahead of time for company and gently reheated. And, yes, four bone-in, skin-on chicken breasts can be used in place of the rabbit.

2 TABLESPOONS VEGETABLE OIL

4 8-OUNCE RABBIT LEG QUARTERS, OR 1 3-POUND RABBIT, QUARTERED

1½ TEASPOONS KOSHER SALT

¼ TEASPOON FRESHLY GROUND BLACK PEPPER

4 SHALLOTS, QUARTERED

8 BABY CARROTS, PEELED

2 CLOVES OF GARLIC, CHOPPED

2 TABLESPOONS SHERRY VINEGAR

3½ CUPS CHICKEN STOCK (PAGE 268) OR LOW-SODIUM CHICKEN BROTH

½ CUP HEAVY CREAM

4 SPRIGS OF FRESH THYME

2 SPRIGS OF FRESH ROSEMARY

4 SPRIGS OF FRESH FLAT-LEAF PARSLEY

1 BAY LEAF

1 TABLESPOON WHOLE-GRAIN MUSTARD

1   In a large, heavy pot with a tight-fitting lid, heat the oil over medium-high heat. Sprinkle the rabbit with the salt and pepper. When the oil is shimmering hot, add the rabbit and sear for 2 to 3 minutes on each side, until golden brown. Remove the rabbit from the pot and set aside.

2   Add the shallots and carrots to the pot and cook for 4 minutes, until the vegetables begin to brown. Add the garlic and cook for 1 minute. Stir in the vinegar and cook until it evaporates. Stir in the stock, cream, thyme, rosemary, parsley, and bay leaf.

3   Return the rabbit to the pot, placing the pieces on top of the vegetables. Bring the liquid to a boil over high heat. Reduce the heat to medium low, cover the pot, and simmer for 45 minutes, or until the vegetables are tender and the rabbit is cooked through. The juices should be golden when the rabbit is pierced with a knife.

4   Use a slotted spoon to transfer the rabbit and vegetables to a bowl. Remove and discard the herb stems and bay leaf. Cover the bowl with foil and set it aside.

5   Increase the heat to medium high and simmer the liquid for 20 minutes, until it reduces to 2 cups. Stir in the mustard. Return the rabbit and vegetables to the pot, heat them through, and serve warm.

BUTTERMILK SORBET

MAKES 1 QUART

Buttermilk makes a slightly creamy and tangy sorbet. It can be frozen for up to one month.

1 CUP SUGAR
1 CUP WATER
2½ TABLESPOONS FRESH LEMON JUICE
1½ CUPS BUTTERMILK

1   In a medium saucepan, bring the sugar and water to a boil, stirring until the sugar dissolves. Pour the sugar mixture into a medium bowl, stir in the lemon juice and buttermilk, cover, and refrigerate until chilled.

2   Freeze the sorbet in an ice cream maker according to the manufacturer's directions. Transfer the sorbet to an airtight container and freeze until firm.

CHOCOLATE SORBET

MAKES 1 QUART

In this sorbet, chocolate supplies a more intense hit of flavor than when it's diluted with milk or cream. It can be frozen for up to one month.

⅔ CUP COCOA
2 TABLESPOONS LIGHT CORN SYRUP
1 CUP SUGAR
3 CUPS WATER
2 OUNCES BITTERSWEET CHOCOLATE, CHOPPED
1 TEASPOON PURE VANILLA EXTRACT

1   Sift the cocoa into a medium heat-proof bowl and set it aside. In a medium saucepan, bring the corn syrup, sugar, and water to a boil, stirring until the sugar dissolves. Pour the sugar mixture over the cocoa and whisk until smooth. Add the chocolate and vanilla and stir until smooth. Cover the bowl and refrigerate until chilled.

2   Freeze the sorbet in an ice cream maker according to the manufacturer's directions. Transfer the sorbet to an airtight container and freeze until firm.

ur-sorbet, or response to something so delicious that, in the warmer weather, could only be improved by a chill. The wild strawberries on our mountain inspire that response, as do the blackberries that are so thick around the farm. We use a small freezer to get the slushy, multi-crystal texture. The formula we use to make sorbet from blackberries can alternatively be used for strawberries, blueberries, huckleberries, raspberries, or any small, soft, berrylike fruit. Similarly, while the honeysuckle sorbet seems, to us, like the essence of a sweet spring night, frozen violets, lily of the valley or rose petals can be used instead—just make sure that the petals are free of pesticide. Buttermilk and chocolate supply a more intense hit of flavor when not diluted with milk or cream; they also seem lighter, as if the buttermilk could pour for hours or the chocolate would never have to stop. The crushed-glass texture and the saturated flavor of the sorbet medium provides a welcome shock. Of all desserts, this really may be the only one that you can imagine eating until you have truly had enough, until you really want no more, even just once.

HONEYSUCKLE SORBET

MAKES 1 QUART

3 CUPS WATER

1 CUP SUGAR

JUICE OF 1 LEMON

2 CUPS HONEYSUCKLE BLOSSOMS, PETALS ONLY WITH NO GREEN LEAVES

1   In a medium saucepan, bring the water and sugar to a boil. Stir until the sugar dissolves, then pour the mixture into a medium bowl and stir in the lemon juice and honeysuckle blossoms. Cover the bowl and refrigerate overnight.

2   Strain the liquid and discard the solids. Freeze the sorbet in an ice cream maker according to the manufacturer's directions. Transfer the sorbet to an airtight container and freeze until firm.

BLACKBERRY SORBET

MAKES 1 QUART

We have such a profusion of our namesake berry that we've had plenty of chances to perfect this recipe. We found that fewer ingredients mean better blackberry sorbet.

3 CUPS FRESH BLACKBERRIES

2¼ CUPS WATER

1 CUP SUGAR

JUICE OF 1 LEMON

1   Place the blackberries, ¼ cup of the water, and ¼ cup of the sugar in a blender and purée. Strain through a fine-mesh sieve into a medium bowl. Press on the solids in the strainer with a spoon to extract as much of the juice and pulp from the blackberries as possible; you should have about ¾ cup of purée.

2   In a medium saucepan, bring the remaining 2 cups of water and remaining ¾ cup sugar to a boil, stirring until the sugar dissolves. Stir the sugar mixture and lemon juice into the blackberry purée. Cover the bowl and refrigerate until chilled.

3   Freeze the sorbet in an ice cream maker according to the manufacturer's directions. Transfer the sorbet to an airtight container and freeze until firm.

TENDER COALS

The first fire-cooked meal of the year feels festive. Partly, it is the fire itself, its power, its warmth, the glow; partly it is what fire does to food; and partly it is the way we tend to draw close around a fire when the evening is still just a little too cold. Stuffing a breast of veal is not difficult, but the result is impressive and tasty. After a serving of the skillet cake we make from windfall tomatoes, the meat is a fortifying sort of comfort. We love serving it with a raw, crunchy salad—and our irresistible French fries (even if it does mean trotting in and out of the kitchen to fetch fresh batches). The quiet spice of the cupcakes adds the note of warmth that evenings between seasons often want.

ON WINE *The rich, smoky veal breast asks for a rustic wine with an affinity for campfire cookery. A powerful, Tempranillo-based wine fits the bill, and we'd look no further than Ribera del Duero. The Finca Villacresces Nebro Bottling is particularly rich and intense with the distinct note of smoky mint that comes from the tall Anebro trees that grow in that region of Spain.*

GREEN TOMATO SKILLET CAKE

SERVES 8

Fried green tomatoes are a fine thing. Layered with fresh tomato sauce and a sharp fresh cheese and baked, they are even finer. See the photograph on page 261.

2 CUPS VEGETABLE OIL

BEER BATTER (SEE BATTER RECIPE IN MR. FEATHERS'S
    ONION RINGS, PAGE 34)

1 CUP ALL-PURPOSE FLOUR

3 LARGE GREEN TOMATOES, CORED AND CUT CROSSWISE
    INTO ¼-INCH-THICK SLICES

6 LARGE RIPE RED TOMATOES, CORED, SEEDED, AND
    CHOPPED

1 CLOVE OF GARLIC, CHOPPED

½ TEASPOON KOSHER SALT

⅛ TEASPOON FRESHLY GROUND BLACK PEPPER

2 TABLESPOONS EXTRA-VIRGIN OLIVE OIL

¾ CUP CRUMBLED FETA CHEESE

1   In a large cast-iron skillet, heat ½ cup of the vegetable oil over medium-high heat until a pinch of flour sprinkled into the oil bubbles and browns in a few seconds.

2   While the oil is heating, prepare the beer batter and have it in a shallow bowl.

3   Place the flour on a plate. Working in batches and coating only as many green tomatoes at a time as will fit in a single layer in the skillet, dredge the tomato slices in the flour and then coat in the beer batter. Carefully place in the hot oil and fry for about 2 minutes on each side, until golden brown. Remove from the oil and drain on paper towels. Continue frying the tomatoes, adding more vegetable oil to the skillet as needed.

4   Preheat the oven to 350°F.

5   Place the red tomatoes, garlic, salt, and pepper in a food processor and pulse until combined. With the motor running, slowly add the olive oil and process until the mixture is puréed. Pour the sauce into a large bowl and set aside.

6   Arrange one third of the fried green tomatoes in the bottom of a 10-inch cast-iron skillet. Spread ½ cup of the tomato sauce over the fried tomatoes and sprinkle with ¼ cup of the feta. Repeat to make two more layers. Place in the oven for 30 minutes, or until heated through. Remove from the oven and preheat the broiler. Place under the broiler for 5 minutes, until toasty brown on top. Cut into wedges and serve warm.

WOOD-SMOKED VEAL BREAST

SERVES 4 WITH LEFTOVERS

Veal breast is a delicious but underutilized cut of meat. Most butchers stock them. Because so much of this recipe is prepared ahead of time, it makes a good company meal.

I 6-POUND HALF VEAL BREAST

3 TEASPOONS KOSHER SALT

1½ TEASPOONS FRESHLY GROUND BLACK PEPPER

I TABLESPOON VEGETABLE OIL

3 CUPS CHICKEN STOCK (PAGE 268) OR LOW-SODIUM CHICKEN BROTH

I LARGE CARROT, PEELED AND HALVED

I LARGE WHITE ONION, HALVED

I STALK OF CELERY, HALVED

I SPRIG OF FRESH THYME

1   Preheat the oven to 300°F.

2   To make the veal, the day before serving, season the breast with 2 teaspoons of the salt and 1 teaspoon of the pepper. In a very large skillet set over medium-high heat, heat the oil until very hot. Add the veal and sear on both sides for 8 to 10 minutes, until browned.

3   Transfer the breast to a deep roasting pan and add the stock, carrot, onion, celery, thyme, and the remaining teaspoon of salt and ½ teaspoon of pepper. Cover the roasting pan with foil and place in the oven. Roast for about 5 hours, or until the veal is very tender and shreds easily with a fork.

4   Remove the pan from the oven and let the veal and liquid cool to room temperature. Refrigerate the veal overnight in the liquid.

5   The next day, remove the breast from the liquid and place it on a rimmed baking sheet; leave it out on the counter to come to room temperature. Meanwhile, place 2 cups wood chips in a small bowl and add enough water to cover. Soak for 1 hour, then drain and set aside.

6   To smoke the veal, prepare a charcoal or gas grill. When very hot, place the wood chips in a chip box or in a aluminum pie pan and place them over the coals. When the chips are smoking, put the veal breast on the grill, close the lid, and cook for 10 to 15 minutes, turning every now and then, until the veal is heated through and has absorbed a good amount of smoke flavor.

7   To serve, cut the veal breast into 2- or 3-inch squares or rectangles, cutting around the bones and any large pieces of fat. Stack a few pieces of veal on each plate.

SALAD OF PEA TENDRILS IN WILD GARLIC VINAIGRETTE

SERVES 4

Pea tendrils are familiar to those who grow peas; others can check an Asian market, or use mild watercress instead. This salad is also nice served with poached chicken or fish.

2 TABLESPOONS MINCED WILD GARLIC OR REGULAR GARLIC

1 TABLESPOON WHITE WINE VINEGAR

½ TEASPOON KOSHER SALT

⅛ TEASPOON FRESHLY GROUND BLACK PEPPER

¼ CUP GRAPESEED OR VEGETABLE OIL

1 CUP SUGAR SNAP PEAS

3 CUPS PEA TENDRILS

8 ASPARAGUS SPEARS, TOUGH ENDS REMOVED

1 TABLESPOON FINELY CHOPPED FRESH MINT LEAVES

1 TABLESPOON MINCED FRESH FLAT-LEAF PARSLEY LEAVES

1   In a small bowl, whisk together the garlic, vinegar, salt, and pepper. Let sit for 5 minutes, then whisk in the oil.

2   Bring a small saucepan of salted water to a boil and have ready a bowl of ice water. Add the sugar snap peas to the boiling water and cook for about 1 minute, just until they turn bright green. Drain and transfer the sugar snap peas to the ice water. When cool, drain again and pat the sugar snap peas dry. Cut them into thin slices on the bias, place them in a large bowl, and add the pea tendrils.

3   Use a vegetable peeler to shave the asparagus lengthwise into thin strips and add them to the peas and tendrils. Stir the mint and parsley into the vinaigrette, pour the mixture over the salad, toss to coat, and serve.

FRENCH FRIES

SERVES 4

I developed this technique for making a crisp and irresistible fry. Because most of the cooking is done two hours in advance, this iteration of French fries can be managed for a company meal. One is well advised to double the recipe, as people eat twice as many of these as they plan. We like serving them in butcher paper on a platter and often season them with black pepper as well as salt.

2 TABLESPOONS PLUS 1 TEASPOON KOSHER SALT

4 LARGE RUSSET POTATOES, PEELED

8 CUPS VEGETABLE OIL

1   In a large bowl, stir together 8 cups hot tap water and 2 tablespoons of the salt, stirring until the salt dissolves. Cut each potato lengthwise into ¼-inch-thick slices and then cut each slice into ¼-inch-wide sticks. Soak the potato sticks in the salted water for 10 minutes. Drain, pat dry with paper towels, then spread in a single layer on a wire rack and set aside to dry for about 15 minutes.

2   In a large, deep pot, heat the oil over medium heat until a deep-fry thermometer registers 250°F. Working in batches and adding only as many potato sticks as can easily float on the surface of the oil in a single layer, fry the potatoes for 3 minutes, or until they just become opaque but not brown. Use a slotted spoon to transfer the fries to a rimmed baking sheet. After all the fries have been cooked, turn off the oil and place the baking sheet in the freezer for 2 hours.

3   About 5 minutes before serving, reheat the oil, this time to 350°F. Working in batches again, fry the potatoes for 3 minutes, or until golden brown and crisp. Remove them with a slotted spoon and drain on paper towels. Sprinkle the hot fries with the remaining teaspoon of salt and serve hot.

SPICED CUPCAKES WITH BROWNED-BUTTER FROSTING

SERVES 12

Cupcakes are a natural for large parties, and the warm spices in these little cakes are perfect for a brisk evening. The browned-butter frosting is light and fluffy but has a deep caramel note. The cakes themselves can be made a day ahead and kept tightly covered at room temperature, but they are best frosted just before serving.

FOR THE CUPCAKES

I CUP CAKE FLOUR

I TEASPOON BAKING POWDER

½ TEASPOON GROUND MACE

½ TEASPOON GROUND NUTMEG

⅛ TEASPOON GROUND CINNAMON

⅛ TEASPOON FINE SEA SALT

4 TABLESPOONS (½ STICK) UNSALTED BUTTER

½ CUP SUGAR

I LARGE EGG YOLK

I LARGE EGG

6 TABLESPOONS MILK

½ TEASPOON PURE VANILLA EXTRACT

FOR THE FROSTING

2 STICKS UNSALTED BUTTER

3 CUPS CONFECTIONERS' SUGAR

3 TABLESPOONS HEAVY CREAM

½ TEASPOON FRESH LEMON JUICE

1   To make the cupcakes, preheat the oven to 375°F. Line a standard 12-cup muffin tin with paper liners and set aside.

2   Sift the flour, baking powder, mace, nutmeg, cinnamon, and salt into a medium bowl and set aside.

3   In the bowl of an electric mixer, beat the butter and sugar together until fluffy. Add the egg yolk and egg and beat until the mixture is thick and pale yellow. Add the flour mixture in three additions, alternating with the milk and beating until well mixed after each addition. Beat in the vanilla.

4   Spoon the batter into the muffin cups, filling each about three-quarters full. Bake for about 20 minutes, until a toothpick inserted into the cupcake centers comes out clean. Cool the cupcakes in the tin on a wire rack for 10 minutes before turning them out on the rack to cool completely.

5   To make the frosting, make an ice bath by placing a small bowl on top of a medium bowl filled with ice. In a small saucepan, cook 12 tablespoons (1½ sticks) of the butter over medium heat, swirling the pan occasionally, for about 7 minutes, until the butter turns a nutty brown. Immediately pour the browned butter into the small bowl sitting in the ice bath. Cool the butter to room temperature, cover, and refrigerate until it solidifies.

6   Transfer the solidified browned butter to a large bowl. Add the remaining 4 tablespoons (½ stick) of butter, the confectioners' sugar, cream, and lemon juice. Beat the frosting with an electric mixer until it is light and fluffy, then spread it over the cooled cupcakes.

SOME BASICS

DOWN TO THE BONES

A slowly simmered stock is the secret behind the intense flavor and full-bodied feel of a good sauce or soup. Chicken and beef stocks are widely used, but no other region of the country has quite so many uses—or quite as large an appetite—for the broth made from the long, slow simmer of a ham hock as ours does. And would anyone who is not a gardening fanatic be sensitive to a vegetable's need for a light-bodied but full-flavored vegetable stock?

A proper stock takes time, it must barely simmer, its surface should simmer like the surface of a pond under a gentle breeze. A stock should never boil. Boiling creates cloudy stocks. But the initial investment of time can change meals for months. Stocks freeze well, so containers can be stockpiled for future soups and braised meals. We also like to reduce stocks and freeze the essence in ice-cube trays to create instant jus and other sauces. To do this, allow the stock to cool to room temperature, uncovered, and then refrigerate. Leave the layer of fat that collects on top of the cold stock in place until you are ready to use it—or strain it and freeze it. Not unlike the paraffin on a jar of homemade jam, the fat protects and preserves the stock.

CHICKEN STOCK

MAKES ABOUT 3 QUARTS

4 POUNDS CHICKEN PARTS AND/OR MEATY BONES
(SUCH AS BACKS, NECKS, CARCASSES, OR WINGS)

16 CUPS COLD WATER

2 LARGE ONIONS, PEELED AND QUARTERED

4 STALKS OF CELERY, ROUGHLY CHOPPED

3 MEDIUM CARROTS, PEELED AND ROUGHLY CHOPPED

2 CLOVES OF GARLIC, CRUSHED

3 BAY LEAVES

¼ CUP LIGHTLY PACKED FRESH FLAT-LEAF PARSLEY
LEAVES AND STEMS

6 TEASPOONS FRESH THYME LEAVES

2 TEASPOONS BLACK PEPPERCORNS

1 TEASPOON KOSHER SALT

1   Rinse the chicken parts, pat dry, and place them in a large stockpot. Add the cold water and bring to a boil over high heat, stirring occasionally and skimming off the white foam that accumulates on top of the stock. Stir in the onions, celery, carrots, garlic, bay leaves, parsley, thyme, peppercorns, and salt. Reduce the heat to low, partially cover the pot, and gently simmer the stock, stirring occasionally, for 3 hours, or until the meat falls off the bones and the bones separate.

2   Strain the stock through a fine-mesh sieve into a large bowl. The stock can be used immediately, or cool it to room temperature, transfer to airtight containers, and refrigerate for up to 3 days or freeze for up to 6 months.

VEGETABLE STOCK

MAKES ABOUT 3 QUARTS

2 LARGE ONIONS, PEELED AND QUARTERED

2 MEDIUM LEEKS, TRIMMED, WASHED, AND ROUGHLY
CHOPPED

2 STALKS OF CELERY, ROUGHLY CHOPPED

2 SMALL PARSNIPS, PEELED AND ROUGHLY CHOPPED

2 SMALL WHITE TURNIPS, PEELED AND ROUGHLY CHOPPED

3 CLOVES OF GARLIC, SMASHED

1 CUP MUSHROOMS OR MUSHROOM STEMS

¼ CUP EXTRA-VIRGIN OLIVE OIL

½ CUP LIGHTLY PACKED FRESH FLAT-LEAF PARSLEY
LEAVES AND STEMS

2 TEASPOONS FRESH THYME LEAVES

1 BAY LEAF

10 PEPPERCORNS

¼ CUP WHITE WINE

2 TEASPOONS SALT

1 TABLESPOON WHITE WINE VINEGAR

1   Preheat the oven to 400°F. In a large roasting pan, stir together the onions, leeks, celery, parsnips, turnips, garlic, and mushrooms. Drizzle the olive oil over the vegetables and toss to coat. Roast for about 45 minutes, stirring occasionally, until the vegetables are lightly browned.

2   Transfer the vegetables into a large stockpot. Pour 2 cups of water into the warm roasting pan and scrape up the browned glaze from the bottom of the pan; pour this mixture into the stockpot. Add 10 cups of water, the parsley, thyme, bay leaf, peppercorns, wine, and salt to the pot. Bring to a boil over high heat, reduce the heat to low, partially cover the pot, and gently simmer the stock for 30 to 45 minutes, until the vegetables are very soft.

3   Strain the stock through a fine-mesh sieve into a large bowl and stir in the vinegar. The stock can be used immediately, or cool it to room temperature, transfer to airtight containers, and refrigerate for up to 3 days or freeze for up to 2 months.

HAM HOCK STOCK

MAKES ABOUT 3 QUARTS

---

3 HAM HOCKS (ABOUT 2 POUNDS)

3 CARROTS, PEELED AND ROUGHLY CHOPPED

2 STALKS OF CELERY, ROUGHLY CHOPPED

1 MEDIUM ONION, QUARTERED

1 BAY LEAF

8 SPRIGS OF FRESH THYME

16 CUPS COLD WATER

1   In a large stockpot, combine the hocks, carrots, celery, onion, bay leaf, thyme, and cold water and bring to a boil over high heat. Reduce the heat to low, partially cover the pot, and gently simmer the stock, stirring occasionally, for about 3 hours, until the ham is tender and starting to fall off the bones.

2   Strain the stock through a fine-mesh sieve into a large bowl. The stock can be used immediately, or cool it to room temperature, transfer to airtight containers, and refrigerate for up to 3 days or freeze up to 6 months. (When the hocks are cool enough to handle, pull the meat from the bones and save it for another use.)

BEEF OR VEAL STOCK

MAKES ABOUT 3 QUARTS

---

6 POUNDS BEEF AND/OR VEAL BONES (SUCH AS KNUCKLEBONES, SHANKS, TAILS, AND NECKS), SAWED INTO 2-INCH PIECES

3 MEDIUM ONIONS, PEELED AND QUARTERED

4 LARGE CARROTS, PEELED AND ROUGHLY CHOPPED

4 CELERY STALKS, ROUGHLY CHOPPED

14 CUPS WATER

½ CUP LIGHTLY PACKED FRESH FLAT-LEAF PARSLEY LEAVES AND STEMS

1 TABLESPOON FRESH THYME LEAVES

1 BAY LEAF

15 BLACK PEPPERCORNS

2 TEASPOONS KOSHER SALT

1   Preheat the oven to 400°F. In a large roasting pan, stir together the bones, onions, carrots, and celery. Roast for 45 minutes, stirring often, until the bones are very brown.

2   Transfer the bones and vegetables into a large stockpot. Pour 2 cups of the water into the warm roasting pan and scrape up the browned glaze from the bottom of the pan; pour this mixture into the stockpot. Add the remaining 12 cups of water, the parsley, thyme, bay leaf, peppercorns, and salt to the pot. Bring to a boil over high heat, stirring occasionally and skimming off the white foam that accumulates on top of the stock. Reduce the heat to low, partially cover the pot and gently simmer the stock, stirring occasionally, for 4 hours, until the meat falls off the bones and the bones separate.

3   Strain the stock through a fine-mesh sieve into a large bowl. The stock can be used immediately, or cool it to room temperature, transfer to airtight containers, and refrigerate for up to 3 days or freeze for up to 6 months.

THE FOOTHILLS PANTRY

Smoking, curing, pickling, and putting foods by has long helped save the bounty of summer for leaner times in this remote region. Whether it is a dash of blackberry vinegar or a great tomato marmalade, these preserves and condiments gave depth and nuance to the dishes. We also like to keep sweet and savory pie crusts in the freezer to pull out for special winter pies. We freeze individual recipes, thaw overnight in the refrigerator, and then roll them out when ready to use.

BASIC PASTRY

MAKES PASTRY FOR TWO 9- OR 10-INCH PIE SHELLS
OR ONE DOUBLE-CRUST 9-INCH PIE

3 CUPS ALL-PURPOSE FLOUR

1 TEASPOON SALT

1 CUP PLUS 3 TABLESPOONS SHORTENING

1 LARGE EGG

⅓ CUP PLUS 1 TO 3 TABLESPOONS ICE WATER

1 TABLESPOON DISTILLED WHITE VINEGAR

1   Place the flour and salt in a food processor and pulse to combine. Add the shortening and pulse until the mixture resembles coarse meal. Transfer to a medium bowl and set aside.

2   In a small bowl, whisk together the egg, ⅓ cup of the ice water, and the vinegar. Pour the egg mixture over the flour mixture and stir with a fork just until the dough comes together. If the dough is too dry, add more water, 1 tablespoon at a time.

3   Turn the dough out onto a lightly floured surface and knead gently into a ball. Divide the ball in half and flatten each piece into a disk about 1½ inches thick. Wrap each disk in plastic and refrigerate for at least 30 minutes, or up to 3 days; the dough can also be frozen for up to 6 months and defrosted overnight in the refrigerator prior to using.

SWEET PASTRY

MAKES PASTRY FOR ONE 9-INCH PIE OR ONE 10-INCH TART

1 CUP ALL-PURPOSE FLOUR

1 CUP CAKE OR PASTRY FLOUR

½ CUP CONFECTIONERS' SUGAR

¼ TEASPOON FINE SEA SALT

8 TABLESPOONS (1 STICK) UNSALTED BUTTER, AT ROOM TEMPERATURE

2 LARGE EGGS

1 LARGE EGG YOLK

1   Place the all-purpose flour, cake flour, sugar, and salt in a food processor and pulse to combine. Add the butter and pulse until the pieces of butter are the size of small peas. In a small bowl, whisk the eggs and yolk together; pour them over the flour mixture and pulse until the mixture forms large clumps.

2   Scoop the dough out of the processor onto a floured surface; knead a few times, just until the dough is smooth. Form the dough into a disk and wrap it in plastic. Refrigerate for at least 30 minutes, or up to 2 days; the dough can also be frozen for up to 6 months and defrosted overnight in the refrigerator prior to using.

BLACKBERRY VINEGAR

MAKES ABOUT 3½ CUPS

This is a very simple vinegar that makes a nice vinaigrette, an interesting finish for beans or greens, or a substitute for cider or even sherry vinegar.

3 CUPS RICE WINE VINEGAR
2 TABLESPOONS SUGAR
1 CUP FRESH BLACKBERRIES

1   In a medium saucepan, heat the vinegar and sugar over medium heat, stirring frequently, until the sugar dissolves.

2   Place the blackberries in a 1-quart glass container and mash with a wooden spoon. Pour the hot vinegar mixture over the berries and stir. Allow the mixture to cool to room temperature, then cover and refrigerate for about 3 days to allow the vinegar to take on the blackberry flavor.

3   Strain the mixture, discard the solids, and return the vinegar to the glass container. Store the vinegar in the refrigerator for up to 2 months.

GREEN TOMATO MARMALADE

MAKES 1 QUART

Serve this tangy marmalade with sharp cheese or use it as an accompaniment to leg of lamb or other rich roasts.

2 GREEN TOMATOES, DICED
1 HEAD ROASTED GARLIC, FLESH REMOVED AND CHOPPED
1 LEEK, WHITE AND LIGHT-GREEN PART, SPLIT, RINSED WELL, AND DICED
1 CUP SUGAR
1 CUP MUSCADINE WINE OR MUSCAT WINE
1½ TEASPOONS GRATED LEMON ZEST
1 TEASPOON VEGETABLE OIL
1 TEASPOON RED PEPPER FLAKES
1 BAY LEAF

1   In a medium saucepan, combine all the ingredients and bring to a boil over high heat. Lower the heat and simmer for 15 minutes.

2   Remove from the heat and discard the bay leaf. Cool the marmalade to room temperature, divide between glass containers, cover, and refrigerate. The marmalade will keep refrigerated for 2 to 3 weeks.

MUSCADINE GRAPE MARMALADE

MAKES ABOUT 3 CUPS

The muscadine is a very local grape, but more and more places are beginning to stock tiny wild grapes for a few brief weeks in the fall. This is delicious with duck and cheese. When cooking with muscadine grapes, be sure to remove the seeds. If bitten into, they are an unpleasant surprise. The skins are important to the success of this jam.

4 CUPS (ABOUT 1½ POUNDS) MUSCADINE GRAPES

¼ CUP SUGAR

¼ CUP BOURBON

1 TEASPOON VEGETABLE OIL

½ VIDALIA OR OTHER SWEET ONION, THINLY SLICED

¼ CUP WHITE WINE

1   Preheat the oven to 350°F.

2   In a medium bowl, toss the grapes, sugar, and bourbon together. Spread the mixture onto a greased baking sheet and roast for about 20 minutes, until the grapes are very soft. Remove from the oven and let cool. Once cool, chop the grapes coarsely and pick out the seeds with your fingers. Set the grapes and their juices aside.

3   In a medium saucepan, heat the oil over medium-high heat. Add the onion and cook, stirring frequently, until lightly browned, about 10 minutes. Remove from the heat, cool slightly, and then coarsely chop the onion. Return the onion to the pan and add the grapes and their juices. Stir in the wine, place over medium heat, and simmer the mixture for 5 to 6 minutes, until most of the wine has evaporated. Serve the marmalade warm, or cool to room temperature, transfer to an airtight container, and refrigerate for up to 2 weeks.

CLOVED WATERMELON PICKLE

MAKES 1 QUART

This pickle is great with duck, turkey, or game and is terrific with charcuterie.

½ CUP KOSHER SALT

4 CUPS ½-INCH CUBES PEELED WATERMELON RIND, WHITE PART ONLY, WITH ALL PINK FLESH REMOVED

3 CUPS SUGAR

½ CUP RICE-WINE VINEGAR

2 TEASPOONS WHOLE CLOVES

1 CINNAMON STICK

ZEST AND JUICE OF 1 LEMON

ZEST AND JUICE OF 1 LIME

1   In a large bowl, combine the salt and 1 gallon (16 cups) water and stir until the salt dissolves. Add the watermelon rind and refrigerate 8 hours or overnight.

2   Drain the rind and place it and the lemon and lime juice in a large cast-iron pot or Dutch oven with 3 cups of fresh cold water. Bring to a boil over high heat, then lower the heat and simmer, uncovered, for 45 minutes, or until the rind is tender when pierced with a fork. Drain and set aside.

3   Rinse out the pot the rind cooked in and add the sugar, vinegar, cloves, cinnamon, and lemon and lime zests along with 3 cups of fresh water. Bring the mixture to a boil and cook, stirring, for about 5 minutes, until the mixture is slightly syrupy. Add the watermelon rind back to the pot and simmer, uncovered, about 40 minutes more, until the rind becomes transparent.

4   Place a large strainer or colander over a bowl and drain the rind; cool the rind and syrup separately. When cooled, place the rind in a large airtight container and pour just enough syrup over it until it is completely submerged. The rind will keep refrigerated for about 2 months.

GREEN TOMATO PICKLE

MAKES 2 QUARTS

Any green tomato can be used, but the ones we like best are Speers Tennessee Green, Green Zebra, and Arkansas Travelers. This can be used on a platter of crudité, served with charcuterie or minced and added to a remoulade sauce for fried fish.

2 POUNDS (ABOUT 5 SMALL) GREEN TOMATOES

3 CUPS WHITE VINEGAR

3 CLOVES OF GARLIC, PEELED

2 BAY LEAVES

1 TEASPOON PICKLING SPICE

¾ TEASPOON CRUSHED RED PEPPER FLAKES

4 TEASPOONS KOSHER SALT

1 TABLESPOON SUGAR

1   Cut the tomatoes in half width-wise, and using a small spoon or your fingers, scrape out and discard the seeds. Slice the tomatoes into ¼-inch-thick slices and divide them between two 1-quart jars and set aside.

2   In a medium saucepan, combine the vinegar, garlic, bay leaves, pickling spice, pepper flakes, salt, sugar, and 1½ cups water and bring to a boil over high heat. Boil and stir until the sugar and salt are dissolved, then immediately pour the hot liquid over the tomatoes in the jars. Let cool to room temperature, then cover the jars and refrigerate for at least 4 days to allow the flavors to blend. The tomatoes will keep for about 2 months.

PRESERVED LEMONS

MAKES ABOUT 1 QUART

This recipe is called for in the Fall Salad of Shaved Fennel and Celery Root. Preserving lemons allows you to enjoy them, especially seasonal varieties such as Meyer lemons. This versatile condiment can be used with anything from fish to starch. My favorite is preserved lemon and asparagus risotto. The blanching is a very important step in this process. The recipe takes more than twenty-four hours but keeps for a very long time—up to a year.

8 LEMONS, QUARTERED, PULP AND SEEDS SCOOPED OUT WITH A SPOON AND DISCARDED

2½ CUPS WHITE BALSAMIC VINEGAR

2 CUPS SUGAR

3 SPRIGS FRESH BASIL

1   Bring 6 cups of water to a boil. Add the lemon rinds, bring back to a boil, and cook for about 8 minutes, until the rinds are soft but not mushy. Remove from the water, place in a single layer in a baking pan, and refrigerate, uncovered, overnight.

2   The next day, in a medium saucepan, bring the vinegar, sugar, basil, and 1 cup of water to a boil. Add the rinds to the boiling liquid and cook for 5 minutes. Remove from the heat and let the rinds cool in the liquid. Once cooled, spoon the rinds into a 1-quart jar. Pour in as much of the cooking liquid as needed to completely cover the rinds, close the jar, and refrigerate. They will keep refrigerated for up to a year.

PIMIENTO CHEESE

MAKES ABOUT 4 CUPS

Pimiento cheese has been referred to as the Southern pâté. In the South, it is often added to just about everything, from hamburgers to grits to cheese dips. Most often, it is served with crackers as an appetizer. The key to good pimiento cheese is pickle juice. Following are some of our favorite versions.

6 TABLESPOONS MAYONNAISE

2 TABLESPOONS PICKLE JUICE

1½ TEASPOONS DIJON MUSTARD

1 TEASPOON HOT SAUCE, PREFERABLY FRANK'S RED HOT SAUCE

1 TEASPOON MINCED GARLIC

½ TEASPOON KOSHER SALT

1 TEASPOON FRESHLY GROUND BLACK PEPPER

1 ROASTED RED PEPPER, SKINNED, SEEDED, AND CHOPPED

½ CUP PIMIENTO PIECES, DRAINED

1 POUND GRATED MILD OR MEDIUM-SHARP CHEDDAR CHEESE

In a medium bowl, stir together the mayonnaise, pickle juice, mustard, hot sauce, garlic, salt, and pepper until smooth. Fold in the red pepper, pimiento, and Cheddar. Chill for at least 30 minutes before serving.

SPICY PIMIENTO CHEESE

MAKES ABOUT 5 CUPS

½ POUND GRATED EXTRA-SHARP CHEDDAR CHEESE

½ POUND GRATED MILD CHEDDAR CHEESE

1 (7-OUNCE) JAR PIMIENTO PIECES, DRAINED

1 (7-OUNCE) JAR ROASTED RED PEPPERS, DRAINED

2½ TABLESPOONS MAYONNAISE

1 TABLESPOON WORCESTERSHIRE SAUCE

4 OUNCES CREAM CHEESE, CUT INTO CHUNKS

2 TABLESPOONS DRAINED PICKLED JALAPEÑO SLICED

In a food processor, combine both Cheddars, the pimiento, roasted red pepper, mayonnaise, and Worcestershire and blend until well combined. Add the cream cheese a little at a time, pulsing between additions, and then blend the mixtures for about 1 minute, until you have a very smooth, creamy dip. Add the jalapeño slices and blend for 1 more minute. Chill for at least 30 minutes before serving.

CORNMEAL LAVOSH

MAKES ABOUT 100 (2-INCH) CRACKERS

Lavosh is a classic Armenian flatbread. We used cornmeal to give it a regional twist and use it for croutons, crackers, and on cheese plates; we serve it with charcuterie and pimiento cheese as well. The key to successful lavosh is not overworking the dough.

2¼ TEASPOONS (¼-OUNCE PACKAGE) DRY YEAST

1 CUP WARM (NOT HOT) WATER

2 CUPS BREAD FLOUR OR ALL-PURPOSE FLOUR

½ CUP CORNMEAL

½ CUP MASA HARINA OR CORN FLOUR

1 TABLESPOON UNSALTED BUTTER, SOFTENED

1½ TEASPOONS SUGAR

¼ TEASPOON CAYENNE PEPPER

1 TEASPOON KOSHER SALT, PLUS MORE FOR SPRINKLING

2 TABLESPOONS MELTED UNSALTED BUTTER

1   Place the yeast in a medium bowl, stir in the warm water and let the mixture sit at room temperature 5 to 7 minutes, until it starts to foam. Stir in the bread flour, cornmeal, masa harina, softened butter, sugar, cayenne, and 1 teaspoon of the salt. Stir until the dough begins to hold together, then turn it out onto a lightly floured surface and begin to knead it with lightly floured hands. Knead it just until it begins to feel smooth and uniform in texture, about 30 seconds. Gather the dough into a ball, cover with a damp kitchen towel, and let rest 15 minutes. Preheat the oven to 375°F.

2   Using a rolling pin, roll half the dough out on a well-floured surface until paper thin. Poke the dough all over with a fork, then carefully lift the dough and transfer it to a greased baking sheet. Use a pastry brush to brush it lightly with half the melted butter and sprinkle with kosher salt. Repeat with the remaining dough. Bake the lavosh 7 to 10 minutes, until golden brown.

3   Cool the lavosh on the pans, then break it into whatever size you like (2-inch cracker squares are good for snacking and dipping). Will keep for 2 days in an airtight container.

BLACK-EYED PEA HUMMUS

MAKES ABOUT 6 CUPS

This dish is a variation on a Middle Eastern dish, yet the ever-present black-eyed pea finds its way into the mix again. Black-eyed pea hummus is great as a dip, on bread, or as a spread on a sandwich, and it can also be fried as a vegetarian option. This recipe makes a lot but can easily be halved. Good tips when making this is to use a food processor instead of a food mill whenever possible, and process the peas while hot.

2 CUPS DRIED BLACK-EYED PEAS

1½ TABLESPOONS CHOPPED GARLIC

¾ CUP EXTRA-VIRGIN OLIVE OIL

¼ TEASPOON CAYENNE PEPPER, OR TO TASTE

GRATED ZEST AND JUICE OF 2 LEMONS

¼ CUP CHOPPED FRESH FLAT-LEAF PARSLEY

2 TABLESPOONS CHOPPED CHIVES

4 TEASPOONS KOSHER SALT, OR TO TASTE

1   Soak the black-eyed peas overnight in 8 cups of water. The next day, drain the peas and transfer them to a large pot. Add enough water to cover by 1 inch and bring to a boil over high heat. Reduce the heat and simmer the peas, uncovered, about 45 minutes, until tender.

2   Drain the peas, immediately transfer them to a food processor, add the garlic, and process until smooth. Add the remaining ingredients and pulse until combined. Transfer to an airtight container and refrigerate until chilled. Serve with bread, crackers, or crudite. The hummus will keep refrigerated for about 5 days.

RESOURCES

Just as no painting can be made without paint and brushes, no meal can be made without the best ingredients and equipment. Some of our sources mail-order directly to customers and we want to share them with you.

ANSON MILLS
803-467-4122
www.ansonmills.com
Our friend Glenn Roberts founded his company both to save heritage varieties of grains and to insure that the grains be properly ground and packaged. His stone-ground grits are the secret to our delicious version.

BENTON'S COUNTRY HAM
423-442-5003
www.bentonshams.com
For the smokiest bacon and some of the finest ham in the country, call on our local smoker. Warning: the waiting list can be quite long.

BLACKBERRY FARM
865-984-8166
www.blackberryfarm.com
We often have seasonal items from our larder—pickles, jams, and chutneys from our garden and preservation kitchen, up to twenty different traditional hams and sausages, and, of course, our cheeses—available through our Website. We also offer our homemade granola as well as some of our favorite tableware, and, for the holidays, rare assemblages of artisan foods in gift baskets.

D'ARTAGNAN
973-344-0565 or 800-327-8246
www.dartagnan.com
For wonderful, domestic foie gras, as well as truffles, duck confit, and game meats.

JB PRINCE
800-473-0577
www.jbprince.com
We used to have to wait for trips to New York City to buy hard-to-find pastry molds, odd-shaped knives, great kitchen aprons, and other professional-quality kitchen gear. But now, JB Prince sells its vast array of professional kitchen tools online.

KORIN
212-587-7021 or 800-626-2172
www.korin.com
Japan has a history of making state-of-the-art knives and other kitchen tools. We use Japanese-style knives for filleting, mincing, shaving, and doing many things that require the sharpest edge and the lightest tough.

LAUREL CREEK FARM
865-680-1739
www.laurelcreekmeat.com
Our friends at Laurel Creek are a wonderful source for southern mountain grass-fed beef, pork, and poultry.

MAUVIEL COPPER
302-326-4803
www.mauviel.com
Copper is known for its superior ability to distribute heat evenly across the surface of a pot or pan and to hold that heat. Mauviel is the premier maker of French copper and is now beginning to sell retail through its Website. (Also purchase Mauviel from www.chefresource.com and Amazon.com.)

MUDDY POND SORGHUM
931-445-3509
www.muddypondsorghum.com
Our friends the Guenther family at Muddy Pond Farm produce sorghum the old-fashioned way, which insures a clean, robust flavor.

SUNBURST TROUT
800-673-3051
www.sunbursttrout.com
For high-quality smoked wild trout and domestic caviar, we call on our friends at Sunburst.

SWEET GRASS DAIRY
229-227-0752
www.sweetgrassdairy.com
Our friends at Sweet Grass make wonderful cheeses that complement our own and also make a wonderful cheese tray.

VIKING KITCHEN EQUIPMENT
662-455-1200 or 888-845-4641
www.vikingrange.com
In addition to some of the stoves we swear by, the Viking Company produces fine pots, pans, knives, and counter-top appliances and sells them retail at both their stores and on their Website.

ACKNOWLEDGMENTS

To all of the chefs who have been an important part of Blackberry's past, including Bob Carter and John Fleer, and especially to our current team of Josh Feathers, Joseph Lenn, and Adam Cooke, I offer thanks. They have contributed a piece of their hearts while helping to make our culinary program truly unique in the epicurean world.

I am also grateful to our food artisans—the gardeners, livestock managers, bakers, foragers, cheese makers, butchers, chocolatiers, and sommeliers. Our neighbors and purveyors, often one and the same, help us maintain the integrity and reflect the identity of this place that we love on our table every day. Thank you, as well, to our longtime guests, who give us purpose and an opportunity to share our daily inspirations and life's work. Your thoughts guide us and your interest inspires us.

Sarah Elder, Andy Chabot, and Heather Anne Thomas truly went above and beyond in their efforts for this book. We also wish to thank our editor, Aliza Fogelson, whose enthusiasm for the work is almost matched by the talent and perseverance that she brought to it.

Most important, my deepest gratitude goes to my wife, Mary Celeste, and our children Cameron, Sam, Rose, and Josephine. Thank you for taking care of me and for putting up with odd hours, late nights, test foods, and dirty kitchens.

INDEX

Note: Page numbers in *italics* refer to recipe photographs.

Angel Biscuits, 61
Apple(s):
    Bourbon, Fried Pies, 110, *111*
    Crisp, Skillet, *98, 99*
    Stack Cake, 122, *123*
    Stewed Spiced, 138
Asparagus:
    and Country Ham Salad with Muscadine
        Vinaigrette, 235, *235*
    Salad of Pea Tendrils in Wild Garlic
        Vinaigrette, 263

Bacon:
    Benton, about, 195
    -Glazed Carrots on Wilted Romaine, 107, *107*
Barbecue, notes about, 29
Barbecue Sauces:
    Blackberry, 37
    Coffee, 37
    Peach, 36
Basil, Opal, Syrup, Lemon Chess Pie with, *248,*
    249
Beall, Cameron, 9
Beall, Kreis, 7, 8, 14, 132–33
Beall, Sandy, 7, 8, 29, 132–33
Bean(s):
    Baked, Sam Beall's, 33
    Barbecued Quail with Black-Eyed Pea Salad,
        40, *41*
    Black-Eyed Pea Hummus, 275
    Sam's Cassoulet, 182, *183*
    White, Fennel, and Sun-Dried Tomato
        Ragout, Country Ham–Wrapped Sturgeon
        with, 162, *163*
Beef:
    Autumn Lamb Roast, 93
    Braised Short Ribs, 199
    Grilled Chili-Rubbed Rib Roast, 66, *67*
    Stock, 269

Beet(s):
    Carpaccio with Summer Chanterelles and
        Chives, 20, *21*
    Raw Winter Vegetable Salad, 175
Benton, Allan, 195
Berries. *See also* Blackberry
    Blueberry and Apple Green Tea, 44, *45*
    Buttermilk Panna Cotta with Wild
        Strawberries, 224, *225*
    Dried Cherry and Cranberry Sauce, 138
    Raspberry Red Oz Tea, 44, *45*
    Rhubarb Tart with Wild Raspberry Cream,
        214
    Strawberry-Citrus Lemonade, 44, *45*
Biscuits:
    Angel, 61
    Blackberry Farm, *60,* 61
    preparing, notes about, 60
Blackberry:
    Barbecue Sauce, 37
    Cobbler, *24, 25*
    Sorbet, 254
    Vinegar, 271
Black-Eyed Pea Hummus, 275
Black-Eyed Pea Salad, Barbecued Quail with, 40,
    41
Black Walnut Soup, 119, *119*
Blini, Corn, 166, *167*
Blueberry and Apple Green Tea, 44, *45*
Bourbon Apple Fried Pies, 110, *111*
Bourbon-Braised Pork Belly on Grits with
    Caramelized Onions, 170, *171*
Bourbon Butterscotch Sauce, 77
Bourbon Zabaglione, 231
Breads:
    Angel Biscuits, 61
    biscuits, notes about, 60
    Blackberry Farm Biscuits, *60,* 61
    Corn, Lacy, 127
    Corn, Skillet, *126,* 127
    corn bread, in Southern cooking, 126
    Cornmeal Lavosh, 275

Bread stuffings and dressings:
    Beall Family Oyster Dressing, 139, *139*
    Roast Turkey with Corn Bread Stuffing and
        Gravy, 136–37
Brussels Sprouts, Pecan, *121,* 122
Buttermilk:
    Dressing, Kale Salad with, 100
    Panna Cotta with Wild Strawberries, 224, *225*
    Sorbet, 253
    –Vanilla Bean Ice Cream, 74
Butterscotch Pudding, Baked, 179
Butterscotch Sauce, Bourbon, 77

Cabbage:
    Skillet Slaw, 188
    Sweet and Spicy Foothills Coleslaw, *32, 33*
Cakes:
    Apple Stack, 122, *123*
    Coconut, *172, 173*
    Roasted Pineapple Upside-Down, *164, 165*
    Spiced Cupcakes with Browned-Butter
        Frosting, 264, *265*
Carpaccio:
    Beet, with Summer Chanterelles and Chives,
        20, *21*
    Citrus, with Chocolate-Covered Clementines,
        200
Carrot(s):
    Bacon-Glazed, on Wilted Romaine, 107, *107*
    Raw Winter Vegetable Salad, 175
    Soufflé, Sam's, 140, *141*
    Sweet and Spicy Foothills Coleslaw, *32, 33*
Caviar, notes about, 166
Celery Root:
    and Potato Purée, 199
    Raw Winter Vegetable Salad, 175
Chard, Creamed, 219
Charlesworth, Haesel, 87–90
Cheese:
    Curd and Pea Shell Salad, 19
    Green Tomato Skillet Cake, 259, *261*
    made at Blackberry Farm, 240–42

Cheese (*continued*):
    Pimiento, 274
    Pimiento, Spicy, 274
    Sam's Carrot Soufflé, 140, *141*
    Summer Squash Casserole, 70, *71*
    Tennessee Corn and Truffle Flan, 161
Cherry, Dried, and Cranberry Sauce, 138
Chess Pie, Lemon, with Opal Basil Syrup, *248*,
    249
Chicken:
    Buttermilk-Brined Fried, with Sage, *53*, 54
    Chili-Cured, Batter-Fried, *53*, 57
    Poussin Roasted with Sumac-Ginger Butter,
        176, *177*
    Smoky Mountain Skillet-Fried, *53*, 56
    Southern-style fried, about, 52
    Spring, Herb-Roasted, 236, *236*
    spring, notes about, 234
    Stock, 268
    Sweet Tea–Brined Fried, *53*, 55
    Tennessee Fire-Fried, Kreis's, 53
Chiles:
    Chili-Cured, Batter-Fried Chicken, *53*, 57
    Grilled Chili-Rubbed Rib Roast, 66, *67*
Chocolate:
    -Covered Clementines, Citrus Carpaccio with,
        200
    Sorbet, 253
    Spiced Fudge Sauce, 77
    White, Ice Cream Sandwiches, 58, *59*
    White, Toasted, Ice Cream, 58
Cider-Basted Venison, *186*, 187
Citrus Carpaccio with Chocolate-Covered
    Clementines, 200
Clementines, Chocolate-Covered, Citrus
    Carpaccio with, 200
Cobbler, Blackberry, 24, *25*
Coconut Cake, *172*, 173
Coffee:
    Barbecue Sauce, 37
    -Rubbed Duck Breast with Wine Marmalade,
        121
    Warm Café-au-Lait Sabayon with Creole
        Kisses, 237
Coleslaw, Sweet and Spicy Foothills, *32*, 33
Collard Greens, Wilted, 102
Collards, Kimchee, 103
Collards, Pot Likker, 102
Condiments:
    Blackberry Vinegar, 271
    Cloved Watermelon Pickle, 272
    Green Tomato Marmalade, 271
    Green Tomato Pickle, 273

Muscadine Grape Marmalade, 272
    Pimiento Cheese, 274
    Preserved Lemons, 273
    Spicy Pimiento Cheese, 274
Cookies:
    Creole Kisses, 237
Corn. *See also* Cornmeal; Grits; Hominy
    dried, about, 115
    fresh, about, 114–15
    gritted, about, 115
    with Roasted Hen-of-the-Woods Pudding, *250*,
        251
    Soup, Chilled, with Garlic Custard, 65
    and Truffle Flan, Tennessee, 161
Corn Bread:
    Lacy, 127
    Skillet, *126*, 127
    in Southern cooking, 126
    Stuffing and Gravy, Roast Turkey with,
        136–37
Cornmeal:
    about, 115
    Corn Blini, 166, *167*
    Herbed Spoonbread, 224
    Lacy Corn Bread, 127
    Lavosh, 275
    Roasted Hen-of-the-Woods with Corn
        Pudding, *250*, 251
    Skillet Corn Bread, *126*, 127
    Tennessee Corn and Truffle Flan, 161
Coykendall, John, 11–15
Coykendall, Karen, 14
Cranberry and Dried Cherry Sauce, 138
Cress, Wild, with Warm Ham Vinaigrette, 219
Crisp, Skillet Apple, *98*, 99
Cruze, Earl, 54
Cucumber, Lemon, Soup, *18*, 19
Cupcakes, Spiced, with Browned-Butter Frosting,
    264, *265*
Custard, Garlic, Chilled Corn Soup with, 65

Dandelion Green(s), 218
    about, 217
    Salad, Braised Rabbit with, 245
Desserts. *See also* Cakes; Ice Cream; Sorbet;
    Tarts
    Baked Butterscotch Pudding, 179
    Blackberry Cobbler, 24, *25*
    Bourbon Apple Fried Pies, 110, *111*
    Bourbon Butterscotch Sauce, 77
    Bourbon Zabaglione, 231
    Buttermilk Panna Cotta with Wild
        Strawberries, 224, *225*

Citrus Carpaccio with Chocolate-Covered
    Clementines, 200
Lemon Chess Pie with Opal Basil Syrup, *248*,
    249
Peach Shortcake, 72, *73*
Skillet Apple Crisp, *98*, 99
Spiced Fudge Sauce, 77
Sweet Potato Pie, 142, *144*
Warm Café-au-Lait Sabayon with Creole
    Kisses, 237
White Chocolate Ice Cream Sandwiches,
    58, *59*
Dips and spreads:
    Black-Eyed Pea Hummus, 275
    Pimiento Cheese, 274
    Spicy Pimiento Cheese, 274
Dressing, Oyster, Beall Family, 139, *139*
Drinks:
    Blueberry and Apple Green Tea, 44, *45*
    Raspberry Red Oz Tea, 44, *45*
    Strawberry-Citrus Lemonade, 44, *45*
Duck(s):
    Breast, Coffee-Rubbed, with Wine Marmalade,
        121
    Sam's Cassoulet, 182, *183*
    Wine-Roasted, 94, *95*

Eggplant Mousseline with Roasted Tomatoes,
    96

Feathers, Josh, 34, 54
Fennel:
    Fresh and Pickled, Rye Whiskey–Cured Trout
        with, 229
    Stuffed Pork Roulade, 246, *247*
    and Sun-Dried Tomato White Bean Ragout,
        Country Ham–Wrapped Sturgeon with,
        162, *163*
Fig Tart, *190*, 191
Fish:
    caviar, notes about, 166
    Country Ham–Wrapped Sturgeon with Fennel
        and Sun-Dried Tomato White Bean Ragout,
        162, *163*
    Oil-Poached Salmon with Radish Salad and
        Parsley Coulis, 22, *23*
    Oven-Baked Trout with Ramps and Morels,
        212, 213
    Rye Whiskey–Cured Trout with Fresh and
        Pickled Fennel, 229
Flan, Tennessee Corn and Truffle, 161
Fleer, John, 55
French Fries, 263

Fruit. *See also* Berries; *specific fruits*
    Citrus Carpaccio with Chocolate-Covered
        Clementines, 200
Fudge Sauce, Spiced, 77

Garlic Custard, Chilled Corn Soup with, 65
Garlicky Greens, Wilted, 218
Grains. *See* Cornmeal; Grits; Rice
Grape, Muscadine, Marmalade, 272
Green Goddess Potato Salad with Garden
    Radishes, 49
Green(s). *See also* Cabbage
    Asparagus and Country Ham Salad with
        Muscadine Vinaigrette, 235, *235*
    Bacon-Glazed Carrots on Wilted Romaine,
        107, *107*
    Butter Lettuce with Sheep's Milk Dressing, 169
    cold-weather, cooking notes, 100
    Collard, Wilted, 102
    Creamed Chard, 219
    creasy, about, 217
    Dandelion, 218
    dandelion, about, 217
    Dandelion, Salad, Braised Rabbit with, 245
    Kale Salad with Buttermilk Dressing, 100
    Kimchee Collards, 103
    Oven-Roasted Kale, 100
    pokeweed, about, 217
    Pot Likker Collards, 102
    spring, preparing, 217
    Wild Cress with Warm Ham Vinaigrette, 219
    Wilted Creasy, and Crisp-Roasted Morels,
        Ten-Hour Braised Lamb Neck with, 222,
        223
    Wilted Garlicky, 218
Grits, about, 115
Grits, Bourbon-Braised Pork Belly on, with
    Caramelized Onions, 170, *171*
Guenther, John and Emma, 143

Ham:
    Country, and Asparagus Salad with Muscadine
        Vinaigrette, 235, *235*
    Country, –Wrapped Sturgeon with Fennel and
        Sun-Dried Tomato White Bean Ragout,
        162, *163*
    Hock Stock, 269
    Vinaigrette, Warm, Wild Cress with, 219
Hatter, Ila, 205–9
Herbed Spoonbread, 224
Herb-Roasted Spring Chicken, 236, *236*
Hesse, John, 84
Holbrook, Kristian, 87, 240–42

Hominy, about, 115
Hominy, Pan-Roasted, Giblet, and Black
    Trumpet Ragout, Buttered Quail with, *108,*
    109
Honeysuckle Sorbet, 254
Hummus, Black-Eyed Pea, 275

Ice Cream:
    Buttermilk–Vanilla Bean, 74
    Peach, 76
    Sandwiches, White Chocolate, 58, *59*
    in Southern states, 74
    Spiced Pecan, 75
    Toasted White Chocolate, 58
Iced Tea:
    Blueberry and Apple Green Tea, 44, *45*
    Raspberry Red Oz Tea, 44, *45*

Kale:
    cooking methods, 100
    Oven-Roasted, 100
    Salad with Buttermilk Dressing, 100
Kimchee Collards, 103

Lamb Neck, Ten-Hour Braised, with Wilted
    Creasy Greens and Crisp-Roasted Morels,
    222, 223
Lamb Roast, Autumn, 93
Lavosh, Cornmeal, 275
Lemonade, Strawberry-Citrus, 44, *45*
Lemon Cucumber Soup, *18,* 19
Lemon(s):
    Chess Pie with Opal Basil Syrup, *248,* 249
    Preserved, 273
    Strawberry-Citrus Lemonade, 44, *45*
Lettuce:
    Asparagus and Country Ham Salad with
        Muscadine Vinaigrette, 235, *235*
    Bacon-Glazed Carrots on Wilted Romaine,
        107, *107*
    Butter, with Sheep's Milk Dressing, 169

Main dishes:
    Autumn Lamb Roast, 93
    Barbecued Quail with Black-Eyed Pea Salad,
        40, *41*
    Bourbon-Braised Pork Belly on Grits with
        Caramelized Onions, 170, *171*
    Braised Rabbit with Dandelion Green Salad,
        245
    Braised Short Ribs, 199
    Buttered Quail with Pan-Roasted Hominy,
        Giblet, and Black Trumpet Ragout, *108,* 109

Buttermilk-Brined Fried Chicken with Sage,
    53, 54
Chili-Cured, Batter-Fried Chicken, *53,* 57
Cider-Basted Venison, *186,* 187
Coffee-Rubbed Duck Breast with Wine
    Marmalade, 121
Country Ham–Wrapped Sturgeon with Fennel
    and Sun-Dried Tomato White Bean Ragout,
    162, *163*
Deep-Fried Turkey, *134,* 135
Fricassee of Rabbit in Mustard Cream, 252
Grilled Chili-Rubbed Rib Roast, 66, *67*
Herb-Roasted Spring Chicken, 236, *236*
Kreis's Tennessee Fire-Fried Chicken, 53
Oil-Poached Salmon with Radish Salad and
    Parsley Coulis, 22, *23*
Oven-Baked Trout with Ramps and Morels,
    212, 213
Peach-Glazed Baby Back Ribs, 36
Poussin Roasted with Sumac-Ginger Butter,
    176, *177*
Roast Turkey with Corn Bread Stuffing and
    Gravy, 136–37
Rye Whiskey–Cured Trout with Fresh and
    Pickled Fennel, 229
Sam's Cassoulet, 182, *183*
Smoky Mountain Skillet-Fried Chicken, *53,* 56
Stuffed Pork Roulade, 246, *247*
Sweet Tea–Brined Fried Chicken, *53,* 55
Ten-Hour Braised Lamb Neck with Wilted
    Creasy Greens and Crisp-Roasted Morels,
    222, 223
Wine-Roasted Ducks, 94, *95*
Wood-Smoked Veal Breast, 260, *261*
Marmalade, Green Tomato, 271
Marmalade, Muscadine Grape, 272
Meat. *See also* Beef; Pork
    Braised Rabbit with Dandelion Green Salad,
        245
    Cider-Basted Venison, *186,* 187
    Fricassee of Rabbit in Mustard Cream, 252
    Sam's Cassoulet, 182, *183*
    Ten-Hour Braised Lamb Neck with Wilted
        Creasy Greens and Crisp-Roasted Morels,
        222, 223
    Veal Stock, 269
    Wood-Smoked Veal Breast, 260, *261*
Michaels, Tom, 158
Morels:
    Crisp-Roasted, and Wilted Creasy Greens,
        Ten-Hour Braised Lamb Neck with, *222,*
        223
    and Ramps, Oven-Baked Trout with, *212,* 213

Muscadine Grape Marmalade, 272
Mushroom(s):
    Beet Carpaccio with Summer Chanterelles and
        Chives, 20, *21*
    Buttered Quail with Pan-Roasted Hominy,
        Giblet, and Black Trumpet Ragout, *108,* 109
    Oven-Baked Trout with Ramps and Morels,
        212, 213
    Roasted Hen-of-the-Woods with Corn
        Pudding, *250, 251*
    Ten-Hour Braised Lamb Neck with Wilted
        Creasy Greens and Crisp-Roasted Morels,
        222, 223
    Tennessee Corn and Truffle Flan, 161
    truffles, notes about, 158
    Wild, Soup, 213

Nuts. *See also* Pecan(s)
    black walnuts, about, 118
    Black Walnut Soup, 119, *119*
    Peanut Soup, 134

Okra, Skillet, 69
Onion(s):
    Caramelized, Bourbon-Braised Pork Belly on
        Grits with, 170, *171*
    Rings, Mr. Feathers's, 34, *35*
Oranges:
    Citrus Carpaccio with Chocolate-Covered
        Clementines, 200
Oyster Dressing, Beall Family, 139, *139*

Pancakes:
    Corn Blini, 166, *167*
    Lacy Corn Bread, 127
Panna Cotta, Buttermilk, with Wild Strawberries,
    224, 225
Parsley Coulis and Radish Salad, Oil-Poached
    Salmon with, *22, 23*
Parsnips, Roast, 188
Pastry, Basic, 270
Pastry, Sweet, 270
Peach:
    Barbecue Sauce, 36
    -Glazed Baby Back Ribs, 36
    Ice Cream, 76
    Roasted, Tart, 43
    Shortcake, 72, *73*
Peanut Soup, 134
Pea(s):
    Black-Eyed, Hummus, 275
    Black-Eyed, Salad, Barbecued Quail with, 40,
        41

Salad of Pea Tendrils in Wild Garlic
    Vinaigrette, 263
Shell and Cheese Curd Salad, 19
Pecan(s):
    Brussels Sprouts, *121,* 122
    Creole Kisses, 237
    Spiced, Ice Cream, 75
    Tart with Sorghum, 143, *145*
Pepper(s):
    Barbecued Quail with Black-Eyed Pea Salad,
        40, *41*
    Chili-Cured, Batter-Fried Chicken, *53,* 57
    Grilled Chili-Rubbed Rib Roast, 66, *67*
    Pimiento Cheese, 274
    Roasted Bell, Salad, 94, *95*
    Spicy Pimiento Cheese, 274
Pickle, Cloved Watermelon, 272
Pickle, Green Tomato, 273
Pies:
    Fried, Bourbon Apple, 110, *111*
    Lemon Chess, with Opal Basil Syrup, *248,*
        249
    Sweet Potato, 142, *144*
Pimiento Cheese, 274
    Spicy, 274
Pineapple, Roasted, Upside-Down Cake, *164,* 165
Pork. *See also* Ham
    Bacon-Glazed Carrots on Wilted Romaine,
        107, *107*
    Belly, Bourbon-Braised, on Grits with
        Caramelized Onions, 170, *171*
    Benton bacon, about, 195
    Peach-Glazed Baby Back Ribs, 36
    Roulade, Stuffed, 246, *247*
    Sam's Cassoulet, 182, *183*
Potato(es):
    and Celery Root Purée, 199
    French Fries, 263
    Grill-Roasted, *67,* 69
    Salad, Green Goddess, with Garden Radishes,
        49
    Sweet, Pie, 142, *144*
    Whipped Mashed, 140, *140*
Poultry. *See also* Chicken
    Barbecued Quail with Black-Eyed Pea Salad,
        40, *41*
    Buttered Quail with Pan-Roasted Hominy,
        Giblet, and Black Trumpet Ragout, *108,* 109
    Coffee-Rubbed Duck Breast with Wine
        Marmalade, 121
    Deep-Fried Turkey, *134,* 135
    Roast Turkey with Corn Bread Stuffing and
        Gravy, 136–37

Sam's Cassoulet, 182, *183*
    Wine-Roasted Ducks, 94, *95*
Poussin:
    Herb-Roasted Spring Chicken, 236, *236*
    Roasted with Sumac-Ginger Butter, 176, *177*
Puddings:
    Baked Butterscotch, 179
    Roasted Hen-of-the-Woods with Corn, *250,*
        251

Quail:
    Barbecued, with Black-Eyed Pea Salad, 40, *41*
    Buttered, with Pan-Roasted Hominy, Giblet,
        and Black Trumpet Ragout, *108,* 109

Rabbit:
    Braised, with Dandelion Green Salad, 245
    Fricassee of, in Mustard Cream, 252
Radish(es):
    Garden, Green Goddess Potato Salad with, 49
    Salad and Parsley Coulis, Oil-Poached Salmon
        with, *22, 23*
Ramp(s):
    and Morels, Oven-Baked Trout with, *212, 213*
    notes about, 227
    Risotto, Smoky Mountain, with Jack Daniel's,
        230, *231*
Raspberry, Wild, Cream, Rhubarb Tart with, 214
Raspberry Red Oz Tea, 44, *45*
Rhubarb Tart with Wild Raspberry Cream, 214
Rice:
    Smoky Mountain Ramp Risotto with Jack
        Daniel's, 230, *231*
    Risotto, Smoky Mountain Ramp, with Jack
        Daniel's, 230, *231*
Roberts, Glenn, 126
Ross, Jeff, 205, 209
Rye Whiskey–Cured Trout with Fresh and
    Pickled Fennel, 229

Sabayon, Warm Café-au-Lait, with Creole Kisses,
    237
Salads:
    Asparagus and Country Ham, with Muscadine
        Vinaigrette, 235, *235*
    Black-Eyed Pea, Barbecued Quail with, 40, *41*
    Butter Lettuce with Sheep's Milk Dressing,
        169
    Dandelion Green, Braised Rabbit with, 245
    Kale, with Buttermilk Dressing, 100
    Pea Shell and Cheese Curd, 19
    of Pea Tendrils in Wild Garlic Vinaigrette,
        263

Potato, Green Goddess, with Garden Radishes, 49

Radish, and Parsley Coulis, Oil-Poached Salmon with, 22, 23

Raw Winter Vegetable, 175

Roasted Bell Pepper, 94, 95

Summer Squash, 34

Sweet and Spicy Foothills Coleslaw, 32, 33

Salmon, Oil-Poached, with Radish Salad and Parsley Coulis, 22, 23

Sandler, Pat, 205, 209

Sauces:

Barbecue, Blackberry, 37

Barbecue, Coffee, 37

Barbecue, Peach, 36

Bourbon Butterscotch, 77

Dried Cherry and Cranberry, 138

Fudge, Spiced, 77

Sausages:

Sam's Cassoulet, 182, 183

Seafood. See Fish; Oyster Dressing

Shellfish. See Oyster Dressing

Shortcake, Peach, 72, 73

Shuckman, Lewis, 166

Side dishes. See also Salads

Bacon-Glazed Carrots on Wilted Romaine, 107, 107

Beall Family Oyster Dressing, 139, 139

Beet Carpaccio with Summer Chanterelles and Chives, 20, 21

Celery Root and Potato Purée, 199

Creamed Chard, 219

Dandelion Greens, 218

Eggplant Mousseline with Roasted Tomatoes, 96

French Fries, 263

Green Tomato Skillet Cake, 259, 261

Grill-Roasted Potatoes, 67, 69

Heirloom Tomato Terrine, 39

Herbed Spoonbread, 224

Kimchee Collards, 103

Mr. Feathers's Onion Rings, 34, 35

Oven-Roasted Kale, 100

Pecan Brussels Sprouts, 121, 122

Pot Likker Collards, 102

Roasted Hen-of-the-Woods with Corn Pudding, 250, 251

Roast Parsnips, 188

Sam Beall's Baked Beans, 33

Sam's Carrot Soufflé, 140, 141

Skillet Okra, 69

Skillet Slaw, 188

Smoky Mountain Ramp Risotto with Jack Daniel's, 230, 231

Stewed Spiced Apples, 138

Summer Squash Casserole, 70, 71

Whipped Mashed Potatoes, 140, 140

Wild Cress with Warm Ham Vinaigrette, 219

Wilted Collard Greens, 102

Wilted Garlicky Greens, 218

Winter Squash Purée, 179

Sorbet:

Blackberry, 254

Buttermilk, 253

Chocolate, 253

Honeysuckle, 254

Soufflé, Sam's Carrot, 140, 141

Soups:

Black Walnut, 119, 119

Corn, Chilled, with Garlic Custard, 65

Lemon Cucumber, 18, 19

Peanut, 134

Sunchoke, 185

Wild Mushroom, 213

Spinach:

Wilted Garlicky Greens, 218

Spoonbread, Herbed, 224

Squash:

Raw Winter Vegetable Salad, 175

Summer, Casserole, 70, 71

Summer, Salad, 34

Winter, Purée, 179

Stocks:

Beef or Veal, 269

Chicken, 268

freezing, 267

Ham Hock, 269

Vegetable, 268

Strawberries, Wild, Buttermilk Panna Cotta with, 224, 225

Strawberry-Citrus Lemonade, 44, 45

Stuffing, Corn Bread, and Gravy, Roast Turkey with, 136–37

Sturgeon, Country Ham–Wrapped, with Fennel and Sun-Dried Tomato White Bean Ragout, 162, 163

Sullivan, Michael, 87, 150–55

Sunchoke Soup, 185

Sweet Potato Pie, 142, 144

Tarts:

Fig, 190, 191

Pecan, with Sorghum, 143, 145

Rhubarb, with Wild Raspberry Cream, 214

Roasted Peach, 43

Tea:

Green, Blueberry and Apple, 44, 45

Red Oz, Raspberry, 44, 45

Sweet, –Brined Fried Chicken, 53, 55

Tomato(es):

Green, Marmalade, 271

Green, Pickle, 273

Green, Skillet Cake, 259, 261

Heirloom, Terrine, 39

Roasted, Eggplant Mousseline with, 96

Sun-Dried, White Bean, and Fennel Ragout, Country Ham–Wrapped Sturgeon with, 162, 163

Trout, Oven-Baked, with Ramps and Morels, 212, 213

Trout, Rye Whiskey–Cured, with Fresh and Pickled Fennel, 229

Truffle and Corn Flan, Tennessee, 161

Truffles, notes about, 158

Turkey, Deep-Fried, 134, 135

Turkey, Roast, with Corn Bread Stuffing and Gravy, 136–37

Vanilla Bean–Buttermilk Ice Cream, 74

Veal Breast, Wood-Smoked, 260, 261

Veal Stock, 269

Vegetable(s). See also specific vegetables

Raw Winter, Salad, 175

Stock, 268

Venison:

Cider-Basted, 186, 187

Sam's Cassoulet, 182, 183

Vinegar, Blackberry, 271

Walnut, Black, Soup, 119, 119

Walnuts, black, about, 118

Watercress:

Wild Cress with Warm Ham Vinaigrette, 219

Watermelon Pickle, Cloved, 272

White Chocolate:

Ice Cream Sandwiches, 58, 59

Toasted, Ice Cream, 58

Wine-Roasted Ducks, 94, 95

Wood-Smoked Veal Breast, 260, 261

Zabaglione, Bourbon, 231